Contemporary Issues in Marketing and Consumer Behaviour

This third edition of *Contemporary Issues in Marketing and Consumer Behaviour* has been revised and updated to reflect the fast-changing world we live in. The new state-of-the-art chapter on digital marketing digs deeply into two new frontiers of marketing which have significant impact on contemporary social life: influencer marketing and online gaming. Other new topics help us to understand how marketing can perpetuate local and global inequality through creating and sustaining hierarchies of knowledge and influencing norms of race, disability, gender and sexual orientation.

Topics new to this edition include:

- Digital Markets and Marketing
- Hierarchies of Knowledge in Marketing
- Marketing Inequalities: Feminisms and Intersectionalities
- The Ethics and Politics of Consumption

New case studies include:

- Emerging Economy Brands
- The Fairtrade Brand
- Disappearing Influencers
- Decolonising the Media

Written by four experts in the field, this popular text successfully links marketing theory with practice, locating marketing ideas and applications within wider global, social and economic contexts. It provides a complete and thought-provoking overview for postgraduate, MBA and advanced undergraduate modules in marketing and consumer behaviour and a useful resource for dissertation study at both undergraduate and postgraduate levels.

Online resources include chapter-by-chapter PowerPoint slides.

Elizabeth Parsons is Professor of Marketing at the University of Liverpool, UK.

Pauline Maclaran is Professor of Marketing and Consumer Research at Royal Holloway, University of London, UK.

Andreas Chatzidakis is Professor of Marketing at Royal Holloway, University of London, UK.

Rachel Ashman is Senior Lecturer in Marketing at the University of Liverpool, UK.

Contemporary Issues in Marketing and Consumer Behaviour

Third Edition

Elizabeth Parsons, Pauline Maclaran,
Andreas Chatzidakis and Rachel Ashman

Routledge
Taylor & Francis Group

LONDON AND NEW YORK

Designed cover image: Анатолий Тушенцов

First published 2023
by Routledge
4 Park Square, Milton Park, Abingdon, Oxon OX14 4RN

and by Routledge
605 Third Avenue, New York, NY 10158

Routledge is an imprint of the Taylor & Francis Group, an informa business

British Library Cataloguing-in-Publication Data
A catalogue record for this book is available from the British Library

ISBN: 978-1-032-06199-3 (hbk)
ISBN: 978-1-032-06200-6 (pbk)
ISBN: 978-1-003-20115-1 (ebk)

DOI: 10.4324/9781003201151

Typeset in Corbel
by Apex CoVantage, LLC

Access the Support Material: www.routledge.com/9781032062006.

Contents

Figures

Tables

1

INTRODUCTION

How has Marketing Changed?

It has been six years since the second edition of this book was published. Much has changed in this time. Climate change has increased the frequency of natural disasters. Environmental instability intersects with war and conflict to magnify the effects of poverty, deepen humanitarian risks and result in displaced populations. The resource-rich regions of the Middle East and North Africa (MENA) have been particularly hard hit, where environmental degradation and internal conflict continue to erode health, education and other critical systems. In tandem with these events, the outbreak of the Coronavirus disease in December 2019 (Covid-19) resulted in a global pandemic whose effects were far reaching, with total confirmed deaths of over 6.5 million by November 2022, although estimates that include unreported deaths suggest this figure should be tripled. Against this backdrop of conflict, crisis and accelerated change, the search for viable and sustainable solutions has prompted a re-evaluation of the functioning of the economy. Suggestions that we return to potential 'alternative economies' which could deliver a better balance of social wellbeing and equality and support a more sustainable way of living are becoming increasingly popular. Within this nexus, the marketing approach and activities of businesses have also been significantly re-evaluated. As we explore later in this book, businesses are recognising that issues of sustainability, equity, inclusivity and diversity are no longer only important as mere side issues to the business of profitability, they are now integral to it. With this in mind, in the sections that follow, we re-visit the questions we asked in the second edition of this book: how has marketing changed? How have consumers changed? And how should marketing relate to society?

How Has Marketing Changed?

Because marketing is essentially about managing and responding to knowledge and information about markets and consumers, digital communication has revolutionised marketing practices and reach. Increasingly complex data storage, processing and analytical capabilities combined with a rise in consumer use of digital communications, in particular, social media, has vastly increased companies'

DOI: 10.4324/9781003201151-1

ability to engage with, relate to and communicate with consumers on an increasingly intimate and personal level. These developments are commonly referred to as digital marketing, which is a broad term which encapsulates:

> the application of data, ICT-based technology (*e.g.* artificial intelligence), platforms (*e.g.* social networks), media and devices to extend the scope of marketing within both physical and virtual spaces, for the purpose of improving customer relationships by empowering, informing, influencing, and engaging consumers.
>
> (Krishen et al., 2021, p. 184)

With this ability comes power, which, as marketing scholars observe, can have both positive and negative effects. On the positive side, marketing scholars have spent much time and effort charting the range of opportunities that digital communications offer. In their detailed review of the emergence and scope of academic studies of digital marketing, Krishen et al. (2021) highlight five stages, each with a key focus (see Table 1.1). Broadly speaking, the last ten years has seen the increasing recognition of digital marketing as a co-creative effort not only involving the company and the consumer but also opening out to include a network of stakeholders, which has been termed an 'ecosystem'. Second, a focus on not only engaging consumers through relatable content but also facilitating consumer generation of content, thus involving the consumer in the 'work of production', further blurring the boundary between the organisation and the consumer. Third, extending the network of influence of digital marketing to embrace objects as well as people. This is exemplified in the internet of things (IoT), where a range of devices that can sense and collect data are linked together in an ecosystem. An example of this in practice would be the 'smart home', where the ecosystem might include music systems, lighting, home security, thermostats and so on, which may be controlled by a smartphone or PC. Finally, the emergence of Big Data, which refers to the very large and complex data sets brought about by developments in digital technology (see Erevelles et al., 2016, for an overview). Significant expertise is required to adequately analyse

Table 1.1 Development of Digital Marketing Studies 2000–2019

Year	Key Focus of Digital Marketing Studies
Up to 2000	customer trust, internet marketing, telemarketing, online advertisement, internet forums
2000–2005	customer satisfaction, online communities
2006–2010	customer satisfaction, online reviews
2011–2015	co-creation, customer engagement, e-tourism, data mining
2016–2019	Big Data analytics, customer engagement, content generation, video advertisement, IoT applications

Source: Adapted from: Krishen et al. (2021, p. 188)

and draw meaningful and valuable conclusions from Big Data, and its development has spawned a whole industry of information management specialists and analysts. In marketing, one specific application of Big Data is via consumer analytics, which includes the collection of data on consumer activity, the analysing of this data to extract 'consumer insights', and then the application of these insights to an area of marketing activity. Consumer insights may include, for example, the identification of an unmet need, a new perspective on how consumers are using existing products and services in unexpected ways, or observations on an emerging consumer trend. For example, the online retailer Amazon uses Big Data to inform their pricing, termed dynamic pricing. Amazon uses real-time information on shopping patterns, the popularity of products and competitor pricing to constantly adjust their prices in much the same way that airlines do. Netflix, the online TV and film streaming service, uses Big Data to personalise viewing experience by collecting data on viewing habits and offering recommendations.

However, not everyone views digital marketing as delivering positive outcomes. While some see digital marketing as offering opportunities and empowering consumers in giving them more choice and control, others argue that it introduces surveillance into consumers lives, disempowering and manipulating them in the interests of the company (and profit). For example, the information and content we engage with online is significantly shaped and filtered in ways that we are often not aware of. As Airoldi and Rokka observe:

> it is worth asking if what we buy online or eat for dinner has become less a matter of our choice and more the computational result of digital platforms' 'production of prediction' (Mackenzie 2015). Also, to what extent is our musical taste a mere consequence of *YouTube* or Spotify's automated recommendations (Airoldi 2021)?
> (Airoldi and Rokka, 2022, p. 411)

One of the key critiques of digital marketing revolves around Big Data which uses forms of machine learning combined with complex algorithms to shape, predict and ultimately manipulate consumer choices. So companies have the knowledge not only of what the consumer might choose or do next but they also have the ability to actually shape those decisions and activities. Some argue that ultimately digital marketing merely perpetuates surveillance capitalism (Zuboff, 2019) in which consumer manipulation, the erosion of privacy and 'hypernudging' are all intensified (Darmody and Zwick, 2020).

Perhaps both positive and negative views of digital marketing co-exist because it contains a contradiction bringing both empowerment for consumers but at the same time control over them. Airoldi and Rokka put forward a view which helps to understand how this paradox might work in practice. They argue that while consumers may well be disempowered, they may also have more of a role than often realised:

On the one hand, platform algorithms control and constrain us, by ordering the social world. On the other hand, the algorithmic articulation happens recursively and always in relation to behaviors and reactions of the 'humans in the loop' (Mühlhoff, 2020). This means that algorithms are also subject to consumer adaptation, negotiation, and new forms of resistance to marketers' control.

(Airoldi and Rokka, 2022, pp. 419–420)

How Have Consumers Changed?

The current generation of young people (those born between 1995 and 2010, Generation Z) have played a central part in the marketing digital revolution. In *Generation Z: A Century in the Making*, Seemiller and Grace (2018) identify the key features of this generation: integrity, openness, tenacity and care. This generation is also racially diverse and has greater gender fluid identification than previous generations. They have grown up in a digital world, where curating your identity online is second nature, and they have an innate understanding of how social media shapes their view of both themselves and of others.

Generation Z, many exist in two different places at the same time. Their 'real life' identity and online identity can reflect two entirely different people, one for each setting. And, some may even be managing several different identities online.

(Seemiller and Grace, 2018, p. 31)

Although, as studies show, while they are aware of this, their ability to act reflexively on this knowledge is often limited and this generation has been described as the 'worried generation' with high rates of anxiety and depression.

Generation Z are also known for their level of civic engagement, seen as problem solvers and creative change makers. One of the foci for this generation has been collective action with the intention to affect social and environmental change. Examples of this include the Generation Z Swedish climate activist Greta Thunberg, who has organised school climate strikes, spoken publicly at events and rallies across the globe and engaged in social media activism. In 2019, at age 16, Thunberg was named as the youngest ever *TIME* magazine's Person of the Year. Also, Malala Yousafzai, the Pakistani education activist who was shot in the head by a Taliban gunman as she rode home from school on the bus after speaking out about the right of girls to learn. Malala established the Malala Fund charity to continue to fight for the future of girls in developing countries and was awarded a Nobel Peace prize in 2014 at age 17, becoming the youngest ever Nobel laureate. These examples epitomise the tenacity and determination of Generation Z and their drive to make a difference.

Understanding the values and priorities of Generation Z helps to understand some of the wider parallel trends playing out through the market. The market has increasingly been viewed as offering potential for connection, with individuals searching for alternatives to a conventional market-based economy to bring social change and societal wellbeing. Generation Z have become disillusioned with the ability of the conventional market to deliver wellbeing and prosperity with a tendency to be less well off than their parents' generation. This factor combined with the wider series of health, economic and environmental challenges outlined at the start of this chapter has resulted in a questioning of the existing 'mainstream' economy to deliver and prompted the search for alternatives. Indeed, alternative economies are often seen as a form of resistance to the effects of a mainstream economy:

> the mainstream economy is typically conceived to extract value from local communities, externalize governance and lead to crises and social stratification. Alternative economies have (re-)emerged in local communities where various groups and social movements are working towards localized development driven by their hope to improve human conditions.
>
> (Campana et al., 2017, p. 125)

Campana et al. (2017) point towards the importance of local communities and grassroots activism in providing the bedrock for alternative forms of exchange that extend beyond the purely economic. One example is timebanking, where time is exchanged as opposed to money. The UK Timebanking website, a national charity set up to support timebanking, describes the process as:

> Timebanking is a way of exchanging skills without any money changing hands. With timebanking, you do what you love, when you want to . . . and get a little help when you need it. For every hour you spend helping someone, you earn an hour back from your time bank.
>
> (Timebanking UK)

Because an intermediary, community-based 'time bank' is used, rather than being based on individual reciprocity, this scheme is focused on building bonds within a community network. Other examples of alternative forms of community exchange in the UK include shared allotments, community shops, food larders and toy and tool libraries. Indeed, alternative economies are hugely complex and diverse, including a global tapestry of motivations, logics of organisation and institutional contexts (Campana et al., 2017). In India, for example, the Deccan Development Society (DDS), an agricultural cooperative of nearly 5,000 Dalit (oppressed caste) and Adivasi (Indigenous) women emerged from a context of extreme malnutrition and social and gender discrimination. The cooperative integrates biodiversity conservation with agricultural livelihoods. They were awarded the United Nations' prestigious Equator Award in 2019. Or the Indigenous Quechua communities of the Peruvian Andes who protect the 'biocultural heritage' of the Parque de la Papa (Potato Park) in Pisac,

Cusco, conserving more than 1,300 varieties of potato and distributing potatoes to communities in need (see Kothari, 2021, for more details). These initiatives are examples of alternative economies concerned with re-localising and preserving food systems to produce food sovereignty so that they reduce their reliance on the mainstream economy for their livelihood.

The previous examples all require a different orientation of the consumer to the market and also a variety of forms of non-economic relations of exchange. Consumer researchers have been particularly interested in the forms these relations might take as well as their underlying logics. For example, the sharing economy which – rather than being characterised as an 'alternative' to the mainstream economy – focuses on the practices of exchange therein (sharing via the economy). More than a decade in the making, the sharing economy has also been characterised as 'coming of age', and as such, a stream of recent work has focused on examining what this new phenomenon actually is, how it relates to previous instances of 'the economy' and what its potential for disruption of these earlier forms might be. Gandini draws on the work of Pais and Provasi (2015) in helpfully outlining the range of practices involved in the sharing economy:

> rental schemes (for example, Zipcar), asset rental (for example, Airbnb), service brokerage (for example, 'gig work' platforms such as Uber or Deliveroo), non-monetary sharing exchanges (for example, timebanks), peer production (for example, open source and free software communities) and financial transactions (for example, crowdfunding practices).
>
> (Gandini, 2019, p. 377)

Eckhardt et al. (2019) outline the implications of the sharing economy for a range of market actors observing the increased role for the consumer in these economies who takes on some of the 'work of production' that may previously have been the preserve of the company or organisation (see also Scaraboto and Figueiredo, 2022). Thinking about how consumers engage with these platforms, we can identify a series of practices which relate to sharing. These include timebanking (as discussed previously), bartering, renting and crowdfunding. Crowdfunding is an interesting case because rather than sharing an end product or service, instead, sharing is located in the beginning of the process (i.e. in the arena of concept development and innovation).Crowdfunding is defined as:

> an open call, essentially through the internet, for the provision of financial resources either in the form of donation or in exchange for some form of reward and/or voting rights in order to support initiatives for specific purposes.
>
> (Schwienbacher and Benjamin, 2012, cited in Drozdova et al., 2019, p. 164)

Crowdfunding is a key way in which entrepreneurs seek funding for their projects, choosing to go direct to interested parties rather than rely on financial institutions which may view highly innovative projects as too high risk. In this way, consumers (backers) can be involved in choosing between and supporting new ideas and innovations. Backers typically receive benefits for their support, such as being early adopters of a product or service, discounts and, in some cases, opportunities to receive equity. As such, crowdfunding involves founders, or entrepreneurs, and backers (those who fund the projects) but is also reliant on the digital platform (usually managed by a third party) that facilitate the process, 'hosting' crowdfunding initiatives. One successful example is Kickstarter.com which has features built into the platform which mean that only high-quality and innovative projects end up being funded. This is because if a project doesn't gain traction and reach its initial fundraising goal, then it doesn't receive any funds and backers are not charged. At the time of writing, new projects appearing on the platform website were as diverse as board games, podcasts, short films, theatre productions, music and arts festivals, DIY craft kits, comics and cookery books. Projects were proposed by individuals but also charities and community groups. In this respect, crowdfunding operates in a variety of forms and could be seen as supporting individual entrepreneurial activity but also communal efforts directed towards building bonds within the community for wider societal benefit. The crowdfunding phenomenon then is a good example of the distinctly hybrid forms that the sharing economy is taking.

Consumer researchers are also interested in the sorts of logics that underlie the sharing economy in its various forms. Gandini (2019) observes that exchange within the sharing economy rests on reputation, specifically 'reputation systems'. Reputation systems are made up of reviews, feedback and points elements on platforms which are often then translated into rankings and/or ratings. These ratings are intended to be used for building trust and as a basis for making predictions, therefore, guiding transactions which are often between strangers. However, 'reputation' also allows some access and excludes others from the sharing exchange. Gandini draws on Polanyi's (1944/2001) earlier concept of the 'fictitious commodity' to argue that reputation might be seen as an 'essential organising principles' of the sharing economy:

> In other words, just as the [Polyani's] fictitious commodification of labor, land and money represented the social precondition of the emergence of the modern market economy and its vital organizing principle, so the fictitious commodification of reputation represents the essential organizing principle of the sharing economy and the social precondition to its existence as a form of hybrid exchange whereby market and non-market features coexist.
>
> (Gandini, 2019, pp. 380–381)

In this way, Gandini urges us to look back in history and learn from earlier understandings of exchange in order to understand this new hybrid form of exchange but also to really excavate the (digital/technical) conditions in and through which the sharing economy operates. Indeed, Belk et al. (2019) warn us about the dangers of seeing the sharing economy in a nostalgic light, observing that reputation metrics can be as much disempowering and individualising as productive of a shared sense of community.

> While it may be a nostalgic exaggeration, many of those participating in the sharing economy describe it as being reminiscent of an earlier time when people really did help one another and share hospitality and favors. In making such a claim, they ignore the prices paid, rules imposed, mutual judgments of the reputation economy, and all the smiles, conversations, and emotional labor that are offered primarily in order to get good ratings and thereby enhance future bookings.
>
> (Belk et al., 2019, p. 5)

What Is Marketing's Role in Society?

In the previous two sections, we have outlined some of the changes that have occurred in relation to marketing and consumers since we published the second edition of this text in 2017. In this section, we explore how these elements intersect in considering the potential role that marketing might play in society both now and in the future. Positive and hopeful views of marketing tend to call for a focus on 'responsible research' in marketing, highlighting its potential to address wellbeing and inequality. For example, a recent special issue of the *Journal of Marketing* titled 'Better Marketing for a Better World' argued that while marketing has a dark side: 'Marketing has the power to improve lives, sustain livelihoods, strengthen societies and benefit the world at large'. These studies tend to see potential in marketing's ability to prompt individual and societal behaviour change. The broad view is that with access to more marketing information, the consumer can make better and wiser choices (Ozanne et al., 2021). Indeed, the academic Transformative Consumer Research (TCR) movement (see Davis et al., 2016, for an overview) views marketing as having significant potential as a 'Force for Good'. Their focus is on the wellbeing that marketing can bring: 'TCR strives to bring together scholars and stakeholders (e.g. managers, policy makers, consumer advocates, consumers) to promote actionable marketing solutions that help improve individual and societal well-being' (Mende and Scott, 2021, p. 116).

One recent example of marketing's potential to make a difference is the concept of brand activism, where brands align themselves with issues and values that may be seen as political. A recent survey of marketing leaders (The CMO Survey 2018, 2020) asked the question, 'Do you believe it is appropriate for your brand to take a stance on politically-charged issues?' In the 2018 survey, 17.4% indicated 'yes', and this rose to 18.5% in the February 2020 survey (Moorman, 2020, p. 388). To delve deeper into the practices that might constitute

Table 1.2 How Marketing Leaders Rate Different Types of Political Activism

Type of Political Stances	% Report Appropriate
Allowing employees to speak out on political issues	52.8%
Making changes to products and services in response to political issues	47.2%
Having executives speak out on political issues	33.3%
Using marketing communications to speak out on political issues	27.8%
Selecting partners on the basis of political stance	23.6%

Notes: Results from The CMO Survey (2020).

Source: Moorman (2020, p. 389)

'taking a stance', Moorman and colleagues added in an extra question in the 2020 survey. The results are shown in Table 1.2.

While brand activism has been widely discussed in the academic literature, it seems that companies are still very wary of getting involved with politics. Table 1.2 suggests that companies are happier to allow individual employees to take a stand on political issues than they are to incorporate politics in their advertising or have those higher in the company speak out about them.

While proponents of marketing as a positive potential force tend to stress its ability to promote wellbeing at the individual and societal levels, other views are somewhat more negative. Bleak views of marketing reference the embedding of marketing in consumerist capitalism which is predicated on the need for constant growth. They observe that a constant expansion of consumer need and consistent rise in consumer standards of living 'is running up against the critical thresholds of the complex Earth Systems' capacity to support this total economic exploitation of the environment' (Carrington et al., 2016, p. 21). As Carrington et al. (2016) insightfully observe, marketers have become obsessed with the potential of ethical consumption and, in particular, the attitude-behaviour gap. The attitude-behaviour gap encompasses the idea that while consumers often subscribe to ethics in their attitudes, they often don't follow these up in their buying behaviour. The logical conclusion stemming from this view is that if only consumers followed through with their ethical attitudes in the marketplace through their consumption choices, all would be well. This view responsibilises the consumer, mistakenly seeing them as sovereign and agentic (having the ability to make a real difference), but also mistakenly rests on 'the hopelessness of enacting real change through the same system that is the cause for ethical transgressions and misery in the first place' (Carrington et al., 2016, p. 32).

Others observe that the ethical and ecological commitments in marketing operate as a veneer or 'semiotic surface' (Ahlberg et al., 2022). Examples of this can be found in critiques of marketing practice as forms of 'washing', or 'value signalling', in which values are cited for effect rather than underpinning any substantive activity. See, for example, Marcet Alonso et al.'s (2022) study of employer branding in the retail industry. Here, they observe how the employer branding process acts a form of 'career-washing', where values of the ideal career are promoted with little substantive evidence to support them and further that they also act as a form of distraction from the poor state of retail careers. In Sobande's (2019) analysis of intersectional advertising, she finds a practice of woke-washing, where brands make use of feminist and Black social justice activist issues to build their appeal. She also finds that these adverts:

> predominantly uphold/s the neoliberal idea that achievement, social change and overcoming inequality requires individual ambition and consumption, rather than structural shifts and resistance.
>
> (Sobande 2019, p. 2724)

Woke-washing then again emerges as a form of distraction, glossing over the need to address underlying structural inequalities. In calling for more nuanced approaches to ethical standards in advertising, Sobande argues that brands should be held to account. When promoting concerns of inequality and social justice, they need to provide clear, substantive evidence that they are taking action to address these concerns (2019, p. 2470).

Outline of the Book

Having broadly considered some of the key recent developments in how we think about marketing and consumption, the task in this book is to choose some of the key issues to explore in more depth. This task is one we grappled with in the second edition, and given the breadth of marketing and its ever-evolving nature, this was never going to be easy. In the first two chapters, we explore two key contemporary trends in marketing practice ('Building Brand Cultures' and 'Digital Marketing'). The next two chapters foreground the ethical and political dimensions of consumption and marketing ('Ethical Debates in Marketing Management' and 'The Ethics and Politics of Consumption'). We have devoted significant attention to these because the structures of markets and marketing are now more than ever before central to the problems of planetary and human welfare. This is followed by two chapters which explicitly examine how two sets of theory (feminist and intersectional theories and psychoanalytical theory) are implicated in the history of marketing and how they can shed light on some of the ways inequalities are perpetuated in the marketplace. In the remaining three chapters, we bring together insights from previous chapters on the cultures, ethics and politics of marketing to explore how they play out in Hierarchies of Knowledge, Spaces and Places and on the wider global stage in the Globalised Marketplace.

Brands are everywhere in contemporary society. In Chapter 2, 'Building Brand Cultures', we look at how meaning systems are established around brands and how these can take on a life of their own as the brand intersects with other cultural phenomena such as the art world. We explore earlier moves to a postmodern cultural turn in marketing which creates a backdrop to some more recent moves in branding which rely on a privileging of culture. We explore synergies between organizational and brand cultures, illustrating the important role of employees in building brand culture and then consider how brand cultures are also co-created with consumers and other external stakeholders. Often, communities flourish around consumption of the brand. Thus, the evolution of brand culture is concerned with story-telling but not, as we might expect, just on the part of marketers. Highly successful brands achieve iconic status through responding insightfully to the wider cultural environment and being aware of the stories circulating about them. Other brands are less watchful, however, and become tainted through negative perceptions that arise and over which marketers sometimes have little control. Whether we like them or not, brands play an increasingly significant role in contemporary lifestyles. They are also increasingly coming under attack from the anti-branding movement, which heavily critiques the role of brands and the impact of brand culture on our lives.

In Chapter 3, 'Digital Markets and Marketing', we draw out some key zeitgeists in the contemporary digital world. These include 'influencer marketing and algorithmic culture' and 'gaming and immersive marketing'. Influencer marketing has brought with it a range of benefits, but the pitfalls, as we outline, can be extreme. We have seen a blurring of boundaries of the organisation and a horizontal re-distribution of power between brands and their consumers, such that transparency and authenticity in online brand practice is central to their success. Communication is now entirely networked, and collaboration within, and cultivation of, these networks is key for brands. However, these networks are implicated within a technoculture which relies on algorithms and machine learning. Some commentators see this is as empowering consumers through ever more tailored choice, while others argue that it is the ultimate surveillance and further governing of consumer lives, using complex machine learning to predict and offer them products and services they weren't even aware they needed! The second topic, 'gaming and immersive marketing', represent a major multimillion-dollar global industry in which the stakes are high. We explore one key frontier which is the advent of video game live streaming on platforms such as *Twitch*, highlighting the rise of live streaming as a 'career' and the potential fallouts for streamer wellbeing. Ultimately, we argue just how important it is for marketers to understand the implications of a digital society, particularly because it may be the only society that the next generation experiences.

Chapter 4, 'Ethical Debates in Marketing Management', reviews the debates on marketing ethics, the study of moral principles that guide the conduct of marketers. Here, we include discussion of marketing as a profession and also as a wider societal force. The growing diversity of the socio-cultural environment in which marketers operate means that they will need to be capable of assessing the ethical implications of their actions across an increasingly broad range of contexts and research questions. Marketers have to take into account three key viewpoints – the company, the industry and society – and it's when these groups have conflicting needs and wants that ethical problems arise.

Chapter 5, 'The Ethics and Politics of Consumption' discusses the growth in ethical consumer behaviours and looks at how marketing thinking must change to bring about a more sustainable future. Acknowledging that the intersection of politics with consumption is inherently contentious and multi-dimensional, the chapter identifies three key perspectives. Firstly, it looks at the consequences of everyday consumption and how these are addressed politically through 'individualised collective' choices and actions and through deciding to reduce one's consumption levels altogether. Subsequently, the chapter returns to Marx's notion of 'commodity fetishism', a perspective that has led to distinct politics of consumption centred around ideas of de-commodification, including educating consumers and initiating alternative economies that bring consumers and producers together. Finally, we consider the political role of consumption in a broader sense, as a discourse and a set of logics and practices that are favoured under neoliberal regimes. Implications and avenues for more politically progressive consumer-citizen movements are discussed.

In Chapter 6, 'Marketing Inequalities', we argue that experiences of inequality are inextricably linked with marketplace dynamics. We use a series of theoretical lenses to explore some of the ways in which this has come about. The chapter opens by giving a historical overview of the close links between the emergence and development of the feminist movement and the development of marketing and consumer cultures more generally. We then focus specifically on two recent modes of feminism which have had contemporary influence. These include choice feminism (or postfeminism) and digital (fourth-wave) feminism. The chapter then moves on to examine other sets of theory that have helped us to understand how the market perpetuates inequality. These include intersectional/critical race theory and queer theory. Discussion then moves on to explore how advertising serves to significantly shape received norms (and associated roles) in relation to femininity, masculinity, disability and sexual orientation. Taking this discussion of roles further, we explore how the marketplace provides resources (representations through advertising but also products and services) that shape experiences of motherhood and fatherhood.

Chapter 7, 'Psychoanalysis in Marketing Research and Practice', introduces psychoanalysis, a discipline that has a long and rather controversial relationship with marketing. More recently, as we explain, psychoanalysis has resurfaced as a gateway to understanding various contemporary marketing and consumption-related phenomena. Accordingly, we begin with a brief discussion of the history of psychoanalytic applications in marketing before introducing three key thinkers: Sigmund Freud, Melanie Klein and Jacques Lacan. We explain how some of their psychoanalytic ideas continue to be applied in three broader domains, namely, marketing research, advertising and consumer culture. The benefits and the potential pitfalls of psychoanalytically-inspired understandings to marketing theory and practice are important for marketers to acknowledge in an increasingly complex, consumer-driven marketplace.

In Chapter 8, 'Hierarchies of Knowledge in Marketing', we explore the way in which knowledge systems and regimes of valuation perpetuate knowledge hierarchies specifically on the global stage. The chapter explores the competitive landscape of marketing knowledge, highlighting the role that systems of knowledge (re)production, such as publication and hiring regimes, play in privileging some knowledge forms over others. However, while examining how knowledge production is structured within the marketing discipline, we also explore how hierarchies of knowledge are related to the relationship between 'the production of knowledge *and* the histories of empire, race and capitalism' (Kravets and Varman, 2022, p. 127). This requires a careful consideration of the geopolitics of knowledge focusing on the entrenched differences between the Northern and Southern hemispheres. This is followed by some more practice-based insights from interventions, including decolonising the curriculum and widening participation in education.

Chapter 9, 'Marketing Spaces and Places', focuses on place as a key marketing concept that stretches way beyond simplistic understandings of it as 'background canvas' to all social activity or as one of marketing's four Ps. Place attachments and place-related identities have a powerful effect on consumers, and marketers often attempt to influence these. The spectacular nature of many consumption venues has evolved hugely over the last 150 years, transitioning from shopping arcades and department stores to shopping malls and themed shopping environments. Although the social role of third places may be less spectacular in nature, they may be equally implicated in the reproduction of particular consumption logics and practices. We introduce a typology of different (consumption) spaces and a multi-level perspective to analysing the different dimensions of consumption spaces that is absolute, material and symbolic ones. Altogether, this implies a shift from understanding the consumption *of* place to consumption *in* place.

Chapter 10, 'The Globalised Marketplace', draws on Ritzer's contrasting narratives of grobalization and glocalization to explore the impacts that globalization is having on consumer culture. The narrative of grobalization argues that in a drive for growth, multinational corporations are extending their power and influence across the globe and stifling local cultures and economies. One of the key vehicles facilitating this process is the rise of the global brand. Narratives of glocalization on the other hand suggest that rather than being overwhelmed or stifled, the interaction of the global and the local produces something creative and new – the glocal. In closing, the chapter explores alternatives to these narratives, exploring how individuals and communities are organising themselves in the face of globalization in ways that mean they can stand outside of its effects.

References

Ahlberg, O., Coffin, J., & Hietanen, J. (2022). Bleak signs of our times: Descent into 'terminal marketing'. *Marketing Theory*, 14705931221095604.

Airoldi, M. (2021). The techno-social reproduction of taste boundaries on digital platforms: The case of music on *YouTube*. *Poetics*, *89*, 101563.

Airoldi, M., & Rokka, J. (2022). Algorithmic consumer culture. *Consumption Markets & Culture*, 1–18.

Belk, R. W., Eckhardt, G. M., & Bardhi, F. (2019). Introduction to the handbook of the sharing economy: The paradox of the sharing economy. In R. W. Belk, G. M. Eckhardt, & F. Bardhi (Eds.), *Handbook of the sharing economy*. Edward Elgar Publishing.

Campana, M., Chatzidakis, A., & Laamanen, M. (2017). Introduction to the special issue: A macromarketing perspective on alternative economies. *Journal of Macromarketing*, *37*(2), 125–130.

Carrington, M. J., Zwick, D., & Neville, B. (2016). The ideology of the ethical consumption gap. *Marketing Theory*, *16*(1), 21–38.

Darmody, A., & Zwick, D. (2020). Manipulate to empower: Hyper-relevance and the contradictions of marketing in the age of surveillance capitalism. *Big Data & Society*, *7*(1), 2053951720904112.

Davis, B., Ozanne, J. L., & Hill, R. P. (2016). The transformative consumer research movement. *Journal of Public Policy & Marketing*, *35*(2), 159–169.

Drozdova, N., Kurtmollaiev, S., & Kleppe, I. A. (2019). Crowdfunding the development of new products and services. In R. W. Belk, G. M. Eckhardt, & F. Bardhi (Eds.), *Handbook of the sharing economy*. Edward Elgar Publishing.

Eckhardt, G. M., Houston, M. B., Jiang, B., Lamberton, C., Rindfleisch, A., & Zervas, G. (2019). Marketing in the sharing economy. *Journal of Marketing*, *83*(5), 5–27.

Erevelles, S., Fukawa, N., & Swayne, L. (2016). Big data consumer analytics and the transformation of marketing. *Journal of Business Research*, *69*(2), 897–904.

Gandini, A. (2019). Reputation: The fictitious commodity of the sharing economy? In R. W. Belk, G. M. Eckhardt, & F. Bardhi (Eds.), *Handbook of the sharing economy*. Edward Elgar Publishing.

Kothari, A. (2021). These alternative economies are inspirations for an alternative world. *Scientific American*, June 1. https://www.scientificamerican.com/article/these-alternative-economies-are-inspirations-for-a-sustainable-world/

Kravets, O., & Varman, R. (2022). Introduction to special issue: Hierarchies of knowledge in marketing theory. *Marketing Theory*, *22*(2), 127–133.

Krishen, A. S., Dwivedi, Y. K., Bindu, N., & Kumar, K. S. (2021). A broad overview of interactive digital marketing: A bibliometric network analysis. *Journal of Business Research*, *131*, 183–195.

Mackenzie, A. (2015). The production of prediction: What does machine learning want? *European Journal of Cultural Studies, 18*(4–5), 429–445.

Marcet Alonso, J., Parsons, E., & Pirani, D. (2022). Career-washing? Unpacking employer brand promises on social media platforms. *European Journal of Marketing, 56*(10), 2804–2825.

Mende, M., & Scott, M. L (2021). May the force be with you: Expanding the scope for marketing research as a force for good in a sustainable world. *Journal of Public Policy & Marketing, 40*(2), 116–125.

Moorman, C. (2020). Commentary: Brand activism in a political world. *Journal of Public Policy & Marketing, 39*(4), 388–392.

Mühlhoff, R. (2020). Human-aided artificial intelligence: Or, how to run large computations in human brains? Toward a media sociology of machine learning. *New Media & Society, 22*(10), 1868–1884.

Ozanne, L. K, Stornelli, J., Luchs, M. G., Mick, D. G., Bayuk, J., Birau, M., Chugani, S., Fransen, M. L., Herziger, A., Komarova, Y., Minton, E. A., Reshadi, F., Sullivan-Mort, G., Trujillo, C., Bae, H., Kaur, T., & Zuniga, M. (2021). Enabling and cultivating wiser consumption: The roles of marketing and public policy. *Journal of Public Policy & Marketing, 40*(2), 226–244

Pais, I., & Provasi, G. (2015). Sharing economy: A step towards the re-embeddedness of the economy? *Stato E Mercato, 35*(3), 347–378.

Polanyi, K. (1944/2001). *The great transformation: The political and economic origins of our time.* Beacon.

Scaraboto, D., & Figueiredo, B. (2022). How consumer orchestration work creates value in the sharing economy. *Journal of Marketing, 86*(2), 29–47.

Schwienbacher, A., & Benjamin, L. (2012). Crowdfunding of small entrepreneurial ventures. In D. Cumming (Ed.), *Handbook of entrepreneurial finance.* Oxford University Press, 369–391.

Seemiller, C., & Grace, M. (2018). *Generation Z: A century in the making.* Routledge.

Sobande, F. (2019). Woke-washing: 'Intersectional' femvertising and branding 'woke' bravery. *European Journal of Marketing, 54*(11), 2723–2745.

Timebanking UK. https://timebanking.org/

Zuboff, S. (2019). Surveillance capitalism and the challenge of collective action. In *New labor forum* (Vol. 28). Sage Publications, 10–29.

2

BUILDING BRAND CULTURES

Introduction

Culture refers to the system of symbols and meanings that give human activities significance. Throughout our lives, we are part of many different, often intersecting, cultures, such as national culture, music and literature cultures, lifestyle culture and so forth. These cultures can have a profound influence on the attitudes, beliefs and values that underpin our behaviours. Increasingly, it is recognised that brands, too, can have a powerful influence on us because of the meanings they incorporate and the 'culture' that evolves around them.

Brands are deeply embedded in the meaning systems that we use to make sense of our contemporary world. Take, for example, the golden arches of McDonald's or the Nike swoosh that we encounter daily. These symbols and their meanings are instantly recognisable around the globe, signifying respectively fast-food Americana style and empowerment through sports. Yet not only do brands create their own unique culture but they also draw on other cultural phenomena, such as history, myths, rituals, artworks, the film industry, theatre and television, to convey meanings that resonate in powerful ways with consumers' lifestyles (Schroeder and Salzer-Morling, 2006). This ongoing iteration, between contributing to culture and drawing from it, makes brand culture a complex and multifaceted phenomena. It is much more than just a clever name or logo and also more than the implementation of a successful marketing strategy. Importantly, brand culture is a living entity that evolves and responds to the dynamics of the marketplace. Brand culture is continuously (re)created as the various parties that have an interest in the brand – companies, employees, culture industries, intermediaries, customers – relate stories around their experiences of the brand (Holt, 2004). Indeed, brand culture may also include the role of government agents and politicians as Yalkin's (2018) shows in her study of how soap operas contribute to the Turkish nation brand's culture. Most significantly, however, no matter what parties are involved in its creation, the strength of a brand's culture lies in the collective perception about it rather than the psychological aspects of an individual's response to the brand.

This chapter examines the building blocks of brand culture by looking at how meanings that circulate around a particular brand evolve as

DOI: 10.4324/9781003201151-2

the brand intersects with other cultural phenomena. First, we set the scene with a brief discussion of how postmodernity heralded in a cultural turn with important ramifications for marketing and consumer research. The notion of brand culture emerged from this background. Then we discuss the important synergies between organisational and brand cultures together with the important role of employees in building brand culture before looking at how brand cultures are also co-created with consumers and other stakeholders external to an organisation. We discuss the role of brand communities and how social media are driving their formation. After highlighting the importance of competing in 'myth markets' (Holt, 2004), we illustrate how many highly successful brands achieve iconic status through responding insightfully to the wider cultural environment. Finally, we explore some of the ways that a brand's culture can become tainted through negative perceptions that consumers hold about it and discuss the impact of the anti-branding movement.

Postmodernity and the Cultural Turn

The postmodern era signalled a major change in Western thinking and philosophising. As its name suggests, postmodernity marked the end of modernity – variously referred to as *The Age of Reason* or *The Enlightenment* – a period in Western history running from the mid-eighteenth to the mid-twentieth century. Leading commentators consider that it commenced around the end of the 1950s when the term 'postmodern' was first applied to describe changing characteristics in art and culture (Lyotard, 1984; Jameson, 1991). For example, it was used in architecture to describe the distinct break that occurred during the 1960s with the type of rational thinking that had given rise to modern functionalism (a perspective dictating that the design of an object or building should be determined by its function). In contrast to functionalism, postmodernism focused more on style and, indeed, a mixture of styles that also often playfully harked back to the past. As a cultural movement, postmodernism is characteristically sceptical about many of the key assumptions that have underpinned Western thinking for several centuries. Accordingly, the postmodern critique questions authority, sources of knowledge and many other cultural, social, economic and political, taken-for-granted assumptions in society.

This sceptical questioning is characteristic of the postmodern era, an era that marked the disintegration of what Lyotard (1984) refers to as grand 'metanarratives'. These are systems or ideologies, for example, Christianity and the rationalist thinking of the Enlightenment (see Adorno and Horkheimer, 1973) that set standards to measure dualistic/binary values such as good and bad, high and low, true and false. Hence, a postmodernist perspective challenges traditional value systems with such dichotomous modes of thinking and merges categories in a relativistic way, thereby producing complex mixtures of those binaries. Categories of true and false, genuine and fake, high and low are blurred and mutually dependent. For example, clear demarcations between high and low art no longer exist. An advertisement is just as likely to be labelled an artwork as a Van Gogh painting. In the multicultural world of the twenty-first century, there is no one perspective that is privileged, or one source that provides any absolute 'truth'.

Postmodernism thus spread to affect all disciplines and branches of knowledge, including marketing, where it has made its biggest impact in relation to the understanding of consumers. Indeed, marketing, as the main purveyor of signs, symbols and images has been identified as more or less synonymous with postmodernism, placing the emphasis on product intangibles, such as brand name and overall image, the fantasy aspects that surround a product as opposed to any intrinsic, tangible value in the product itself (Firat and Venkatesh, 1993).

Significantly, during modernism, production and the political economy were privileged over consumption and the domestic sphere. Postmodernism shifted the emphasis from production to consumption, however, privileging culture instead and meaning creation through consumption. The consumer becomes a producer of meanings through his/her/their consumption acts, and, hence, the binary division between production/consumption becomes blurred, with production no longer assuming the privileged position. This has given rise to many new theories around the hedonic and experiential nature of consumption, especially in relation to brands and branding as we now go on to discuss in relation to brand culture.

Building Brand Culture with Employees

Well-known entrepreneurs such as Phil Knight (Nike), Richard Branson (Virgin), Anita Roderick (Bodyshop), Steve Jobs (Apple) and Chrissie Rucker (The White Company) have built strong corporate brand cultures through personal dedication and passion for their enterprises. Their strong, charismatic personalities and missionary zeal can enthuse employees with a sense of their vision for the organisation, often making employees as passionate about the enterprise as the entrepreneurs are themselves. Such entrepreneurial vision intuitively connects corporate identity to organisational mission, a key factor in building a sustainable corporate brand culture.

Following the lead of such inspirational entrepreneurs, many companies are now moving towards corporate branding, as opposed to product branding, in a move to instil a clearer sense of corporate identity and brand culture into their employees, suppliers, customers and other stakeholders. Balmer (2006, p. 34) refers to the growth of the 'corporate brandscape', arguing that brand cultures, and the communities that they engender, are much stronger for corporate brands than those created by product brands. Whether we feel an affinity with them or not, powerful corporate brands, such as Microsoft, IBM, BMW, HSBC and Coca-Cola, convey a rich set of associations in our minds as to what they stand for and who they are. Corporate brand culture is three dimensional, reaching not only inside and outside the organisation but also *across* organisations (Balmer, 2006). Consider the rebellious nature of the Virgin brand and how this is conveyed across many different industries that range from mobile phones to air travel. Embodied in the figure of its flamboyant founder, Richard Branson, the Virgin brand culture is based on the idea of doing things differently, of radical rethinking and of siding with the consumer in the face of bureaucracy and monopoly.

The role of employees in enacting the corporate vision is one of the core building blocks for brand culture, together with the idea that they should 'live the brand' and be empowered to be 'brand champions' (Ind, 2007). From this perspective, the marketing role diffuses throughout the organisation, no longer resting with a specific marketing function or brand manager. Whereas in the past, marketers have been accustomed to thinking of specific externally-focused marketing activities, particularly marketing communications, to convey the brand ethos and values, a corporate brand approach emphasises the customers' brand experience that comes from their dealings with an organisation's employees. From chief executive to delivery driver, all employees' actions can be seen as reinforcing the brand values. These actions are responsible for translating the corporate vision into a reality and embedding the brand culture in all employee/customer interactions, as well as throughout the organisation. In this way, the organisation and all its employees provide the basis for the brand's position in the marketplace vis-à-vis its competitors (Elliott and Wattanasuwan, 1998).

Of course, all this is easier said than done. A corporate branding culture cannot simply be dreamt up in a day or be imposed on an organisation regardless of the existing organisational culture. It requires a subtle touch and a lot of patience to understand and reconcile the different meaning systems that may already exist in an organisation (for example, managerial versus shopfloor cultures). Schultz and Hatch (2006) emphasise that for corporate branding to be successful the strategic vision, organisational culture and stakeholder image must be aligned. Normally, top management dictates the strategic vision, a vision that embodies their aspirations for the future direction of the company. In contrast, organisational culture is 'the internal values, beliefs and basic assumptions that embody the heritage of the company and manifests in the ways *employees* [emphasis in original] feel about the company they are working for' (p. 16). Organisational culture is much more organic than strategic vision, emanating from employees' sense of what the organisation is and their sense of identification with their employer. The culture of an organisation is often taken-for-granted, going unquestioned and expressed in the familiar phrase of 'just the way we do things around here'. If employees' and managements' visions of the organisation are at odds, it will be much more difficult to develop a consistent image with the organisation's customers and other stakeholders.

Successful brands go to great lengths to establish the right culture within their organisation and to ensure that employees believe in the brand. Innocent made itself the fastest-growing business in the UK's food-and-drink sector by building a strong organisational culture that ensures its employees share its strategic vision. In their company headquarters, Fruit Towers in London, the working spaces have been designed to cultivate community and collaboration as well as encourage creativity. To show the company's appreciation of its employees, the Innocent website contains an alumni page detailing the contributions of past employees, a highly original step to reinforce its employee branding.

Of course, from a more critical perspective, we are also right to be sceptical about such seemingly enlightened employer/employee relationships which can be regarded as a form of control, a kind of 'brainwashing'. They can even be seen as establishing a quasi-cult around the brand to ensure that employees internalize the brand values unquestioningly to appear more committed and authentic to the consumer. This in turn helps inscribe the brand into the lifeworld of the consumer (Arvidsson, 2006, p. 43) as they interact with employees. In the next section, we go on to consider the consumer aspects of brand culture in more detail.

Building Brand Culture with Consumers

We have just explained previously how a key aspect of brand culture is to ensure that a common vision unites employees. The other key building block of brand culture is how well the values the organisation embodies match what its customers are seeking. Employees and management may share a similar passion, but if this is not also shared with the customer, then the brand will be doomed to failure. It is now well-recognised that consumers no longer seek just functional benefits from products and services. They seek meanings that help them construct and maintain their identities (Elliott and Wattanasuwan, 1998). By providing us with symbolic resources, brands present us with a multitude of possible ways to express ourselves and with which to gain the approval of our peers.

Brands such as Apple, Benetton, Harley Davidson and Patagonia act as quasi-activists in the sense that they lead us in thinking differently about the world and ourselves (Holt, 2004). Heath and Potter (2005) see this as 'the rebel sell', arguing that it is rebellion, and not conformity, that drives desires in the marketplaces as we seek to differentiate ourselves from others. A good example of this is the Volkswagen Beetle that is remembered as an iconic rebel car in the 1960s and 1970s, when it was seen as a rejection the values of mass society and the showiness of its larger competitors. This iconicity was leveraged successfully by VW in its popular relaunch of the Beetle in the late 1990s.

Social agendas, and the values they represent, can generate deep bonds with consumers who 'buy into them', both literally and metaphorically. The founders of Ben & Jerry's ice cream, Ben Cohen and Jerry Greenfield, have built a strong brand culture around a social and ecological conscience since they launched the brand in 1978. They use sustainable dairy farming programmes ('caring dairy') and aim to achieve a carbon-neutral footprint (or 'hoofprint' as they like to refer to it!). Their consistent commitment to a social agenda has developed a following of highly loyal consumers who see the company as caring for more than just commercial gain. Once again, as Arvidsson (2006) reminds us, we need to maintain a healthy scepticism over such actions. Creating social agendas in this way also enables large corporations to better infuse themselves through every aspect of our lives.

This perceived authenticity of corporate intention and responsibility is becoming increasingly more important to consumers. This is particularly relevant in terms of what Holt (2002) describes as the postmodern branding paradigm, which is 'premised upon the idea that brands will be more valuable if they are offered, not as cultural blueprints, but as cultural resources – as useful ingredients to produce the self as one so chooses'. As people chose brands that have the right meaning for them in terms of how they want to reflect their identity, they need to be confident that the brand is not going to let them down. Choosing brands that they can be sure will enhance their identity helps consumers minimise the purchase risk, and, as we will see later in this chapter, they can become very disillusioned with the brand if they feel it has betrayed their trust.

Consumers are also implicated in nation brands, a type of branding that seeks to create an identity around a country, usually with the aim of securing its position in the global order and enhancing its trading potential. To understand a nation brand's culture, we need to be aware of specific historical and political contexts, as well as any identity tensions these create when consumer co-creation of meanings is involved. For example, soap operas are a huge export market for Turkey and have greatly enhanced Turkey's global reputation not only in economic terms but also as regards its nation brand culture. Soap operas are used as a form of soft power to help the Turkish nation brand emphasise its unique mix of modernity and tradition, a mix that is also reflected in the soap opera narratives that consumers use as a resource to alleviate any tensions consumers between these two elements.

Brand Communities

As we can see, nowadays, brands must be seen to share, rather than manipulate, consumer's passions and emotions. The brand-consumer relationship can be very powerful and include a range of strong emotions, such as love, intimacy and commitment, to the extent that consumers may even experience separation anxiety (Fournier, 1998). Thus, consumers' contribution to brand culture and their role in co-creating meanings not only with marketers but also with other consumers cannot be underestimated. Often, the strength of consumer feeling is experienced collectively and a community forms around the brand, a community that is held together by mutual appreciation and loyalty to the brand. Brand communities are not restricted to any one product category and can be as diverse as the consumer groups who form them. They include commonplace car brands such as Saab, Jeep,

Volkswagen and Mini, as well as more idiosyncratic media productions like *Star Wars*, *X-Files* and *Xena: Warrior Princess*.

A brand community is defined as a 'specialized, un-geographically bound community, based on a structured set of social relationships among admirers of a brand' (Muniz and O'Guinn, 2001, p. 412). Although they differ from traditional communities in terms of their commercial nature, brand communities are held together like their traditional counterparts by three key aspects: consciousness of kind, shared rituals and traditions and moral responsibility. Consciousness of kind is about shared values and how members form in-group/out-group categorisations (see, for example, the Mini case study at the end of this chapter). Shared rituals and traditions are about the community experience and celebrating the brand history. A sense of moral responsibility is about the commitment to other members of the community, helping them with problems or making new members feel at home. In these ways, consumers use their own labour to add cultural and emotional value as they develop interpersonal relationships around the brand (Cova and Dali, 2009). Accordingly, consumers are often drawn to products and services because of their linking value rather than their use value. From this perspective, marketing activities are more about facilitating the 'co-presence and the communal gathering of individuals in the time of the tribes: a kind of "tribal marketing"' (Cova and Cova, 2002).

Social media in particular drive the formation of brand communities, linking physically distant lovers of a brand. More than 50% of the top 1,000 global brands have online brand communities (Manchanda et al., 2012). Such communities enhance consumers' engagement with a brand across seven key dimensions: enthusiasm, enjoyment (affective level), attention, absorption (cognitive level), learning, endorsing and sharing (behavioural level) (Dessart et al., 2015). These types of engagement and intra-community interactions lead to increased loyalty as well as often generating a fervent passion for the brand. Of course, community members have different levels of commitment and loyalty, and not all members participate for the same reasons. A useful typology of significant distinctions in member behaviours has been developed by Kozinets (1999):

Insiders: participate actively on a regular basis and are the most influential community members. They are passionately devoted to the brand.

Devotees: are strongly attached to the brand but less dedicated to the community, and they are not so involved in the social aspects.

Minglers: have strong community ties but are not so attached to the brand. They enjoy the social interactions but may not consume the brand at all.

Tourists: often, they are lurkers and do not have an active relationship with either the brand or the community.

Overall, we can see how the role of the consumer is changing to take a much more active part in the production of value. The firm and the consumer have traditionally been seen as having distinct roles: the role of the firm to create brands offering benefits, the role of the consumer (the target market) being to passively consume those brands and taking no role in actual value creation around the brand. We highlighted earlier the blurred boundaries between traditional binary divisions such as production/consumption. This blurring affects the role of the consumer. Because consumers want relationship with brands they can trust, and with whose values they can identify, they are now influencing much more directly the value systems that a brand embodies and that give it a unique culture. Accordingly to Fournier (1998), we can form relationships with brands that are just as fulfilling as the relationships we have with other people. On this same basis, however, we can put the same pressure on brands that we do on human relationships, and we can expect a lot from them! Consequently, marketers need to spend a lot of effort to co-create brand experiences with consumers, experiences that form a crucial part of building and maintaining brand culture. Through their website, Ben & Jerry's invite customers to suggest new flavours and even to ask for a discontinued flavour or product to be reinstated. This approach shows foresight and acknowledges the power that consumers now have in making demands on a brand. For example, Wispa was an iconic 1980s chocolate bar that was discontinued by social media to lobby Cadbury's for its return. Following this pressure from loyal customers, the bar was reintroduced in 2007. This is by no means an isolated incidence. Other successful campaigns by loyal communities surrounding a brand include the Fiat 500 (ceased production 1975) and the Raleigh Chopper (ceased production 1979) that were both relaunched (2004 and 2007 respectively).

WOM (word-of-mouth/mouse) runs rampant in brand communities, and marketers frequently try to influence consumer-to-consumer (C2C) communications in a variety of ways, including viral and guerilla marketing. Known as a 'seeding' campaign, sometimes marketers place a product with influential consumers (opinion-leading bloggers, for example) to encourage them to post favourable reviews and spread the word to their communities. A study on this by Kozinets et al. (2010) found that bloggers changed marketer messages to make them more relevant and palatable to their community because blatant marketing promotions risk compromising the sharing and caring aspects of communal relations. These authors revealed four key narrative strategies that bloggers used and that were significant for marketers, namely, evaluation, explanation, embracing and endorsement:

Evaluation: avoids mentioning the marketer influence and focuses on product performance.
Explanation: acknowledges the marketer participation and shows awareness of the cultural tension this may produce.
Embracing: emphasises the consumer-marketer co-creation aspects but puts the focus on meeting personal needs with the product.
Endorsement: acts as a quasi-marketer for the product and is happy to pass on all marketing promotions and communications.

The commercial-cultural tension follows a continuum moving from implicit (evaluation) to explicit (endorsement). Whether the message is accepted depends on the product's perceived fit with the blog and communal norms. If there is a mismatch, the community may resist the marketer influence or result in negative WOM. Building brand culture is a delicate balancing act between being seen as authentic (sharing the passion!) and being seen as too self-interested and commercial.

Sometimes a brand community is completely controlled by consumers with no marketer interventions whatsoever. Despite being discontinued by Apple in 1998, the Apple Newton still motivates a lively community of users (see, for example, *http://myapplenewton. blogspot.co.uk/*) who remain dedicated to the brand. They still share knowledge about the product and help each other to maintain their Newtons. Apple launched the Newton in 1993 as the first personal digital assistant on the market. The launch was rushed and the design had many ongoing problems that eventually led to its discontinuation. However, it retained a loyal core of followers who feel abandoned by the parent brand, Apple (Muniz and Schau, 2005). These enthusiasts display a quasi-religious fervor towards their Newtons and rumours even surface from time to time that the Apple Newton will be relaunched (a second coming and narrative of redemption).

Creating Iconic Brands

In Doug Holt's (2004) path-breaking book on cultural branding, he shows how brands become iconic. Icons are representational symbols that embody meanings that we admire and respect. They provide us with templates of what to value and how to behave. In ancient times, icons were mainly religious figures (saints, gods, disciples and so forth) and stories about them were circulated mainly by word-of-mouth, passed down through generations in this way. Now, Holt argues, the circulation of cultural icons has become a key economic activity and takes place through mass communications (i.e. film, books, TV, sports, advertising, PR, etc.). Many icons are film stars such as James Dean and Marilyn Monroe, politicians such as John F. Kennedy and Martin Luther King, or sporting heroes such as Michael Jordan. These figures all represent certain kinds of stories, stories that convey 'identity myths' (Holt, 2004) that people use to address the anxieties and desires they have about their own identity. To illustrate, the 1950s rebel figure, James Dean, defied middle-class conventions of suburban family life and encapsulated the idea that a man could follow his own desires. This myth was especially appealing to the post-war American male who felt tied down by family responsibilities and the dull routine of working for a large and faceless corporation.

According to Holt, iconic brands are the ones that best know how to respond to key cultural tensions that are taking place in the wider socio-cultural environment. A good example of this is Brand Beckham (Milligan, 2004). As a sporting celebrity, David Beckham is also a powerful brand that embodies the core values of dedication, down-to-earth humanity and an impeccable sense of style. Proud of being a loving father, Beckham is well known for being in touch with his feminine side, changing his hair styles regularly and willing to be photographed in a sarong. The identity myth that he represents helps young men carve a path between the perceived 'sissiness' of the feminine and the widespread disapproval of the 'brutish' masculine.

Companies can now be seen as competing in myth markets rather than product markets (Holt, 2004; Thompson and Haytko, 1997). Traditionally, myths make us aware of oppositions that they progressively mediate, such as good/evil, life/death, science/nature, male/female and so forth; their tales take on life's big contradictions and the complexities of being human. It is in this sense they speak across cultures, and similar myths and symbolic associations exist across very different religious beliefs. And so it is that commercial myths can also resonate with us at deep, unconscious levels. A successful brand creates a commercial myth that intersects with both historical and popular memory (Thompson and Tian, 2008). Take, for example, the highly successful Magners Irish Cider campaign that is single-handedly accredited with changing consumer attitudes to cider by transforming it into a fashionable drink. In order to do this, the Magners campaign very successfully taps into beer discourse in order to position and legitimize cider as a masculine and culturally empowering drink. This discourse is about 'challenge, risk and mastery – mastery over nature, over technology, over others in good natured "combat" and over oneself' (Strate, 1992, p. 82). However, a crucial aspect of the campaign's success is that it also draws on nostalgic, age-old images of the Irish male as being in touch with his deeply romantic self, thereby restoring a sense of the 'intense masculinity' that has become displaced and unfashionable in twenty-first-century representations of masculinity. The nature/culture binary is central to the Magners campaign. Maclaran and Stevens's (2009) analysis of the Magners campaign illustrates how the Celtic soul that lies at its core is encouraging young men to negotiate a masculinity that restores ideals of manliness (culture) alongside a celebration of the feminine (nature). Thus, as a commercial myth, this conception of a 'Magners man' conveys a new mythic ideal that draws on many existing cultural myths to achieve its unique 'syncretic blending of narrative and imagistic elements' (Thompson and Tian, 2008).

When the Brand Eludes Control

Identity myths thus have the power to forge deep bonds with consumers, and they are often a crucial part of the relationship we have with a brand. Yet, similar to any meaningful relationship, people can feel very aggrieved when it does not go well. The fact that brands can engender deep emotions in us also means that we can become very dissatisfied if our trust is betrayed, or if we feel let down in some way. For example, when a well-known shopping centre in Dublin was radically refurbished, many consumers felt that they had lost a part of their heritage and were very unhappy with what the management had done to the centre. Some experienced such deep emotions over the changes that they swore never to return (Maclaran and Brown, 2005).

In the current business world, it is almost impossible for a company to control its external brand image. Modern communication technologies, and in particular, the internet, mean that there are very few corporate secrets and any discrepancy between a company's outward image and its internal one swiftly gets revealed. Consumers talk to other consumers all the time and with the use of email, web discussion groups and social networking sites, news can spread very quickly. Consumers also talk to employees and this brings us full circle, back to our previous discussions about the importance of good employee relations. Dissatisfied employees can set up their own websites to reveal home truths about their employer, both to other employees and consumers alike. There is a plethora of boycotting sites to be found on the web, each revealing various dissatisfactions and rallying others to join the boycott. Such actions can seriously damage a company's reputation. Because brand culture is organic, flowing as much from employees and customers as from an organisation's strategic vision, it can also be fragile and not easily controlled by marketers. Brand culture, therefore, can be adversely affected by negative associations, just as easily as it can be enhanced by positive ones.

Many well-known brands have had their reputations severely tainted. Martha Stewart was convicted of illegal stock trading in relation to her own media company. Perrier's crystal-clear water with health-giving properties was contaminated with benzene. The energy company, Enron, was found guilty of accounting fraud. Indeed, transgressions of this nature have become so commonplace that terms such as 'brand rehabilitation strategy' and 'brand repair' are now in frequent use in relation to attempts to avoid irreparable damage to a brand's culture (Kahn, 2005). However, transgressions do not always have to be damaging, and sometimes, they can form an intrinsic part of a brand's culture. Aaker et al. (2004) found that relationships with 'sincere' brands, such as Coca-Cola, Ford and Hallmark, perceived to be traditional and family-orientated, suffered after transgressions. Conversely, relationships with 'exciting' brands such as Virgin, Yahoo and MTV, perceived as more youthful and irreverent, showed signs of reinvigoration.

A brand does not always have to commit a transgression to acquire negative connotations. Brand tainting can also occur because consumers' perceptions change. Recently, there was criticism of the Bodyshop (BBC News, 2006) when L'Oreal took over the company. The Bodyshop was seen as joining the 'enemy' because L'Oreal is 26.4% owned by Nestlé which has been criticised for marketing powdered baby milk in developing countries. Sometimes the most powerful sources for brand tainting exist beyond the control of those who manage the brand, as, for example, with the symbolic associations that may emanate from particular consumer groups that use the brand. The red, white, black and camel check that is synonymous with Burberry led to the brand becoming severely tainted in the UK, where it is associated with a 'chav' image. This image is typified by Danniella

Westbrook, the *EastEnders* soap opera star who gained notoriety for her cocaine addiction and who is a major fan of the Burberry brand. She and her baby were even photographed by the press, both dressed head to foot in Burberry check and with a matching push-chair. Because of negative associations such as these, the Burberry check has been downplayed in recent designs. The baseball cap has been discontinued by the company in an attempt to distance itself from this marginalised 'chav' group. Interestingly, this tainting did not affect the brand's international markets, where Burberry is still seen as an upmarket, very British brand.

Another threat of tainting comes from the many anti-branding movements and campaigns that have been gaining momentum. Works like Naomi Klein's *No Logo* (1999), one of the most influential anti-glo-balization texts, expose how branding techniques are grounded in a profit motive despite the many creative ways in which marketers may try to hide this through appeals to authenticity. In particular, Klein severely critiques such brands as Nike, The Gap, McDonald's, Starbucks, Shell and Microsoft and highlights their many exploitative practices. In addition, successful brands often work to suppress competition in the marketplace. A good example of this is Microsoft, whose software is on 80%–90% of computers around the world (Lury, 2004). A dominant market position, such as Microsoft's, enables a brand culture to be diffused globally with the risk that local cultures are eroded, or even extinguished, in its wake. 'Culture jamming' has become a well-known method of resistance to the pervasiveness of brand culture, made famous by the activist magazine, *Adbusters*. Culture jamming involves transforming advertisements in an ironic way to critique the corpora-tion behind the advertisement's message. Whereas, originally, these activities focused on the ways in which brands manipulated desires, now, they are more likely to expose the hypocrisy 'between brand promises and corporate actions' (Holt, 2002, p. 85).

Summary

In this chapter, we have looked at the different facets of brand cul-ture and explored its many influencing factors. Marketers are by no means the sole source for the meanings that surround a brand and that produce its overall culture. There are many organic influences that marketers cannot control as, for example, those that stem from organisational culture and employee perceptions of the brand. Consumers also play a major role, often co-creating meanings that can be both positive and negative and even forming communities around the brand. The most successful brands built strong cultures that incorporate these organic influences and remain sufficiently flex-ible to adapt to changes in the macro environment. The best brands tell great stories with which we can identify. However, the more we look to brands to guide our beliefs and behaviours, the more they are likely to be held accountable. Activist movements against brands are likely to become more aggressive, as brands play a bigger part in our everyday lives. In the future, as Holt (2002) has indicated, the most successful brands are likely to be those that provide us with the most creative cultural resources.

Case Study: Building a Mini Brand Culture

Like the Volkswagen Beetle, the Mini is an iconic car that dates back to the rebel culture of the 1960s. Just like the mini-skirt and the Beatles, the little car is an enduring symbol of the 'Swinging Sixties'. The Mini was designed by the British Motor Corporation (BMC) in response to the increasing popularity of the smaller and fuel-efficient German 'bubble cars'. Sir Alec Issigonis, the Mini's designer, has become a legend in his own right, famed for his innovative design that allowed both performance and space despite the limitations of size. Sir Alec's history intertwines with that of the Mini, and many stories circulate around him that contribute to the Mini's brand culture and reinforce it as a triumph for British design. Fans relate how Pininfarina, a famous Italian carmaker, once asked Issigonis why he did not style the Mini a little. The reply that Issigonis made to this competitor's taunt has now become part of the Mini myth: 'It will still be fashionable when I'm dead and gone' (Beh, 2008).

The Mini was marketed as a fun car with a cheeky image. 'You don't need a big one to be happy. Happiness in Mini shaped' and 'small is beautiful' are some of its famous straplines. Its brand culture has evolved around this image, an image that made it 'cool' to drive a small, unpretentious car. In challenging prevailing notions of respectability, the Mini was very much a part of the countercultural movement that emerged during the sixties. Heralding the idea of the 'rebel sell' that we have previously referred to, it stood for a youth culture that was hedonistic and fun-seeking. The Mini was continually associated with major celebrities throughout this decade. This enhanced its brand culture significantly, giving it celebrity status by association with stars, such as Peter Sellers, Ringo Starr, Britt Ekland, Lulu and fashion designer Mary Quant. When Marianne Faithful drove to Mick Jagger's drugs trial in her Mini and George Harrison's psychedelic Mini appeared in the Beatles' *Magical Mystery Tour*, the Mini's subversive connotations were enhanced (wikipedia.com). Well-known dare-devil racers, such as Niki Lauder, Enzo Ferrari and Steve McQueen, drove Mini Coopers. In 1969, three Minis featured as get-away cars in *The Italian Job*. The car chase that ensued, with its daring stunt-driving that included descending a set of steps, has become a classic. In 2003, three new BMW MINIs featured in a remake of this film.

Like other iconic brands, the Mini addressed certain tensions in society at the right time. During the post-war 1950s in Britain and the US, size was regarded as a marker of status and this was particularly so in the case of cars. The Suez crisis of 1956 meant that oil prices soared and the size-status equation came under pressure from the need for fuel economy. The Mini car addressed this contradiction and, at the same time, countered the post-war climate of continued austerity with its message that linked fun and size (Beh, 2008). The Mini symbolised a unique blend of hedonism, small size and Britishness, core values that consumers quickly responded to. They bought the Mini not just for its fuel-saving capacity but also because they were buying into these core values. In doing so, they were using the Mini to say something about their own identity: they were cool!

Over the years, although it was a mass-produced car, the Mini brand culture evolved to include a highly individualistic element. This was aided by its many endorsements from celebrities who had specially designed models. It became the custom for individual owners to decorate their Minis in unique ways. Some painted union jacks on the roof or on the bonnet, while others painted colourful stripes or motifs on the bodywork. Still, others kitted out the interior in fanciful décor, sometimes running a theme throughout the car's interior and exterior. This element of creativity and individual self-expression was added to the brand culture by consumers themselves and has now become an important part of the brand's evolving history.

The Mini car finally ceased production in 2000, having become a legend in its own right. A huge following of loyal fans still mourn its loss and remain committed to guarding the Mini's heritage in brand communities around the globe. Many fans also deeply resent the launch of the new BMW MINI in 2001 (BMW bought the Mini brand as part of their takeover of Rover) and argue that it is not an authentic Mini. They perceive one of its core values, Britishness, to have been violated by association with a German manufacturer. In terms of its size also, the design of the new MINI can no longer be regarded as particularly small. There is thus a clash of brand cultures between the values of the old Mini and the new MINI – between old and new brand communities – that is still being played out in the marketplace. Many of the classic Mini clubs that exist will not permit new MINI owners to join and refuse to admit that the new model has any links to them. Despite this opposition, there can be no doubt that the launch of the new MINI has been highly successful. The new design has taken one of the Mini's core values, fun, and used this value very successfully in conjunction with the theme of individualisation. As far as the new MINI manufacturer, BMW, is concerned, there is no disjuncture between the old Mini and new MINI and the brand has simply evolved. The new MINI website (www.mini.co.uk) invites customers to design their own MINI from hundreds of different combinations, alongside this claim:

> Over the years MINI has changed. However the foundations of this small car, its character traits, have remained unchanged from its inception in the 1950s until today. Be it old Mini or the present-day MINI, people just can't stop talking about it.
> Because it's in the genes!

Seminar Exercises

Discussion Topics

1 Outline the three cornerstones of brand culture. Discuss which you think is the most important.

2   What are the different ways in which employees can influence a brand's culture during their interactions with customers? Thinking of your own experiences, identify an incident with an employee that has helped you form an opinion about a brand.

3   How do brands help us create and maintain our identities? Think of your own relationship with brands. What are your favourites, and how do you think these are consistent (or not) with how you see yourself?

4   Identify a brand community and analyse it in terms of the three markers of community as identified by Muniz and O'Guinn (2001).

Group Exercises

1   Take a brand of your choice and put together a presentation about its brand culture.

   • What do you think are the different influences on its brand culture?
   • What are the brand's core values, and how have these evolved?

2   Search through marketing magazines, newspaper reports and marketing websites to identify a recent case of brand tainting (other than those discussed in the chapter).

   • Document what happened to cause the tainting.
   • How could this have been prevented?
   • What should the brand do now to try and overcome the associations of tainting?

3   Investigate more about the classic Mini's history and compare this to the launch of the new BMW MINI.

   • Why is there a potential clash of brand cultures?
   • How do you think BMW could have used the Mini brand community to their advantage?

Internet Resources

An article by Bernard Cova, Olivier Badot and Ampelio Bucci, http://visionarymarketing.com/en/blog/2006/07/beyond-marketing-in-praise-of-societing-by-bernard-cova-olivier-badot-ampelio-bucci/
Mini car forums, www.theminiforum.co.uk/forums/
The famous activist magazine, *Adbusters*, www.adbusters.org
The MINI car website, www.mini.co.uk/

Key Readings

Arvidsson, A. (2006), *Brands, Meaning and Value in a Media Culture*, London: Routledge.
Cova, B., Pace, S., and Skalen, P. (2015), 'Brand volunteering: Value co-creation with unpaid consumers,' *Marketing Theory*, 15 (4), 465–485.

Holt, D. B. (2004), *How Brands Become Icons: The Principles of Cultural Branding*, Boston: Harvard Business Press.

Schroeder, J. E., and Salzer-Mörling, M. (Eds) (2006), *Brand Culture*, London: Routledge

References

Aaker, J., Susan, F., and Adam Brasel, S. (2004), 'When good brands do bad,' *Journal of Consumer Research*, 31, 1–16.

Adorno, T., and Horkheimer, M. (1973), *Dialectic of Enlightenment* (trans. J. Cumming), London: Verso.

Balmer, J. M. T. (2006), 'Corporate brand culture and communities,' in J. E. Schroeder and M. Salzer-Mörling (Eds), *Brand Culture*, London: Routledge, pp. 34–49.

Beh, K. H. (2008), *Unity in Diversity? Relationships in the Mini Brand Community*, Unpublished doctoral dissertation, De Montfort University.

Cova, B., and Cova, V. (2002), 'Tribal marketing: The tribalisation of society and its impact on the conduct of marketing,' *European Journal of Marketing*, 36 (5/6), 595–620.

Cova, B., and Dali, D. (2009), 'Working consumers: The next step in marketing theory?' *Marketing Theory*, 9 (3), 31–339.

Dessart, L., Veloutsou, C., and Morgan-Thomas, A. (2015), 'Consumer engagement in online brand communities: A social media perspective,' *Journal of Product and Brand Management*, 24 (1), 28–42.

Elliott, R., and Wattanasuwan, K. (1998), 'Brands as symbolic resources for the construction of identity,' *International Journal of Advertising*, 17, 131–144.

Firat, A. F., and Venkatesh, A. (1993), 'Postmodernity: The age of marketing', *International Journal of Research in Marketing*, 10 (3), 227–249.

Fournier, S. (1998), 'Consumers and their brands: Developing relationship theory in consumer research,' *Journal of Consumer Research*, 24, 343–373.

Heath, J., and Potter, A. (2005), *The Rebel Sell: How the Counter Culture Became Consumer Culture*, Chicester: Capstone Publishing.

Holt, D. B. (2002), 'Why do brands cause trouble? A dialectical theory of consumer culture and branding,' *Journal of Consumer Research*, 29, 70–90.

Ind, N. (2007), *Living the Brand: How to Transform Every Member of Your Organization into a Brand Champion*, London: Kogan Page.

Jameson, F. (1991), *Postmodernism, or, the Cultural Logic of Late Capitalism*, Durham: Duke University Press.

Kahn, B. (2005), 'Brand rehab: How companies can restore a tarnished image,' *Knowledge@Wharton*, http://knowledge.wharton.upenn.edu/article.cfm?articleid=1279

Kozinets, R. V. (1999), 'E-tribalized marketing?: The Strategic implications of virtual communities of consumption,' *European Journal of Marketing*, 17 (3), 252–264.

Kozinets, R. V., de Valck, K., Wojnicki, A. C., and Wilner, S. J. S. (2010), 'Networked narratives: Understanding word-of-mouth marketing in online communities,' *Journal of Marketing*, 74, 71–89.

Lury, C. (2004), *Brands: The Logos of the Global Economy*, London: Routledge.

Lyotard, J. F. (1984), *The Postmodern Condition: A Report on Knowledge*, Minneapolis: University of Minnesota Press.

Maclaran, P., and Brown, S. (2005), 'The center cannot hold: Consuming the utopian marketplace,' *Journal of Consumer Research*, 32, 311–323.

Maclaran, P., and Stevens, L. (2009), 'Magners man: Irish cider, representation of masculinity and the 'burning Celtic soul',' *Irish Marketing Review*, 20 (2), 77–88.

Manchanada, P., Packard, G., and Pattabhiramaiah, A. (2012), 'Social dollars: The economic impact of consumer participation in a firm-sponsored online community,' *Marketing Science Institute*, 11–115.

Milligan, A. (2004). *Brand It Like Beckham: The Story of How Brand Beckham was Built*. London: Cyan Books.

Muniz, A. M. Jr., and O'Guinn, T. C. (2001), 'Brand community,' *Journal of Consumer Research*, 27 (4), 412–432.

Muniz, A. M. Jr., and Schau, H. C. (2005), 'Religiosity in the abandoned apple newton brand community,' *Journal of Consumer Research*, 31, 737–747.

Schroeder, J. E., and Salzer-Mörling, M. (2006), 'Introduction to the cultural codes of branding,' in J. E. Schroeder and M. Salzer-Mörling (Eds), *Brand Culture*, London: Routledge, pp. 1–12.

Schultz, M., and Hatch, M. J. (2006), 'A cultural perspective on corporate branding: The case of LEGO group,' in J. E. Schroeder and M. Salzer-Mörling (Eds), *Brand Culture*, London: Routledge, pp. 15–33.

Strate, L. (1992), 'Beer commercials: A manual on masculinity,' in S. Craig (Ed), *Men, Masculinity and the Media*, Newbury Park: Sage, pp. 78–92.

Thompson, C. J., and Haytko, D. L. (1997), 'Marketplace mythology and discourses of power,' *Journal of Consumer Research*, 31, 162–180.

Thompson, C. J., and Tian, K. (2008), 'Reconstructing the South: How commercial myths compete for identity value through the ideological shaping of popular memories and countermemories,' *Journal of Consumer Research*, 34, 519–613.

Yalkin, C. (2018), 'A brand culture approach to managing nation-brand,' *European Management Review*, 15 (1), 137–149.

3
DIGITAL MARKETS AND MARKETING

Introduction

Citizens of the world are online. Having just broached the eight-billion milestone in 2022, research shows that internet usage is available to over half the world's population (Digital, 2022, 2022). While not baked into its initial design, with the development of Web 2.0, networked sociality has become the norm (Hackl, 2022). Brands of all sorts from tool manufacturers to makeup makers all have a presence on popular social media channels like *Instagram*, *Facebook* and *YouTube*. The explosive success of social media is unprecedented. No other technological milestone has taken off at such a pace. It took radio technology 38 years to reach 50 million followers, TV took 13 years to achieve the same, whereas *Facebook* added 100 million users in nine months (Srivastava, 2013). While there have been some bumps in the road, as governments attempt to protect their citizens from its potential harms, there is no denying that consumer desire for social media technologies is boundless.

In response to the digitalisation of society and the new structures this has created, marketing has adapted into a digital form. This has not been an easy transition. Brands have needed to learn how to deal with a re-distribution of control from the marketer to the consumer, and there has been a shift away from marketing to big data, algorithms and data analytics (Belk, 2020). Nevertheless, for now at least, the lively pulse of marketing and consumption beats through the screens of laptops, smartphones and iPads. As a result, marketing practice is mutating alongside technologically driven consumer culture into a digital form.

Digital marketing encapsulates a broad church of activities, including social media advertising, search engine optimisation, website and platform design, word-of-mouth marketing, re-marketing, algorithmic marketing and influencer marketing alongside many more (Chaffey and Smith, 2022). Further, markets are also changing, with traditional barriers of geography and time no longer constraining how and when consumers buy things and interface with brands. In this way, with consumers able to access any corner of the world's market around the clock, consumers have a greater choice in where and how they shop. With intensifying competition and transparency, brands

DOI: 10.4324/9781003201151-3

are required to meet higher standards and are not able to dupe consumers, making them more accountable for their actions.

What Are Digital Markets and Marketing

Digital marketing encompasses a plethora of different techniques
which take place online. These techniques engage and influence customers, encouraging them to browse, connect and buy goods within
a participatory culture (Jenkins, 2009). Digital marketing is the use of
digital technologies to create integrated, targeted and measurable
communications which help to acquire and retain consumers while
building deeper relationships with them (Digital Marketing Institute,
2022). Digital marketing is targeted because the affordances of the
technology allow it to be, and it is measurable because this is inherent in the use of digital technology, through clicks, timestamps, likes,
traffic counts and so on. These qualities contribute to the datafication of social behaviour as marketers have a heightened ability to
track the effects of their campaigns and integrate these findings into
insight-driven practice (Aimé et al., 2022). This withstanding, there
remains a rich qualitative side to digital marketing, whereby natural-
istic insights into consumers' culturally driven thoughts and feelings
can be traced and understood within online communities (Kozinets,
2019). Importantly, qualitative insights offer deeper meaning to the
marketing function for those who tune in and listen. Social listening
through qualitative methods, such as netnography, can offer benefits
to brands and marketers, including understanding consumer needs,
brand perceptions, customer segmentation, competition and insights
around ROI.

Chapter Outline

As outlined previously, digital markets and digital marketing encapsulate an array of practices and activities. Rather than describe them
all, this chapter illuminates two new frontiers of digital markets
and marketing which are prolific and disruptive, experiencing rapid
growth and increasing scholarly interest. These include 'influencer
marketing and algorithmic culture' and 'gaming and immersive marketing'. Within these areas, this chapter offers a brief review of marketing theory that is shaping the way these practices and activities
are understood. Firstly, we offer a brief history of how content creation on the internet has developed over time, including an overview
of technoculture. Secondly, we cover influencer marketing and algorithmic culture. Influencer marketing is a significant development in
digital marketing in the last five years. It has become one of the major
sources of marketplace information and discovery for consumers and
a significant source of revenue for retailers and marketing agencies
(Grandview Research, 2022; Leung et al., 2022). Thirdly, the landscape
of gaming and immersive marketing is described, setting into context the steep rise in gaming cultures among users of the internet,
particularly illustrating the phenomenon of live streaming, which is

altering the way in which consumers interact with brand advertising and real-time media. We describe how platform and gaming culture is changing, how consumers and influencers spend and make money (Cutolo and Kenney, 2021) through block chain and crypto currencies and how this relates to the market economy. Within these new frontiers, the datafication of marketing is increasing, with Big Data sets offering marketers more opportunities for precise targeting but leaving them open to vulnerabilities, such as the changing design of hidden algorithms (Kozinets and Gretzel, 2021). Far from being divorced from the marketing function, increasingly, datafication is automating processes which would have traditionally been undertaken by humans. Finally, within our chapter summary, we discuss these two frontiers and consider their implications on networked consumption, suggesting how disruptive marketing technologies benefit and harm consumer sociality.

Web 1.0, 2.0 and 3.0 . . .

In understanding digital markets and marketing, it is important to set into context how content on the internet has developed over time. Digital interfaces and their technologies are typically contextualised in this way by considering their development as a numbered series of 'webs', termed Web 1.0, Web 2.0 and Web 3.0. These webs are useful in understanding the development of e-business and digital marketing. These are now described in turn, according to definitions provided within Hackl et al. (2022).

Web 1.0 represents the period when '"the internet connected the world" information systems, which changed how consumers make purchasing decisions and engage with brands' (p. 30). During this time, the web served as a publication medium, its main function being to transfer content from an authority source to a larger audience of users, much akin to reading a book, during the period between roughly 1989–2005. Following this period, Web 2.0 represents the 'rise of social media, eCommerce, the sharing economy, and user content creation. This is where we see the rising importance of followers, likes, shares and subscribers' (p. 30). During this time, emerging initially around 2004, the web enabled user participation and created an enhanced role for the audience. For example, within a social network, each additional user added value for other users, hence, why it has been called a 'participatory culture' (Jenkins, 2009). Web 3.0 is the next point of significance 'when technology will interconnect people, places and things in real and digital worlds' (Hackl, 2022, p. 30). This was created in 2014 by a cryptocurrency co-founder, Gavin Wood. Web 3.0 encompasses an innovation called the metaverse, which is not a new idea but is experiencing renewed interest. The metaverse has lots of differing definitions depending on authors' viewpoints, but largely, it is agreed that it is a convergence of our physical and digital selves, where we can share immersive experiences with other. A definition states that 'the metaverse represents the top-level hierarchy of persistent virtual spaces that may also interpolate in real life, so that social, commercial

and personal experience emerge through web 3.0 technologies'
(Hackl et al., 2022, p. 26). For marketing, this convergence of the digital and non-digital means that consumers will no longer be a target
for marketing communications but rather will be immersed into joint
value creation, where companies and consumers intra-act, emerging
together without limits on their form or materialities.

Technocultural Marketing

Technoculture is a term within the field of digital marketing and technology research which encompasses how consumer culture alters amid
widespread technological innovation (Green, 2002). The term acknowledges that technology is a powerful force in society, never not neutral
but active in shaping societies' structures, politics, media and information. It is certainly hard to deny that our contemporary society depends
on computer networks, which are comprised of desktops, laptops,
iPads, smartphones, servers, networks, websites and platforms as well
as human actors, such as programmers, marketers, consumers and followers. As consumers, we intermingle within the networks that these
technologies enable and become hopelessly addicted to their alluring
design. Offering intermittent rewards for its usage, such as likes and
follows, consumers are repeatedly enlivened with 'nuggets of endor-
phin' (Thompson and Patterson, 2023). Further, when considering how
society was re-ordered at the start of the Covid-19 pandemic, without
the use of technology to maintain a social connection, there would
have been a mass shut down and subsequent crash in many organisations and economies. Instead of this, society at large remained connected and productive through using technology. Technoculture and its
'affordances, actors and assemblages' has spread in the same way that
a virus or bacteria might and 'literally become part of the social and cultural body' (Kozinets, 2023, p. 153).

Consequently, the use of technology and its embedding of technoculture have inculcated new facets of consumer culture into the fabric
of consumers lives. Examples of technoculture include memes, hashtags, emojis, viral videos, certain languages and practices, for example, taking selfies and posting pictures of food online (Kozinets et al.,
2017). Further, increasingly intimate relationships, whether sexual or
platonic, are mediated by facets of technoculture and have created a
new frontier in dating and relating to others. For example, platforms
like *Tinder* have given rise to practices like 'ghosting', whereby a person disappears from a relationship without warning, leaving no trace
of themselves as they move on with their lives. Furthermore, communities like *Reddit* connect people around a multiplicity of topics, using
specific cultural practices such as upvoting, downvoting, stealth bans
and self-reverence. As marketers, understanding novel elements of
complex relationality such as these are important in empathetically
situating ourselves within the hearts and minds of consumers so that
they can best be understood and served.

Further, considering what happens to consumers' relationships
with their bodies in the wake of technocultural changes is important.

For example, the book *Neuromancer* by William Gibson (1984) illustrates some early facets of technoculture and how its assimilation into our lives changes the way we understand our bodies. When writing about the body in relation to texts such as this and others, Dyens (2000, p. 1) notes that 'the human body entangled in technology wavers between life and non-life, between biology and matter, between the finite and infinite'. Certainly, these possibilities and the re-framing of boundaries, whether this be around bodies, employment or relationships with others in terms of digital markets and digital marketing, are difficult to conceive but critical to engage with in understanding societies' worldmaking and connected consumption.

Influencer Marketing and Algorithmic Culture

The internet has enacted a 'horizontal revolution' for all kinds of information (Tuten and Solomon, 2017). Traditionally, product-based information would be offered from brands to consumers via sales agents, marketing materials and adverts. As such, brands experienced little recourse if they did not fulfil the many promises they made when selling their products and services. However, with the advent of social media, this is no longer the case. Social networks provide a public forum where consumers can give voice to the problems they experience with products and services or discuss a brand's conduct. With the availability and accessibility of social networks, consumers have unprecedented access to each other through forums, brand websites and review sites. In using these, consumers can speak and be spoken to by everyone present in a network and individuals can be highly disruptive in expressing their thoughts and feelings about their brand experiences. Power, which used to be held by brands, has been re-distributed horizontally within consumer networks, with businesses becoming much more accountable for their actions. Consequently, there has been a shift in how brands build consumer trust. Perceived authenticity is a difficult to achieve. Perceived authenticity is consumers' amorphous sense that the brand is genuine and meaningful (Canavan, 2021). Consumers trust each other far more readily than they trust brands and are happy to listen to each other's experiences online. Every review and piece of recommender material counts towards a brand's reputation with a wide range of publicly available metrics, such as likes, stars and comments, all providing an assessment of how well a brand is serving its consumer base. If a company receives many negative reviews, restoring a positive online reputation can be challenging. Companies can easily fall prey to an algorithmic negativity bias (Zhu et al., 2021). This is the contextual backdrop within which influencer culture has risen to prominence in the last 15 years. Spending time dwelling in rich content on social networks and listening to the views of trusted others is a normal part of everyday life.

Realising the precarity of their positions within the new normal of the internet, brands have cottoned on to the insatiable trust and solidarity consumers have with one another. Brands have become particularly attuned to entrepreneurial individuals who have built a loyal following of likeminded others whom they influence to buy products. Initially known as market mavens, early adopters or opinion leaders, influencers are individuals who traditionally rose to prominence via blogging, then vlogging and nowadays, via 'content creation' of varying sorts. Influencers are individuals who have grown an organic followership or community around themselves as personal brands, through creating compelling content, such as photos, videos, blog posts, reels, stories, shorts or podcasts. Through these activities, over time, influencers can become an algorithmically favoured and socially recognised, authentic opinion leader. Influencers are highly attractive and valuable to brands who wish to partner with them for campaigns and sponsorships. Through their efforts to develop a devoted following, influencers can create a platform upon which to communicate with an audience of willing-to-listen consumers (Ashman et al., 2021).

Through their content creation, influencers build strong relationships between consumers and brands and generate revenue (Audrezet et al., 2020) for themselves and their sponsors. Initially beginning on *YouTube*, a site specialising in video content, which is the world's most popular video-sharing network, influencer marketing has spread through blogs, *Instagram*, *TikTok* and many other algorithmically driven platforms. For influencers, working within algorithmic consumer culture in presenting new and exciting content can evolve into a lucrative, high-flying career. Of course, on the flip side, for every one influencer who makes it, earning millions for their opinions, there are thousands more who languish in relative anonymity (Ashman et al., 2018).

The Era of Influence within Algorithmic Marketing Environments

Social media are online means of communication, collaboration and cultivation among interconnected and interdependent networks of people, communities and organisations enhanced by technological capabilities and mobility (Tuten and Solomon, 2017). Far from being simple environments, social media networks are complex and advancing in a state 'permanent beta'. Social media environments are designed by software developers in addicting ways to ensure that consumers keep visiting, oftentimes with an obsessive passion. Social media platform developers and designers learn about consumers through collecting their data and then capitalise on aggregated data sets by selling advertising and re-selling the data to third parties. A large part of this strategy rests on the design and usage of algorithms. Algorithms mathematically frame how a group of data behaves and, in doing so, order how posts and search results are ranked (Gillespie, 2014). Algorithms control the innermost workings of a platform and specify what a consumer sees when they log on. The use of algorithms in social networks is varied. For example, on *Instagram*, the site's original premise was to order what consumers saw when they logged in by the network of friends they cultivated (Leaver et al., 2020). Consumers would see only what their friends posted in a historically designed timeline, and once a consumer had seen all this content, there was no more to view. This has changed in recent years, and the platform has become driven by algorithmic hierarchies (Leaver et al., 2020). Since these changes, there is no end to the content a consumer can see on *Instagram*. The stream is endless. The platform still maintains the networked friend-pool element, but it also has a page, whereby consumers can be shown content from others whom the platform considers relevant, driven principally by an algorithmically decided formula. Other platforms, such as *TikTok*, are fully driven by an AI-controlled algorithm which chooses consumer content based on their swipes, pauses and general behaviour, learning about a consumer over time and feeding them the content the algorithm sees fit (Stokel-Walker, 2021). These changes imbue algorithms with a power in generating what a consumer sees and alters the way researchers are understanding agency within social networks (Kozinets et al., 2017). Within techno-mediated social networks, consumers are not in charge of their own viewing environment, as algorithms 'silently structures our lives' (Martin, 2019, p. 835). Since an average consumer spends over two hours per day on social media platforms (Oberlo, 2022), this sets into context how much agency consumers are ceding to amorphous mathematical formulas and machines which influence consumption decisions and opinions.

Influencer Marketing in Marketing Theory

In recent years, researchers working in the marketing discipline have paid greater attention to studying and writing about influencer marketing. In doing so, researchers are getting to grips with the affordances and drawbacks of influencer cultures and learning how influencing functions within digital marketing. Topics of interest include conceptual work around influencer marketing effectiveness (Leung et al., 2022), how influencers enact emotional labour and tribal entrepreneurship (Mardon et al., 2018), how influencers fit into the neoliberal agenda through their unconventional activities (Ashman et al., 2018), their design thinking activities (Ashman et al., 2021) and their many facets of authenticity (Abidin, 2022) and how influencers manage their endorsement relationships, sometimes unsuccessfully (Cocker et al., 2021), among many others.

Leung et al. (2022, p. 228) offer a conceptual view of influencer marketing and sketch a terrain which describes the sorts of creative control a brand expects when partnering with an influencer. They view influencer marketing as a strategy 'in which a firm selects and *incentivises* online influencers to engage their followers on social media in an attempt to leverage these influencers unique resources to promote the firms' offerings, with the ultimate goal of enhancing firm performance'. Conceiving influencer marketing as distinct from a celebrity endorsement, whereby a brand has complete control over the messages being communicated, they propose that influencer marketing can exhibit high levels of originality and reap creativity benefits which enhances marketing communication effectiveness.

However, they also caution that creative freedom placed into the hands of influencers can be a threat which could deviate from an official brand message. These threats comprise part of the reason why an industry has emerged to manage influencer marketing, with agencies specialising in this area enacting complex practices, such as scoring, advanced searching technologies and ongoing influencer relations, to ensure that influencers are strategically matched with brands and managed throughout the campaign activation process.

Moral Transgressions and Influencer Culture

A key theme in influencer marketing research is understanding the nuances of building and relating to a followership of consumers. In exploring the tribal relations which influencers create, Mardon et al. (2018) discover how emotional bonds are formed and characterised between beauty influencers and their consumer followings. In doing this, they find that there is a moral element to the emotional labour that influencers enact through managing their relations with the public, with a fine balance to be struck in creating close communal relationships so as not to transgress finely balanced community boundaries. This research speaks to the earlier days of influencer marketing, whereby the explicit promotion of branded content was not as commonplace as it is today. The moral transgressions found by the researchers include attempts to 'cover up' brand sponsorships or sneakily 'get round' the rules of explicitly being paid to use a product. Influencers perform significant emotional work in appearing genuine and authentic to their followers by carefully curating their life's lows and revealing negative emotions (Mardon et al., 2018). Influencers also enact regular bouts of gratitude to their followership as an acknowledgement of the importance of the consumer/viewer/follower in the influencer's own successes.

A more recent study in the same vein by Cocker et al. (2021) moves deeper into the notion of transgressing branded sponsorship deals. This work untangles the multifaceted nature of appearing authentic in an online marketing environment. The study uncovers instances, whereby social media influencer endorsements are perceived as transgressive by their fellow community members. Based on a netnographic study of *YouTube* beauty influencers, the findings of this study offer a description of five ways an influencer can act in a transgressive manner when engaging in brand sponsorships. These include underhand endorsement, over endorsement, over-emphasis, over-saturation and over-indulgence (Cocker et al., 2021). These transgressive endorsements are now described in turn.

Firstly, underhand endorsement is when influencers transgress their followers' expectations of presenting honest and unbiased reviews of products and services. Over time, as influencer marketing has become a commonplace marketing promotion, followers have come to accept explicit brand deals as part of the influencer marketing offering, with communities tolerant of watching a personalised advert within a video in return for watching an entertaining piece of content. Nevertheless, where these endorsements are underhand and not explicitly communicated to followers, this failure to disclose results in the influencer being perceived as secretive and deceptive.

Secondly, over-endorsement is when influencers engage in too high of a frequency of brand deals, tipping the balance of the community's tolerance for adverts. Even though followers have come to accept brand sponsorships, they still prefer that, for the most part, influencers' content remains organic versus sponsored.

Thirdly, when influencers over-emphasise brand deals as part of their offerings, they break their moral responsibility to provide valuable content for the community. A brand sponsorship will be accepted by followers if they do not detract from the audience's enjoyment of the content. For example, if an influencer posts a seven-minute video and four minutes of it is an endorsement, this is seen as negatively impacting the experience of watching a video. Visible and verbal over emphasis in brand endorsements will lead to followers feeding back with negative comments.

Fourthly, over-saturation of branded content occurs when brands partner with multiple social media influencers within the same community and request them to post similar endorsements for the brand in quick succession. This happens frequently in the influencer marketing landscape, where a group of influencers promote the same product at once. While the individual influencer cannot be held responsible for the actions of a brand in this respect, these actions result in the erosion of community members' enjoyment of content and leave them feeling that their trust has been betrayed in favour of repetitive content.

Finally, over-indulgence is when influencers agree to excessive incentives from brands, so much so that community members feel they are less likely to speak honestly about a product. For example, if a brand offers an overly lucrative deal to an influencer, which is not uncommon given the significant power of influencers to sway consumer option, this could potentially disadvantage other community members by reducing their access to honest, unbiased product recommendations. These five forms of transgressive endorsement speak to the reality and practicalities of the influencer marketing terrain and show the complex pathway that influencers must tread in balancing the demands of their consumer following, versus offering a brand a space within their channels to promote their products and services.

Influencers Caught within the Neoliberal Network

While influencers are conceived as having significant agency in the studies previously mentioned, particularly in Leung et al. (2022), other studies paint a darker picture. For example, in a study by Ashman et al. (2018), influencers are framed as fodder for the neoliberal online market. They posit that influencers are required to cede significant agency to the gold rush of building a successful online presence and often receive very little in terms of reward. Speaking to influencers about their activities, both at an individual level and within group discussions at conferences, their participants revealed the efforts behind their glossy social media feeds. Influencers often felt the need to conform to the expectations of their followers and to the algorithmic ruling of the platforms. Influencers navigated the complexities of being an individual at the centre of a community. One of their participants commented:

> Even if you try your best . . . cure with kindness as they say, it can get worse. Like you get comments that . . . it just becomes more and more extreme, and it actually becomes upsetting, and it can make you feel like you are in danger.

This study demonstrates the individual perspectives of influencers and the experiences of creating a social media presence. Clearly, building a loyal and kind followship is a highly skilled and complex task, not for the faint of heart.

Gaming and Immersive Marketing

Although they sit at the frontier of recent digital marketing innovations, video games and live streaming are not new. Live streaming was used principally during the first presidential webcast held in 1999 from George Washington University. Moving through many technological advancements since then, live streaming companies now enable all consumers to have their own streaming platform, provided they own a microphone and webcam. *YouTube* and *Twitch* are the foremost companies working at this interface, having been live streaming since 2008. Live streaming has benefitted greatly from the pandemic, spurred on by the force of Covid-19, locking down consumers in their homes with little to do. Since then, live streaming has escalated in popularity, with a larger uptake of consumers starting their own streams or tuning in to watch the activities of others. In this year, the rampant use of *Twitch* has seen 7.8 million unique creators streaming each month with an average of 93,800 average concurrent streamers (Twitch Tracker, 2022). Set in this context, live streaming represents a significant evolution in technology usage and creates a new terrain for marketing practice, which will re-shape the way that markets function within the digital ecology. Certainly, both watching and streaming live content rest on finding pleasure in the vicarious, experienced in the imagination through the feelings and actions of another person.

Video Game Live Streaming as a New Frontier

Liveness is characteristic in many traditional media forms, including radio, theatre shows and in-store service. Recently, live experiences have become more commonplace in social media networks (Auslander, 2008). Live streaming is when a consumer/influencer/gamer casts their activities through a technologically mediated, algorithmically managed environment. Through sharing live experiences, consumers are networked together in real time.

An increasing number of consumers are spending large amounts of their free time dwelling within live environments. For example, on average, users spend roughly 95 minutes per day on platforms such as *Twitch* (Business of Apps, 2022). With consumers spending their time on streaming platforms, marketers and researchers are working to understand how to tap into this economy and how to best reach market segments through live streaming. Advances in live streaming bring back into relevance notions of interruption-based marketing, as some of the marketing opportunities 'on stream' include adverts, which cannot be skipped past, played at regular intervals.

Live streaming also creates implications for marketing work and changes the notion of the influencer. For example, on *Twitch*, due to the liveness of the stream, there is a raw and effervescent quality to the content being produced. For example, in contrast to traditional content on *YouTube*, content on live streaming platforms is not edited and uploaded in an asynchronous fashion. When performing live, there are 'front-stage' pressures on the streamer, such as always maintaining their online authentic persona. Where influencers can painstakingly edit and curate their images, live streamers are always performing. Further, influencer content is traditionally much shorter. Most videos are around 10–30 minutes long, with longer videos of up to an hour being the exception, although not unheard of. For live streamers, their revenue is earned based on how many subscribers they have to the channel, and it is well known that the more a live streamer is online, the more successful they are likely to be. The algorithm on platforms such as *Twitch* favours those who stream for longer periods of time more regularly. This creates a culture of 'needing' to live stream not only regularly, for example, daily, but also for long periods of time, creating significant implications for live streamers' wellbeing at work whilst also increasing the pressure of them needing to perform well *and* to game as much as possible. Running a live stream online is mostly associated with gaming. Live streaming, however, is not just as simple as playing a game whilst others watch. A gamer must simultaneously read and respond to the chat function, whereby the followership interacts with the streamer and they must narrate their activities, joining in to create the collective effervescence of the game. Such multi-tasking and immersion into the game whilst live streaming to the world over long periods of time can be problematic for those wishing to be successful gamers and popular live streamers.

There are also issues of gender and discrimination in the online gaming world, particularly in eSports games (Paul, 2018). Recent research on gaming cultures and the online communities within them has focused on their potentially toxic nature and the gendered implications of gaming (Drenten et al., 2022). A paper in this area by Drenten et al. (2022) describes how gaming cultures are exclusionary to women, despite women making up 48% of total gaming consumption.

The Implications of a Digital Society

As the previous paragraphs illustrate, digital and social media market-ing are creating new frontiers in marketing and are arguably the most important developments in marketing since the 1990s technological revolution (Srivastava, 2013). Today, digital technologies are central within consumers' lives and taken-for-granted by younger genera-tions. For example, children are typically using iPads from infancy and are consuming advertising and media through streaming services, within social networks and through communication via video calls and instant messaging. This has physiological implications as well as social ones. Physiologically, consumers' postures are altering (think 'text head') due to the prolific use of digital technology, with head, neck and eye strain becoming common maladies, with an increas-ing amount of screen time altering consumers' ability to hold their attention for long spans of time (Pandya and Lodha, 2021). Digital technologies alter and place a toll on our bodies, minds and chemical makeup, with headaches and numbness in the extremities abound-ing. Socially, digital technologies are increasing our knowledges and understanding, changing the way we consume information, creating improvements in industry and employment and offering humanity a world-wide interconnectedness as a result of globalization. Such widespread interconnectedness can be a double-edged sword. For example, research shows that an over reliance on digital technolo-gies for social connectedness during the Covid-19 pandemic has led to an atrophy of social skills with peers, with respect to a loss of the nuances and understanding of the delicate nature of what it means to be within others' physical presence (Pandya and Lodha, 2021). Fur-ther, as the research previously on gaming demonstrates, there are significant issues with digital technologies replicating the structural biases of society through their programming, for example, racism.

Chapter Summary

This chapter considers digital markets and marketing from the per-spective of new frontiers, focusing on two recent waves of marketing practice, namely, influencer marketing and live streaming. By con-centrating on these two developments, we offer insights into some of the studies which are nuancing our understanding of networked and mediated sociality. This chapter has only scratched the surface of these topics. Digital marketing has many different activities within it and, in some ways, cannot be accurately considered as an isolated form of marketing because our society is no longer analogue. It is inherently affected by the digital in all its activities. For example, during the Covid-19 pandemic, it was shown in high relief how much technology can help us to keep society and the social moving, even when we cannot be physically together. Understanding how technol-ogy is impacting our consumer culture is the first step in learning how to be a good digital marketer. Without an understanding of the lively cultures happening online, it is hard to relate to consumers who are acting within the net. Selfies, reels, videos, texts, tweets, posts, hashtags, emojis, swipes, likes and comments are new metrics of success in a digital world. Marketing can benefit from the traces left behind by online sociality, both by qualitative and quantitative feedback on how consumers feel, what they think, how they laugh and emote and where they spend their time and money. This is one of the greatest opportunities marketing has ever experienced.

Case Study: Disappearing Influencers

One of the hallmark practices of influencer marketing is the need to maintain a presence online, creating content according to a regular schedule. Whether influential 'market makers' promise to post one *YouTube* video per week ('every Sunday at 7pm!!') or post a stream of consciousness via *Instagram* stories each weekday, their followers soon expect to see a familiar face. Over time, through following a regular content creation schedule which typically includes a pattern of activities over various social networks, influencers seek to build a committed organic followership. An influencer's followership plays a symbiotic role in their online activities, feeding back their likes and dislikes, indicating which sort of content they should produce (Ashman et al., 2021). Each online community dwelling around an influencer has its own personality and enacts varying roles. Shaped by this symbiosis, a community develops its own idiosyncrasies, accepted behavioural norms and languages. Some communities can be supportive and loving, others active in discussion about a certain lifeway, whilst some can be touchy and easily offended. Sensitive and easily unbalanced communities are far more likely to have trolls.

Trolling

Trolls are individuals who spend their time maliciously harassing or cyberbullying others within online communities. For example, two of the most famous UK influencers who rose to prominence in the first wave of *YouTube* success, Anna and Jonathan Saccone-Joly, have long documented their struggles with trolls, saying that trolls 'try to destroy our lives every day' by contacting brands, family and their children's school with various attempts to dramatise their lives.

It is hard to pinpoint what makes an influencer more prone to being trolled, but it certainly seems that some channels are more vulnerable as a troll's target. These influencer channels might take an overtly political stance on a topic, for instance, being staunchly against cruelty to animals. The influencer might be part of a marginalised group, be battling a health problem, such as an eating disorder, or may feature a family member who falls into a marginalised category. It might simply be that the influencer translates over camera in a way which some find unpalatable. For sure, being on the receiving end of a lot of controversy or being trolled online is upsetting and serious for influencers, causing them to suffer mental health issues and, in some cases, lead them to leave the profession altogether, disappearing from the internet.

Disappearing Acts

There are certainly other reasons why influencers might disappear. Oftentimes, an influencer will simply 'burn out' due to the pressure of needing to produce content on a consistent schedule. Influencers can also experience a 'drying up' creatively, whereby they run out of ideas about what sort of content to make. Sometimes influencers also feel that they no longer want to produce content their followership want to watch. For example, influencers can take to their cameras to bemoan the audiences' desires to see yet another 'what I eat in a day' video, preferring to produce more creative and diverse content. This can upset the followership and cause friction between themselves and their favourite influencer. For example, another well-known UK influencer, *Helen Anderson*, has taken to camera to defend her choices in creating content her way, almost berating her followers for not always watching her more innovative videos. Sometimes it isn't clear why an influencer ceases to post or disappears from the internet, but usually, if a consumer is an ardent fan of a channel, they will have an inkling of why they left or may have witnessed the slow demise of the influencer slowly stopping to hit their regular schedule or becoming less passionate over time. This has happened with *YouTube* sensation Emma Chamberlain, whose recent decline in mental health has been obvious as she becomes disconnected with the world, playing out on her videos. In late 2022, Emma has slowly stopped posting on her channel with 11.9 million subscribers, often leaving gaps of over a month at a time.

The Effects of Online Disappearance

Disappearing influencers are an issue for multiple agents acting within the attention economy – including influencers, consumers, brands and social media platforms. Disappearing influencers, first and foremost, raises issues of wellbeing for the influencer themselves. Influencers are typically self-employed individuals who are working within social media networks and their livelihoods depend entirely on their actions. There is no safety net for influencers who decide to stop posting content. If they do not make new content, any income related to these activities will stop immediately. Also, once an influencer ceases to post, it puts the followership at risk of transferring to another influencer and watching their content instead. The loss of a popular influencer can also have emotional impacts on a devoted fanbase, as they feel the loss of the influencer in their lives akin to losing a close friend or even member of family. The nature of parasocial relationships has been well documented, defined as being one-sided relationships that a consumer makes with a media personality. Parasocial relationships have regularly been discussed in relation to influencer marketing, but they do not fully capture the closeness felt between an influencer and devoted fan. There is a need to engage with a more human under-standing of the influencer-consumer relationship. The word 'para' suggests that the relationship is somewhat odd or parasitic or even unreal – but the opposite is the case. The relationships developed between consumers and influencers are in fact intimate and close, and they engender feelings for both parties, which should be valued. This unique relational quality is perhaps why influencers have been recognised as so valuable by brands.

Being Well Online

Witnessing the public decline of an influencer's wellbeing is common-place. Monami Frost is an example of a disappearing influencer who rose to prominence in the online environment over several years but then she suddenly quit *Instagram* due to the large amount negativity and trolling she was receiving. Monami has experienced significant backlash in her choice for her family to follow a vegan diet and for her baby to be breastfed. In response to this, after reporting a decline in her mental health, she has deleted her entire catalogue of successful *YouTube* videos and, in doing so, has broken up the community that for the most part supported her. Through listening to her follower-ship, she designed and launched two vegan restaurants which sadly fell prey to the harsh conditions of the Covid-19 pandemic and then the cost-of-living crisis. Initially incredibly successful, the expansion of these restaurants was too rapid, and she shut them down in 2022. Unfortunately, the only trace of Monami Frost left on *YouTube* (as of December 2022) is a stream of hate videos created by her trolls.

In sum, disappearing influencers is a common yet relatively undis-cussed online phenomenon. Beginning to unpick some of the nuances of this topic serves to demonstrate how complex navigating the social media realm can be. Predominantly an issue for disappointed consumer fans and influencer wellbeing, disappearing influencers are also an issue for brands who wish to promote their products and services through an influencer's followership. Further, managing the disappearance of an influencer, particularly one with a significant fol-lowing, is an issue for social media platforms. Social media platforms fundamentally rely on a network of discrete individuals and their abil-ity to generate traffic. If this sharply declines through the loss of a successful influencer, so, too, does their power in selling advertising space and collecting consumer data.

Seminar Exercises

Discussion Topics

Can you think of an instance of when you have experienced influencer disappearance?
How did it make you feel? Why do you think it happened?
What do you think could be done to increase influencer wellbeing?
Do you feel that influencers have power within social networks or are they fodder for the attention economy?

Group Exercise

Within a group, take a moment to think about influencers you might enjoy and individually create a list of your favourite influencers. Share them with the group and see if anyone likes the same genre of influencer! Have an open discussion about the pros and cons of influencers and think about what changes would need to be made to turn some of the negative factors into positives, through considering the design of social media platforms.

Internet Resources

CAP – www.asa.org.uk/static/uploaded/3af39c72-76e1-4a59-b2b47e81a034cd1d. pdf

Saccone-Joly's – www.dailymail.co.uk/femail/article-7277269/Vlogger-Father-year-reveals-plagued-online-trolls-call-police-home.html

Key Readings

ABIDIN, S.C., 2017. Influencer extravaganza: Commercial "lifestyle" microcelebrities in Singapore. In *The Routledge Companion to Digital Ethnography*. London: Routledge, pp. 184–194.

Ashman, R., Patterson, A., and Kozinets, R.V., 2021. Netnography and design thinking: development and illustration in the vegan food industry. *European Journal of Marketing*, 55(9), pp. 2491–2514.

Kozinets, R.V., 2019. Consuming technocultures: An extended JCR curation. *Journal of Consumer Research*, 46(3), pp. 620–627.

Patterson, A., and Ashman, R., 2020. Getting up-close and personal with influencers: The promises and pitfalls of intimate netnography. In *Netnography Unlimited*. London: Routledge, pp. 241–248.

References

Abidin, C., 2022. Grief hypejacking: Influencers, # thoughts and prayers, and the commodification of grief on *Instagram. The Information Society*, pp. 1–14.

Aimé, I., Berger-Remy, F., and Laporte, M.E., 2022. The brand, the persona and the algorithm: How datafication is reconfiguring marketing work ☆. *Journal of Business Research*, 145, pp. 814–827.

Ashman, R., Patterson, A., and Brown, S., 2018. 'Don't forget to like, share and subscribe': Digital autopreneurs in a neoliberal world. *Journal of Business Research*, 92, pp. 474–483.

Ashman, R., Patterson, A., and Kozinets, R.V., 2021. Netnography and design thinking: Development and illustration in the vegan food industry. *European Journal of Marketing*, 55(9), pp. 2491–2514.

Audrezet, A., De Kerviler, G., and Moulard, J.G., 2020. Authenticity under threat: When social media influencers need to go beyond self-presentation. *Journal of Business Research*, 117, pp. 557–569.

Auslander, P., 2008. *Liveness: Performance in a Mediatized Culture*. London: Routledge.

Belk, R., 2020. Resurrecting marketing. *AMS Review*, 10(3), pp. 168–171.

Business of Apps, 2022. *Twitch Statistics*, available at: www.businessofapps. com/data/twitch-statistics/

Canavan, B., 2021. Post-postmodern consumer authenticity, shantay you stay or sashay away? A netnography of RuPaul's Drag Race fans. *Marketing Theory*, 21(2), pp. 251–276.

Chaffey, D., and Smith, P.R., 2022. Digital marketing excellence: Planning. In *Optimizing, and Integrating Online Marketing* (5th ed.). London and New York: Routledge Taylor & Francis Group.

Cocker, H., Mardon, R., and Daunt, K.L., 2021. Social media influencers and transgressive celebrity endorsement in consumption community contexts. *European Journal of Marketing*, 55(7), pp. 1841–1872.

Cutolo, D., and Kenney, M., 2021. Platform-dependent entrepreneurs: Power asymmetries, risks, and strategies in the platform economy. *Academy of Management Perspectives*, 35(4), pp. 584–605.

Digital 2022, 2022. *Digital 2022 Global Overview Report*, available at: https://datareportal.com/reports/digital-2022-global-overview-report

Digital Marketing Institute, 2022. *Digital Marketing*, available at: https://digitalmarketinginstitute.com/

Drenten, J., Harrison, R.L., and Pendarvis, N.J., 2022. More gamer, less girl: Gendered boundaries tokenism and the cultural persistence of masculine dominance. *Journal of Consumer Research*, https://doi.org/10.1093/jcr/ucac046

Dyens, O., 2000. Cyberpunk, technoculture, and the post-biological self. *CLCWeb: Comparative Literature and Culture*, 2(1), p. 1.

Gibson, W., 2019. Neuromancer (1984). In *Crime and Media*. London: Routledge, pp. 86–94.

Gillespie, T., 2014. The relevance of algorithms. In T. Gillespie, P.J. Boczkowski, and K.A. Foot (Eds), *Media Technologies*. Cambridge: MIT Press, pp. 167–194.

Grandview Research, 2022. Available at: www.grandviewresearch.com/industry-analysis/fashion-influencer-marketing-market.

Green, L.R., 2002. *Technoculture: From Alphabet to Cybersex*. Crows Nest, Australia: Allen & Unwin.

Hackl, C., Lueth, D., and Di Bartolo, T., 2022. *Navigating the Metaverse: A Guide to Limitless Possibilities in a Web 3.0 World*. Hoboken: John Wiley & Sons.

Jenkins, H., 2009. *Confronting the Challenges of Participatory Culture: Media Education for the 21st Century*. Cambridge: The MIT Press, p. 145.

Kozinets, R.V., 2019. *Netnography: The Essential Guide to Qualitative Social Media Research*. Thousand Oaks: Sage.

Kozinets, R.V., 2023. Understanding technoculture. In R. Belk and R. Llamas (Eds), *The Routledge Guide to Digital Consumption*. London: Routledge, pp. 152–165.

Kozinets, R.V., and Gretzel, U., 2021. Commentary: Artificial intelligence: The marketer's Dilemma. *Journal of Marketing*, 85(1), pp. 156–159. https://doi.org/10.1177/0022242920972933

Kozinets, R.V., Patterson, A., and Ashman, R., 2017. Networks of desire: How technology increases our passion to consume. *Journal of Consumer Research*, 43(5), pp. 659–682. https://doi.org/10.1093/jcr/ucw061

Leaver, T., Highfield, T., and Abidin, C., 2020. *Instagram: Visual Social Media Cultures*. Cambridge: Polity Press.

Leung, F.F., Gu, F.F., and Palmatier, R.W., 2022. Online influencer marketing. *Journal of the Academy of Marketing Science*, 50(2), pp. 226–251.

Mardon, R., Molesworth, M., and Grigore, G., 2018. *YouTube* Beauty Gurus and the emotional labour of tribal entrepreneurship. *Journal of Business Research*, 92, pp. 443–454.

Martin, K., 2019. Ethical implications and accountability of algorithms. *Journal of Business Ethics*, *160*, pp. 835–850.

Oberlo, 2022. *How Much Time Does the Average Person Spend on Social Media?* (2012–2022), available at: www.oberlo.co.uk/statistics/how-much-time-does-the-average-person-spend-on-social-media#:~:text=your%20free%20trial-,average%20time%20spent%20on%20social%20media, also%20the%20highest%20ever%20recorded.

Pandya, A., and Lodha, P., 2021. Social connectedness, excessive screen time during COVID-19 and mental health: A review of current evidence. *Frontiers in Human Dynamics*, *3*.

Paul, C.P., 2018. *The Toxic Meritocracy of Video Games: Why Gaming Culture is the Worst*. Minneapolis: University of Minnesota Press.

Srivastava, M., 2013. Social media and its use by the government. *Journal of Public Administration and Governance*, *3*(2), pp. 161–117.

Stokel-Walker, C., 2021. *TikTok Boom: China's Dynamite App and the Superpower Race for Social Media*. Kingston: Canbury Press.

Thompson, K., and Patterson, A., 2023. A 'thumbs up' and 'thumbs down' for thumb culture; The paradoxical nature of smartphones. In R. Belk and R. Llamas (Eds), *The Routledge Guide to Digital Consumption*. London and New York: Routledge, pp. 255–266.

Tuten, T.L., and Solomon, M.R., 2017. *Social Media Marketing*. Thousand Oaks: Sage.

Twitch Tracker, 2022. *Statistics*, available at: https://twitchtracker.com/statistics

Zhu, J.J., Chang, Y.C., Ku, C.H., Li, S.Y., and Chen, C.J., 2021. Online critical review classification in response strategy and service provider rating: Algorithms from heuristic processing, sentiment analysis to deep learning. *Journal of Business Research*, *129*, pp. 860–877.

4
ETHICAL DEBATES IN MARKETING MANAGEMENT

Introduction

In the context of the current deepening global environmental crisis, marketing is under increased scrutiny in its role as the engine for continuing economic growth at the expense of the world's resources. In addition, recent developments in digital technology, coupled with the opening up of previously closed economies in the transformation of some countries to free market systems, have further exacerbated ethical challenges in marketing. While there are positive signs that marketing leaders are recognising the need to prioritise social and environmental responsibility over profits (Gifford, 2019), in practice, this may not be that easy to achieve. The ethical landscape is a complex one, as Brenkert (2008, p. 4) observes, 'we harbour, as a society, a deeply divided consciousness over marketing'. Many of those living in developed countries readily embrace the array of goods that are the consequence of the efficient operation of markets. At the same time, some feel a sense of unease at the cost of this abundance.

This chapter first considers the definition and scope of research on marketing ethics, identifying where gaps exist. This is followed by a brief discussion of the ethical theories (deontology and teleology) which underpin the two main approaches to ethics in marketing. The first of these 'the normative approach' puts forward a series of recommendations regarding marketing best practice norms or codes which are based on an assessment of fairness for all stakeholders involved. Whereas 'the positive approach' sets out a series of frameworks in order to better understand ethical decision making in marketing in context and is thus more process based and reliant on individual circumstances rather than promoting a set of universal norms or codes for behaviour. Although conceived in the 1980s and 1990s, recent research finds that these approaches still act as a basis on which ethical marketing decisions are made today (Eagle et al., 2021). Having set out the key building blocks of ethics in marketing, the chapter then explores how ethics plays out in practice in the ethical brand and the moralized brandscape. In closing, the chapter considers the rise of Fairtrade, arguing that it might be seen as one of the first prominent examples of an ethical brand.

DOI: 10.4324/9781003201151-4

Marketing Ethics: A Definition and Scope

Surprisingly, few authors offer an actual definition of marketing ethics. Drawing from Aristotelian moral philosophy for inspiration, Gaski observes that marketing ethics could be considered as 'standards of conduct and moral judgement applied to marketing practice' (1999, p. 316). Murphy (2017) opens this out to include both individuals and organisations and identifies the role of integrity and fairness in ethical marketing practice:

> Ethical marketing refers to practices that emphasize transparent, trustworthy, and responsible personal and/or organizational marketing policies and actions that exhibit integrity as well as fairness to consumers and other stakeholders.
>
> (Murphy, 2017, p. 85)

However, ethical standards typically vary from one institutional environment to the next and from one culture to the next, which makes a universal application of a set of ethical marketing codes problematic. Complications also emerge from differing perspectives on ethics. In this respect, Laczniak et al. (1995) found that the views of American consumers and chief executive officers differed widely, with consumers being far more pessimistic than CEOs about the ethical climate of businesses.

Defining the scope of marketing ethics is also difficult, as the literature on marketing ethics is both complex and extensive. At several intervals over the past 30 years, scholars have made attempts to summarise and review this body of work. Murphy and Laczniak (1981) locate initial debate on marketing ethics in the 1930s, although they observe that more significant developments occurred in the 1960s (i.e. Bartels, 1967). This latter work was largely concerned with highlighting a general, global approach to marketing ethics. It was not until the 1970s that work began to focus on specific issues, such as marketing research, consumer issues, managerial issues and marketing education issues. In a review of studies, Nill and Schibrowsky (2007) identify a series of topics that have been covered in published work on marketing ethics (see Table 4.1). Note that the studies may typically encompass more than one of these categories.

Since Nill and Schibrowsky's audit in 2007, we have seen a further increase in interest in marketing ethics. Eagle et al. (2021) observe that in the period from 2000–2019, 11,300 journal articles were published on the topic, compared to 1,377 in the period from 1980–1999. While the topics in Table 1.1 remain salient, research has intensified more recently in the areas of resource depletion and sustainability (Eagle and Dahl, 2015) and issues of data privacy and security brought about by the rise of digital marketing and the use of Big Data. One particular concern is the access that children and young people have to the digital world, in particular, the rise of new advertising formats designed to persuade children and young people (Daems et al., 2019).

Table 4.1 Topical Areas of Marketing Ethics

	Issues related to:
Functional areas	Product Price Placement Promotion
Sub-disciplines of marketing	Sales Consumers/consumption International marketing Marketing ethics education Marketing research Social marketing Internet marketing Law and ethics
Specific ethics related topics	Ethics and society Ethical decision-making models Ethical responsibility towards marketers' stakeholders Ethical values Norm generation and definition Marketing ethics implementation Relationship between ethics and religion Discrimination and harassment Green marketing Vulnerable consumers

Source: Nill and Schibrowsky, 2007, p. 258

Commentators also make suggestions for where we could undertake more research into marketing ethics. To this end, Laczinak and Murphy (2019) observe that there is more to be done to understand the base of pyramid issues (i.e. the potential for marketing to address poverty and inequality with a focus on less affluent emerging economies). They also make a call to return to corporate social responsibility with a long-term view and, in a global economy, return to issues of power and responsibility in marketing channels to address the exploitation of other stakeholders in the production chain to include those working in the mines, fields and factories (Laczinak and Murphy, 2019, p. 406).

What Role for Marketing Ethics?

The role marketing ethics ought to play, both in relation to the individual and the organisation, has been a key topic for debate. Authors have questioned the extent to which marketing ethics might offer guidelines to marketers (Gaski, 1999, 2015; Smith, 2001). They have also been concerned with how theories of marketing ethics might translate into application (Robin and Reidenbach, 1987, 1993; Smith, 1995; Thompson, 1995). In addressing these issues, studies have been undertaken from two key perspectives: the normative approach, which aims to prescribe ethical standards and offer guidelines regarding marketing practice; and the positive approach, which aims to describe and understand ethical practices through empirical work. Before exploring these perspectives, however, it is useful to summarise their underpinning philosophies, these being primarily deontological and teleological theories.

Deontological Theories

Deontological theories focus on the behaviours of the individual, specifically the principles used to arrive at the ethical decision. Murphy and Laczniak (1981, p. 252) give the example of Kant's categorical imperative as a deontological theory 'that persons should act in such a way that their maxim for action could be a universal law'. In this perspective, the focus is on the behaviour itself and actions are judged by their inherent wrongness or rightness. As Hunt and Vitell observe, 'For deontologists the conundrum has been to determine the "best" set of rules to live by' (1986, p. 6). The principles for these rules may come from a range of sources, such as the family, religion, politics and so on.

Teleological Theories

In contrast, teleologists place emphasis on perceived outcomes rather than behaviours. They propose that individuals should make judgements based on an evaluation of the likely consequences of their actions. Teleological theories differ, however, on the issue of whose good one ought to promote:

- *Ethical egoism* suggests that individuals should act in their own interests (i.e. choose an act that results in the most favourable consequences for the individual).
- *Utilitarianism* strives to produce the greatest good for the greatest number of people. Here, an act should be judged on an evaluation of the balance of good consequences over bad consequences it provides for all individuals (Hunt and Vitell, 1986, pp. 6–7).

Although this discussion of the two sets of theories is a simplification, it is important to understand their principles, as they provide the basis for most normative work, and some positive work, on marketing ethics. This work is explored next.

A Normative Role for Marketing Ethics

Authors working from a normative perspective have been concerned to provide a series of recommendations regarding marketing practice (Laczniak, 1983; Laczniak and Murphy, 1985, 1993, 2006; Smith and Quelch, 1993; Chonko, 1995, Murphy et al., 2005). These recommendations are concerned with 'what marketing organizations or individuals ought to do or what kinds of marketing systems a society ought to have' (Hunt, 1976, p. 20). Laczniak and Murphy, in describing normative marketing ethics, observe that 'exchange, because it is *social*, must have its outcomes evaluated in terms of fairness or rightness on all marketplace parties' (2006, p. 154, emphasis in original). In examining the role of ethics in marketing management, Smith (1993) observes that the marketing manager often has little direct authority and has to rely on the cooperation of other functions within the organisation. This means that marketing managers are typically exposed to a range of competing pressures. Chonko (1995) explores how marketing professionals might deal with unethical behaviour. In his evaluation, it seems that whistle blowing (or threatening to blow the whistle) and negotiation are potentially the most advantageous courses of action. He also usefully identifies some reasons why professionals sometimes engage in unethical behaviour. The first issue is diffusion of responsibility, where elaborate organisational structures mean that responsibility is so diffused that accountability is difficult to pinpoint. A second issue is rationalization, through which wrong decisions can often easily be explained away. Chonko observes that four commonly held beliefs about behaviour might facilitate this:

- A belief that the behaviour is within reasonable ethical and legal limits – that is, the behaviour is *not really* immoral or illegal.
- A belief that the behaviour is in the best interests of the individual, the organisation or both – the individual would somehow be *expected* to undertake the behaviour.
- A belief that the behaviour is *safe* because it will never be found out or published, the classic crime-and-punishment issue of discovery.
- A belief that because the behaviour helps the organisation, the organisation will *condone* it and even protect the individual who engages in the behaviour (Gellerman, 1986, cited in Chonko, 1995, p. 114)

A key issue is that managers are not aware that marketing ethics can be learned. Instead, they seem to think that ethics are merely a product of their upbringing, religious beliefs and social circle. To this end, theorists (particularly normative theorists) are at pains to develop marketing ethics education at business-school level. Laczniak and Murphy observe the following:

> The role of relativism and the attitude that all marketing practices are flexible depending on circumstance and personal opinion – views often expressed by business students – seem overstated given the articulated norms and values of marketing professionals, as well as specific codes developed through the consensus of peer practitioners.
>
> (2006, p. 171)

They argue further that these codes ought to be taught in business schools, although students should be taught to improve the ethical cultures of their organisations rather than merely to preach ethics (2006, p. 172). To try and bridge the gap between seemingly abstract codes of ethics and the everyday decisions that marketing managers face, Laczniak and Murphy have developed a set of perspectives to guide marketing activity. The seven basic perspectives (BP) are as listed in the next section:

- BP1: Ethical marketing puts people first.
- BP2: Ethical marketers must achieve a behavioural standard in excess of the law.
- BP3: Marketers are responsible for whatever they intend as a means or ends as a marketing action.
- BP4: Marketing organisations should cultivate better (i.e. higher) moral imagination in their managers and employees.
- BP5: Marketers should articulate and embrace a core set of ethical principles.
- BP6: Adoption of a stakeholder orientation is essential to ethical marketing decisions.
- BP7: Marketing organisations ought to delineate an ethical decision-making protocol. (Laczniak and Murphy, 2006, p. 157)

Laczniak and Murphy observe that taken in isolation, these perspectives are difficult to apply. For example, in the societal perspective in BP1, whose interests ought marketers to put first? They suggest that this can be addressed by referring to BP6, the adoption of a stakeholder orientation. They highlight a series of further relationships between the perspectives and suggest that while each basic perspective is a useful guideline in itself, they work together to form a holistic approach to marketing management. Overall, in taking a normative approach to marketing ethics, Murphy et al. (2005, p. 47) chart a middle path between ethical theory, individual judgement and societal standards:

> In the final analysis, ethics still requires considerable prudential judgement that comes from the intuition of the marketing manager (hopefully, grounded in virtue ethics), but it is tempered by a knowledge of ethical theory as well as corporate, industry and societal standards.

Clearly, the normative approach is not without its challenges. As Gaski (2015) observes, the multiplicity of perspectives it embraces can lead to conflict between norms and ambiguity in offering guidance.

A Positive Role for Marketing Ethics

While normative approaches to marketing ethics have traditionally held sway, positive approaches to marketing ethics have recently become increasingly popular. Over the years, authors have developed a series of frameworks in order to better understand ethical decision making in marketing (Ferrell and Gresham, 1985; Hunt and Vitell,

1986; Thompson, 1995). The most widely used of these frameworks has undoubtedly been Hunt and Vitell's (1986, 2006, see also Vitell and Hunt, 2015) *general theory of marketing ethics*. The model attempts to 'explain the decision making process for problem situations having ethical content' (1986, p. 5). Since publication, the framework has been applied in a range of contexts, with most authors finding significant support for the model (Mayo and Marks, 1990; Hunt and Vasquez-Parraga, 1993; Mengue, 1998; Vitell et al., 2001).

In their *general theory of marketing ethics*, Hunt and Vitell recognise that when making decisions, marketers draw on both teleological and deontological evaluations and, thus, they build both of these elements into their model (see Figure 4.1). They observe that the cultural, industrial and organisational environments, as well as past personal experiences, impact upon the individual's perception of the ethical problem. These factors also impact on the perceived alternatives available to them. They suggest that both a deontological and teleological evaluation of these alternatives takes place. In the deontological evaluation, they posit that the individual evaluates alternatives against a set of norms, including personal values and beliefs. They also observe that these norms include issue-specific beliefs, such as 'deceptive advertising, product safety, sales "kickbacks," confidentiality of data, respondent anonymity and interviewer dishonesty' (1986, p. 9). In the teleological evaluation, four constructs are considered. These include '(1) the perceived consequences of each alternative for various stakeholder groups, (2) the probability that each consequence will occur to each stakeholder group, (3) the desirability or undesirability of each consequence, and (4) the importance of each stakeholder group' (1986, p. 9). They also note that individuals will differ in the stakeholder groups they identify and the relative importance of these.

Figure 4.1 General theory of marketing ethics (Hunt and Vitell, 1986, p. 8)

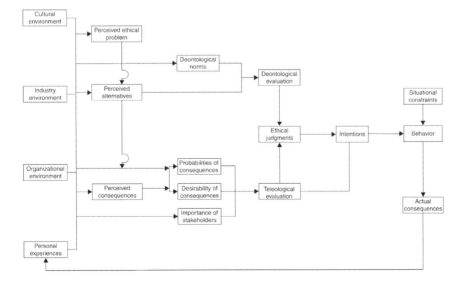

The key part of the model is the combination of these two sets of evaluations. The model posits that 'an individual's ethical judgement (for example, the belief that a particular alternative is the most ethical alternative) is a function of the individual's deontological evaluation (i.e. applying norms of behaviour to each of the alternatives) and the individual's teleological evaluation (i.e. evaluating the sum total of goodness versus badness likely to be produced by each alternative)' (1986, p. 9). Hunt and Vitell then introduce an intentions construct, 'the likelihood that any particular alternative will be chosen' (1986, p. 9), which intervenes between ethical judgment and actual behaviour. They argue that intentions may often differ from ethical judgements due to the influence of teleological evaluations. For example, an individual may reach a conclusion regarding the most ethical course of action but chooses another course due to preferred consequences either to themselves or perhaps to the organisation. In these cases, the individual may well feel guilt depending on their individual ethical norms and beliefs. The action taken is also dependent on situational constraints, such as opportunities, and these may also result in behaviours that do not match intentions and ethical judgements. Hunt and Vitell also include a learning construct, the 'actual consequences' of the chosen alternative. These actual consequences feed back into personal experiences and, therefore, highlight the possibility that individuals may, to an extent, become conditioned by their organisational context (i.e. through the operation of punishments and rewards). It is important to note that the cultural, industrial and organisational environments and past personal experiences, as well as affecting the perceived ethical problem and alternatives available, also affect deontological norms, perceived consequences, probability of consequences, desirability of consequences and importance of stakeholders. Thus, the model takes account of situational and contextual factors both in the formulation of the problem and the resulting action or behaviour. In fact, more recently, Vitell and Hunt (2015) argue that the model needn't be confined to marketing managers. If we exclude the industrial and organizational environments, the model may apply to understand the ethics of consumer behaviour more generally.

Thompson (1995) introduces a further model of marketing ethics, arguing that 'the current models of marketing ethics do not sufficiently address the multitude of contextual influences that, from a contextualist perspective, are intrinsic to ethical reasoning' (1995, p. 177). While there is not space here to adequately describe Thompson's contextualist model, an overview of its key components is useful in understanding some critiques of earlier perspectives on marketing ethics. In particular, Thompson highlights the 'multiplicity of cultural meaning and value systems' and the fact that the marketing agent is 'culturally situated'. He posits that culturally shared beliefs influence marketing managers' identification of ethical issues, interpretations of the relevant community of stakeholders and evaluations of marketing actions (Thompson, 1995, pp. 183–185). More recently, Ferrell et al. (2015) have provided an overview of a wide range of ethical decision-making models. They develop a synthesized model (2015, p. 57) which suggests that perceptions of ethical issues, individual factors and organizational culture and compliance all impinge on ethical decision making and subsequent ethical behaviour.

Marketing Ethics in Practice: The Ethical Brand

Nowadays, many brands differentiate their identity through focusing on ethical values and social responsibility issues: Ben & Jerry's ice cream, Innocent Smoothies, Green & Black's organic chocolate, Benetton, Dove beauty products and Ecover to name but a few of the best known ones. The ethical brand espouses values such as equality, justice, freedom and environmental protection. For example, Ben & Jerry's values revolve around natural ingredients, employee respect and quality of life. The company also supports a range of causes, including climate justice, Fairtrade and marriage equality. Innocent Smoothies puts sustainable nutrition as its core aim, while Green & Black's are dedicated to ethical sourcing and sustainable cocoa production. Benetton is well known for its social, environmental and economic responsibility and taking a stance to campaign for disadvantaged groups. Dove campaigns against idealised body images for women. Ecover makes cleaning products that replace chemicals with plant- and mineral-based ingredients. These are just a few of the best-known ethical brand names, but there are many others with numbers continuing to proliferate.

One of the oldest and best-loved ethical brands in the UK is without doubt The Body Shop. No high street or shopping centre is complete without one. Founded by the famous entrepreneur and human rights activist, Anita Roddick, The Body Shop's first store opened in 1976. By 1982, shops were opening at the rate of two per month, eventually growing to 2,500 franchises in 61 countries. The brand's ethical reputation was initially established around selling environmentally friendly cosmetics and body-care products in recyclable containers. In 1986, The Body Shop allied itself to Greenpeace's Save the Whales campaign, and thereafter, the brand became associated with social activism. Roddick supported many varied causes, championing environmental issues, challenging traditional beauty ideals and fair trading with the Third World. Her quotes are legendary and include the following: 'There are 3 billion women in the world who don't look like supermodels and only 8 that do'; and 'If you think you're too small to make a difference, you've never been to bed with a mosquito'. Indeed, she was an early pioneer of what is now thought of as corporate social responsibility and continued to be highly critical of standard corporate practices throughout her lifetime. (She died in 2007.) Amid huge controversy, The Body Shop was sold in 2006 to French corporation L'Oreal for £652.3 million. The chain's green credentials were not seen as a good match with those of L'Oreal, often accused of perpetuating false beauty ideals and animal testing (although this latter accusation is strongly denied by L'Oreal). Roddick defended her decision to sell, revealing that she saw herself as a 'Trojan Horse' that was now positioned to influence the cosmetics giant from within. Sadly, she died before she could achieve much in this respect.

One key concern for practices of ethical branding is green-washing, a term given to those companies who just make a token gesture to green concerns in order to boost their image and find another way to attract consumers (Oates, 2021). Superficial green claims by many brands are frequently put to the test and found wanting by the media in the form of newspaper reports, television exposés and websites. Greenpeace has its own dedicated website (www.stopgreenwash. org) where it regularly takes to task the green claims made by big brand names, such as American Airlines and Shell. Green-washing comes in several forms. *Green Spinning* is a PR exercise to manage corporate reputations, usually undertaken in industry sectors that are seen as environmentally polluting, such as oil, chemicals and transport. *Green Selling* occurs when a company promotes an existing product feature as green to climb on the environmental bandwagon and without any intentional development. Finally, *Green Harvesting* refers to whenever a company saves money by cutting back on packaging, energy costs or some other 'green' aspect without passing the savings to consumers. It has now become customary in many hotels, for instance, to ask customers to think about whether they need clean towels each day and to encourage reuse in order to save energy costs. Some hotels offer guests a reward system for compliance but many do not.

Marketing Ethics in Practice: The Moralised Brandscape

The concept of a brandscape refers to the range of brands available in the market, or a particular market segment, when the brands are considered collectively as a cultural phenomenon (Sherry, 1987). The contemporary brandscape increasingly incorporates political and social issues into a multitude of values displayed therein. In this way, the market becomes the main domain for social action. Consumers can celebrate some brands and critique others, using their likes and dislikes to achieve social and political ends. As the brandscape becomes steadily more infused with ideological and ethical values, it becomes what Salzer-Mörling and Strannegård (2007) refer to as the 'moralised brandscape', 'a cultural landscape imbued with images and signs where focus increasingly is put on the expressive side of the brand and where moral statements seem to be an issue in the discourse of both consumers and producers'.

Hence, many brands not previously associated with ethical or green values are espousing moral causes and blurring the boundaries of what is, and what is not, an ethical brand. Coca-Cola's 'Open Happiness' campaign, running from 2009, is a prime example of this. As part of their global marketing message, in 2013, Coke launched their 'Coca-Cola Small World Machine – Bringing India and Pakistan Together' campaign. This saw Coke taking the role of global peacemaker by setting up vending machines in India and Pakistan, two countries with a long history of animosity and violence towards each other. Fitted with high-tech cameras, the vending machines permit consumers to see their counterparts in the neighbouring country. They can then join 'virtual' hands and exchange messages if they wish. Coke's advertising claims that 'A moment of happiness has the power to bring the world closer together'. Although many sceptics argue that this dispensing of happiness around the world is only dispensing money into Coke's coffers, it has proved highly popular with consumers. The success of the campaign earned Coke 20 awards at the 2013 Cannes Lions International Festival of Creativity, including the much-coveted Creative Marketer of the Year Award.

New offerings that link to a moral agenda in unexpected ways are popping up more and more on the contemporary brandscape. Dans le Noir is a restaurant chain that offers a unique dining experience. Diners eat in the dark without being able to see what they are eating or where they are. It was established by the Ethik Investment Group which funds ventures that are socially or environmentally responsible. In the case of Dans le Noir, the restaurant employs a large number of blind staff. Inspired by the creation of diners by blind people for sighted people in the nineteenth century, in 2004, the group created the first Dans le Noir restaurant in Paris. After this proved a successful formula, other restaurants were opened across the globe, at the time of writing there are 13 restaurants in France, UK, Belgium, Luxembourg, Switzerland, Spain, Russia, New Zealand and Egypt. The logo is Dans le Noir? with a question mark and, thus, intended to be ambiguous about who exactly is 'in the dark'. This questioning theme is continued through the website where the question posed alerts potential customers to the nature of the experience available: 'What if sight, the dominant sense, suddenly disappeared for a few hours, would that awaken an unbelievable world of sense, touch, taste and smells?' Research conducted into the experience has shown that customers experience a role reversal when they enter the darkness: it is they who become disabled, whereas the blind staff move with ease and confidence in the black environment (Maclaran et al., 2013).

Adding to the blurring boundaries referred to previously is the rise in cause-related marketing (CRM) which is evident all around us. CRM is whenever a partnership is established between a corporation and a non-profit organisation. By linking to charities or causes, marketers give consumers a more meaningful reason to purchase their products or services. American Express is credited with first using the phrase in 1983 to describe its campaign which donated one cent to the Statue of Liberty every time a customer used their card. Highly successful as a promotional tool, this sponsorship gained American Express 45% new customers and card usage increased by 28%. The company has continued to support historic preservation initiatives and uses these to emphasise its involvement in the community. Since 1990, CRM has gone from a $120 million industry to a $1.62 billion industry in 2010. One survey reported that as many as 89% of respondents said they would switch brands to support a cause if price and quality were the same.

Tesco's 'Free Computers for Schools' is a more recent well-known cause-related partnership enabling parents and friends to collect vouchers to help their local school have new equipment. Pampers and its UNICEF partnership is another high-profile partnership, whereby the manufacturer, Procter & Gamble, donates 4p for every pack of Pampers bought, money that has already given more than 300 million vaccines to children in developing countries. Cadbury's donates a percentage of proceeds from its Wishes chocolates to children's charity Make-A-Wish Foundation. Innocent Smoothies has had a partnership with Age UK for more than eight years. Age UK volunteers knit imaginative hats for Innocent bottles which often feature in promotional campaigns. Every November, Innocent contributes 25p to Age UK for every bottle with a hat.

CRM is seen as a win-win strategy for both profit and non-profit organisations, with the business gaining a halo effect and the cause benefitting from both the donations and, in many cases, the higher profile that big corporation sponsorship can drive. It is not without criticism, however, and charities are warned to be careful how easily they give their name to a cause. Often, it is not clear to the consumer how much the charity will receive, and often, percentages donated are hard to establish (i.e. often couched as percentages of overall profits). In addition, consumers require to believe that a company's good intentions are authentic and not just another instance of green-washing. By putting its head above the parapet in this way, a company may leave itself open to criticism if it is found to be wanting in terms of other ethical behaviours. The power of the internet – particularly social media – to expose firms that do not act in accordance with their stated values is enormous.

Case Study: The Rise of Fairtrade as an Ethical Brand

One of the most instantly recognisable ethical brands around today is Fairtrade. However, Fairtrade did not set out originally to be a brand nor is it comprised of just one organisation. The Fairtrade Movement originated after World War II as a charity sponsored by religious organisations. Its name comes from the fair terms of trade the company ensures for farmers and workers in developing countries. Initially, the ethical ethos of Fairtrade harked back to pre-capitalist notions of a moral economy that linked to eighteenth-century initiatives, focusing on producer rights and boycotting slave goods. The range of products was based mainly around handicrafts and sold through charity shops which meant the brand had a rather dowdy, marginalised image. From the 1990s onwards, however, the movement consciously strove to become more market-orientated, establishing itself more clearly as a brand through the adoption of the Fairtrade Certification Mark and aiming to appeal to mainstream consumer markets.

As a result of this re-positioning strategy, Fairtrade has had a dramatic growth over the last two decades and now has over 4,500 products across a range of categories from flowers to coffee. During this time, it has moved from the margins in the UK at least (Oxfam charity shops) to mainstream retailing (Tesco's supermarkets). Although a core aim is still to re-structure capitalist relations of production, replacing abstract marketing channels with social connections, the idea is to do this from inside rather than outside the market. Fairtrade's success is due in part to its 'branding activity' in using a wider variety of marketing channels. There are still the dedicated Fairtrade brands like Café Direct and Day Chocolate, but the Fairtrade certification system has given the brand more flexibility. The Fairtrade label is now a common sight in well-known supermarket chains, like Sainsbury's, Marks & Spencer and Tesco, who have all adapted some of their own-brand products to meet Fairtrade standards. Major manufacturers like Procter & Gamble, Kraft and Nestlé all now include Fairtrade brands in their product portfolios. In 2010, Nestlé's Kit Kat received Fairtrade certification, a move that resulted in Nestlé being accredited with bringing a better standard of living to Ivory Coast farmers and enabling them to invest in longer-term community-development projects. Fairtrade's expansion has given the brand much higher visibility, and it is now instantly recognisable as the leading brand to espouse trading practices based on economic justice and sustainable development. Of course, there is also criticism and Fairtrade has been accused of helping companies like Nestlé acquire a 'cleaner' image to overcome past tainting from unethical behaviours. Nestlé has long struggled to overcome its negative image from the 1970s, when multinational milk companies were judged to be causing infant illness and death in the Third World by promoting bottle feeding and discouraging breast feeding.

Fairtrade is not just about decent prices and working conditions. One of its central aims is to ensure local sustainability on the basis that 'trade rather than aid' is a better long-term solution to helping developing countries. Fairtrade requirements ensure that small farmers not only obtain a fair price for their produce but also receive a social premium to invest in social, economic or environmental improvements. Thus, by asserting a strict certification system over supply chains to authenticate its moral claims, Fairtrade has managed to translate values of social, economic and environment justice into standards that consumers feel they can trust. The restructuring of interactions right along Fairtrade's supply chains has ensured that economic exchange is embedded in social relations and placed the 'politics of re-connection' (Dolan, 2010, p. 37) at the heart of its value creation. Affluent consumers in industrialised countries are linked to poor producers in developing economies, and hence, consumers feel they are making a more meaningful contribution towards a just society through what they consume. Consumers buy into 'a vision of global social justice' (Dolan, p. 42), a vision that aligns with their own moral identity.

Dolan also problematizes this consumer vision. Marketing strategies are designed to ensure the lives of Third World producers become less remote. Typically, marketers personalise promotional campaigns with depictions of Fairtrade producers who give testimonials relating how Fairtrade has transformed their lives. These provide a type of

myth for middle-class consumers to incorporate into their own identity projects, a myth that they are helping to save the world. Following
Holt (2004), this may resolve certain tensions they are experiencing –
the guilt of contemporary materialism possibly – but may actually
mean the same consumers are less likely to act in other respects to
fight for global justice through major structural changes like supporting higher taxes for more aid to the Third World. In their study
of Oatly, an oat-based milk alternative product, Ledin and Machin
(2020) similarly underline the potential for ethical brands to divert
attention from tangible political activism. In analysing a range of marketing communications channels, including packaging, a poster campaign and a film/social media campaign, they find that Oatly makes
skillful use of this range of channels to communicate a series of intersecting messages which, rather than directly stating ethical values,
nonetheless lead the consumer to believe that their act of purchasing
the product is a political statement. In their words, they reveal:

> how such [ethical] brands do not actually state details of the
> socio-political issue alongside which they align (its causes, pro-
> cess, solutions) yet successfully communicate a compelling sense
> that buying the product is a form of social activism in a way which
> cleverly implicates consumers to internalize its values and give
> them a powerful sense of being part of a political moral order.
>
> (Ledin and Machin, 2020, p. 1)

The problem with this, again, is that ethical (and Fairtrade) brands
have the potential to replace social activism with a form of easy 'ethical shopping'.

Seminar Exercises

Discussion Topics

1 Discuss the pros and cons of taking a deontological approach versus a teleological approach to decisions surrounding marketing
ethics.
2 Using examples, discuss the ethical issues related to green-washing. Explore the implications for consumers, brands and society as
a whole.
3 Referring to Figure 4.1, discuss how cultural, industrial and organizational environments, as well as past personal experiences, might
impact upon an individual's perception of an ethical problem.
4 Argue for and against the following statement: 'ethical brands are
a good thing'.

Group Exercises

1 Using one of the examples listed, prepare a presentation summa-
rising the key ethical debates in the case concerned. Use real-life
examples from marketing magazines, newspaper reports and
marketing websites to illustrate your discussion.

- The promotion and sale of unhealthy or harmful products.
- The targeting of vulnerable segments in advertising campaigns.
- The invasion of consumer privacy in social networking sites.

2 Choose a brand that you believe is part of the 'moralised brand-scape' and analyse how it positions itself using ethical values:

- Compare and contrast two key competitors' strategies.
- Study what consumers are saying about the brand on the web (i.e. using product reviews or web forums) and analyse their main perceptions of the brand.
- What makes the brand's claims authentic, and are there any dangers of 'green-washing' accusations?

3 Consider the following scenario:

Sarah Jones is the marketing manager of a large building company. She is designing an advertisement for a new housing development her company is about to start building. The development is located in a low area which has flooded in the past. The company has recently done some work to reduce the danger of flooding in the future. The fact is that if a flood occurs, the homes are still likely to be flooded with up to five feet of water.
Identify the alternatives available to the marketing manager.
For each of these alternatives:

- Identify the stakeholders that would be affected.
- Identify the probable consequences of the decision for each stakeholder group.
- Identify the desirability of these consequences for each stakeholder group.

Given the previous considerations, identify which alternative you would choose and why.

(scenario adapted from Lund, 2000, p. 334)

Internet Resources

Advertising Standards Authority, www.asa.org.uk/
American Marketing Association. (2020), *American Marketing Association Code of Ethics: Ethical Norms and Values for Marketers*, https://myama.my.site.com/s/article/AMA-Code-of-Conduct
The Academy of Marketing – 'Marketing and Ethics Special Interest Group', https://academyofmarketing.online/ethics-marketing-sig/
The Market Research Society's Code of Conduct, www.mrs.org.uk/standards/code_of_conduct/
The Society for Business ethics, http://sbeonline.org/

Key Readings

Eagle, L., Dahl, S., Pelsmacker, P., and Taylor, C. (2021), Introduction to marketing ethics. In L. Eagle S. Dahl and P. Pelsmacker (Eds), *Introduction to Marketing Ethics*, Thousand Oaks: SAGE Publications Ltd, pp. 3–19.

Laczniak, G.R., and Murphy, P.E. (2019), The role of normative marketing ethics. *Journal of Business Research*, *95*, 401–407.

Vitell, S.J., and Hunt, S.D. (2015), The general theory of marketing ethics: The consumer ethics and intentions issues. In A. Nill (Ed), *Handbook on Ethics and Marketing*, Glos: Edward Elgar Publishing, pp. 15–37.

References

Bartels, R. (1967), A framework for ethics in marketing. *Journal of Marketing*, 20–26.

Brenkert, G. (2008), *Marketing Ethics*, Oxford: Blackwell.

Chonko, L. (1995), *Ethical Decision Making in Marketing*, Thousand Oaks: Sage.

Daems, K., De Pelsmacker, P., and Moons, I. (2019), Advertisers' perceptions regarding the ethical appropriateness of new advertising formats aimed at minors. *Journal of Marketing Communications*, *25*(4), 438–456.

Dolan, C.S. (2010), Virtual moralities: The mainstreaming of Fairtrade in Kenyan tea fields. *Geoforum*, *41*(1), 33–43.

Eagle, L., and Dahl, S. (2015), *Marketing Ethics & Society*, London: Sage.

Eagle, L., Dahl, S., Pelsmacker, P., and Taylor, C. (2021), Introduction to marketing ethics. In L. Eagle S. Dahl and P. Pelsmacker (Eds), *Introduction to Marketing Ethics*, Thousand Oaks: SAGE Publications Ltd, pp. 3–19.

Ferrell, O.C., Ferrell, L., and Sawayda, J. (2015), A review of ethical decision-making models in marketing. In A. Nill (Ed), *Handbook on Ethics and Marketing*, Glos: Edward Elgar Publishing, pp. 38–60.

Ferrell, O.C., and Gresham, L.G. (1985), A contingency framework for understanding ethical decision making in marketing. *Journal of Marketing*, *49*, 87–96.

Gaski, J. (1999), Does marketing ethics really have anything to say? A critical inventory of the literature. *Journal of Business Ethics*, *18*(3), 315–334.

Gaski, J. (2015), The trouble with marketing ethics . . . In A. Nill (Ed), *Handbook on Ethics and Marketing*, Glos: Edward Elgar Publishing, pp. 111–124.

Gellerman, S.W. (1986), Why "good" managers make bad ethical choices. *Harvard Business Review*, 85–90.

Gifford, C. (2019), Top CEOs say social responsibility should be prioritised over profits. *European CEO*, August 20. www.europeanceo.com/finance/top-ceos-say-social-responsibility-should-be-prioritised-over-profits/

Hunt, S.B. (1976), The nature and scope of marketing. *Journal of Marketing*, *40*, 17–28.

Hunt, S.B., and Vitell, S.J. (1986), A general theory of marketing ethics. *Journal of Macromarketing*, *6*(5), 5–16.

Hunt, S.B., and Vitell, S.J. (2006), The general theory of marketing ethics: A revision and three questions. *Journal of Macromarketing*, *12*(26), 143–153.

Hunt, S.D., and Vasquez-Parraga, A. (1993), Organizational consequences, marketing ethics and salesforce supervision. *Journal of Marketing Research*, *30*, 78–90.

Laczniak, G.R. (1983), Framework for analyzing marketing ethics. *Journal of Macromarketing*, *6*(3), 7–18.

Laczniak, G.R., Berkowitz, M., Brooker, R., and Hale, J. (1995), The ethics of business: Improving or deteriorating? *Business Horizons*, *38*(1), 39–47.

Laczniak, G.R., and Murphy, P.E. (1985), *Marketing Ethics: Guidelines for Managers*, Lexington, MA: Lexington Books

Laczniak, G.R., and Murphy, P.E. (1993), *Ethical Marketing Decisions: The Higher Road*, Toronto: Allyn and Bacon

Laczniak, G.R., and Murphy, P.E. (2006), Normative perspectives for ethical and socially responsible marketing. *Journal of Macromarketing*, 12(26), 154–177.

Laczniak, G.R., and Murphy, P.E. (2019), The role of normative marketing ethics. *Journal of Business Research*, 95, 401–407.

Ledin, P., and Machin, D. (2020), Replacing actual political activism with ethical shopping: The case of Oatly. *Discourse, Context & Media*, 34, 100344.

Lund, D.B. (2000), An empirical examination of marketing professionals' ethical behaviour in differing situations. *Journal of Business Ethics*, 24, 331–342.

Maclaran, P., Tissiers-Desbordes, E., and Otnes, C. (2013), Transformation and embodied ritual in a themed servicescape setting. In G. Cornelissen, E. Reutskaja & A. Valenzuela (Eds), European Advances in Consumer Research Volume 10, Duluth, MN: Association for Consumer Research, pp. 182–183.

Mayo, M., and Marks, L. (1990), An empirical investigation of a general theory of marketing ethics. *Journal of the Academy of Marketing Science*, 18(2), 163–171.

Mengue, B. (1998), Organizational consequences, marketing ethics and salesforce supervision: Further empirical evidence. *Journal of Business Ethics*, 17(4), 333–352.

Murphy, P.E. (2017), Research in marketing ethics: Continuing and emerging themes. *Recherche et Applications en Marketing (English Edition)*, 32(3), 84–89.

Murphy, P.E., and Laczniak, G.R. (1981), Marketing ethics: A review with implications for managers, educators and researchers. In *Review of Marketing*, Chicago: American Marketing Association, pp. 251–266.

Murphy, P.E., Lacinak, G.R., Bowie, N., and Klein, T. (2005), *Ethical Marketing*, Upper Saddle River: Pearson Prentice Hall.

Nill, A., and Schibrowsky, J.A. (2007), Research on marketing ethics: A systematic review of the literature. *Journal of Macromarketing*, 27, 256–273.

Oates, C. (2021), Sustainability marketing: Products, fairtrade, and greenwashing. In L. Eagle S. Dahl and P. Pelsmacker (Eds), *Introduction to Marketing Ethics*, Thousand Oaks: SAGE Publications Ltd, pp. 226–237.

Robin, D.P., and Reidenbach, E. (1987), Social responsibility, ethics and marketing strategy: Closing the gap between concept and application. *Journal of Marketing*, 51, 44–58.

Robin, D.P., and Reidenbach, E. (1993), Searching for a place to stand: Toward a workable ethical philosophy for marketing. *Journal of Public Policy and Marketing*, 12(1), 97–105.

Salzer-Mörling, M., and Strannegård, L. (2007), Ain't misbehavin' – Consumption in a moralized brandscape. *Marketing Theory*, 7(4), 407–425.

Sherry, J.F. (1987), Advertising as a cultural system. In *Marketing and Semiotics: New Directions in the Study of Signs for Sale*, Berlin: De Gruyter Mouton, pp. 441–461.

Smith, C. (1995), Marketing Strategies for the ethics era. *Sloan Management Review*, 36, 85–97.

Smith, C. (2001), Ethical guidelines for marketing practice: A reply to Gaski and some observations on the role of normative ethics. *Journal of Business Ethics*, 32(1), 3–18.

Smith, C., and Quelch, J. (1993), *Ethics in Marketing*, Homewood: Irwin.

Thompson, C.J. (1995), A contextualist proposal for the conceptualization and study of marketing ethics. *Journal of Public Policy and Marketing*, 14, 177–191.

Vitell, S.J., and Hunt, S.D. (2015), The general theory of marketing ethics: The consumer ethics and intentions issues. In A. Nill (Ed), *Handbook on Ethics and Marketing*, Glos: Edward Elgar Publishing, pp. 15–37.

Vitell, S.J., Singhapakdi, A., and Thomas, J. (2001), Consumer ethics: An application and empirical testing of the Hunt-Vitell theory of ethics. *Journal of Consumer Marketing*, *18*(2), 153–178.

5
THE ETHICS AND POLITICS OF CONSUMPTION

Amidst ever-increasing instances of abnormal weather tempera-
tures, flash floods, hurricanes and wildfires and innumerable losses
of human and nonhuman forms of life, there is a heightened awareness of the social and environmental effects that contemporary consumer lifestyles bring. Indeed, humanity seems to be on a 'highway to
climate hell with our foot on the accelerator', according to the UN's
secretary general speech in the latest COP27 UN climate summit (the
biggest of its kind).[1] Documented effects, such as the inescapability of
global temperature rises to at least 1.5C,[2] have led to a major growth
in campaign pressure groups, who attempt to influence business and
government to take steps to become more environmentally responsible. Nor is it only in relation to environmental issues, many consumers
now espouse a wide range of causes from human rights and animal
protection to many other philanthropic concerns and solidary behaviours. This has given rise to the notion of the 'ethical consumer', who
uses buying patterns to support certain companies and react against
others. However, ethical consumption is increasingly viewed as the
prerogative of affluent consumers, who try to assuage some of their
middle-class guilt by, for example, simply buying Fairtrade clothing
and carbon offsetting their flights (e.g. Cremin, 2012). In this sense,
ethical consumption can be criticised for reproducing rather than
challenging current consumer practices (albeit of a more 'ethical'
nature) and for being disconnected from the more consequential
realm of organized political action and 'citizenship'.

As we will see in this chapter, however, the binary between consumption and citizenship is problematic, not least because more
sophisticated accounts on the history and politics of consumption
suggest otherwise. Consumer movements, for instance, have been
largely responsible for the abolition of the slavery movement, gender equality and more recently, the advancement of social and environmental justice across commodity supply chains (e.g. Newholm
et al., 2015). Everyday consumers, both through their purchasing
choices and non-choices, and through more organised forms of political participation (e.g. Micheletti and Stolle, 2004) are a fundamental
yet often-neglected actor in the institutional nexus of corporations,
national and transnational institutions, markets, third sector organisations and social movements.

DOI: 10.4324/9781003201151-5

Trying to think about consumption more ethically and politically is further complicated by the fact that what is meant by ethics or politics is inherently contentious and multi-dimensional. For some, it is reduced down to notions of 'ethical' or 'political' consumerism and 'consumption as voting'. Within this paradigm, consumption can be viewed as a new form of marketplace participation, whereby every-day consumers, through their purchases and non-purchases, vote in favour and against particular social, environmental and ideological issues. For many neo-Marxist and critical scholars, however, the point of departure in thinking about consumption is Marx's account of commodity fetishism. As David Harvey (1990), one of the fore-most social theorists, puts it, the grapes we find in our supermarket shelves (and indeed any commodity) are very silent about the social conditions of their production. Accordingly, politics and ethics at that level would require – among other things – cognitive maps that educate consumers about the inner workings of capitalist markets and de-commodification attempts through alternative and solidari-ty-based economies. Finally, one avenue for looking at consumption more politically is by questioning the very role that consumers and consumerism play in contemporary societies. Here, the vocabulary of consumerism, the very essence of consumers' fantasies and subjec-tivities is put to question with a view to uncover why being a 'con-sumer' (as opposed to, for example, a citizen) in neoliberal societies is the preferred mode of social action and mental organisation. In this chapter, we look at these different ways of understanding the ethics and politics of consumption whilst also taking account their respec-tive contradictions and interconnections.

The Rise of the Ethical Consumer

To be sure, thinking about the consequences of everyday consump-tion is not specific to contemporary civilisations. According to some accounts, questions around the ethics and politics of consumption can even be found in the dialogues of Socrates and Plato, whereby the preconditions (that is, acceptance of slavery) for the luxurious life-styles of wealthy Athenians were explicitly contemplated (Bradshaw et al., 2013). More commonly, however, the predecessors to what is now understood as ethical (and political) consumerism are viewed to be the anti-slavery boycotts of the eighteenth and nineteenth cen-turies. Within the UK, for instance, the first 'consumers league' was established in 1897 by Clementina Black to address existing labour concerns (Hilton, 2007). Members of the league were encouraged to boycott the goods of employers who paid unjustifiably low wages and/or allowed intolerable working conditions in their factories. Accordingly, a list of 'fair' employers was created to allow shoppers within the vicinity of Bond Street, Oxford Street and Regent Street to choose more wisely (Ibid.). Eventually, however, the league failed because, as Clementina Black explained, it proved impossible to pro-duce a full and accurate guide for politically minded consumers at a larger level and it could by no means replace the effectiveness of more direct workers' struggles (Ibid.).

Nowadays, of course, it is far less difficult to be informed about the working conditions in the offices and factories of big multinational corporations not least because of the numerous media exposes but also due to the emergence of very sophisticated shopper guides by the likes of UK's *Ethical Consumer* magazine (www.ethicalconsumer. org) and even smartphone applications that provide live information for consumers on the go, such as the Buycott (www.buycott.com). Meanwhile, a variety of labels, from Fairtrade and organic certifications to the recent Edge certification guaranteeing equal gender pay, make civic-minded consumers' shopping trip a far easier task than Clementina Black's supporters back in the late nineteenth century. Accordingly, contemporary ethical consumption is more broadly defined as 'any conscious and deliberate decision to make certain consumption choices due to personal moral beliefs and values' (Crane and Matten, 2004, p. 290). In other words, ethical consumers use their buying patterns in multiple ways to react against certain companies and support others. They may make their decisions to select particular products or services in terms of a company's human rights record, animal protection, environmental friendliness and support for charities to name but a few of the common reasons. Common across such behaviours is the attempt to align one's moral and political values with what they purchase rather than being guided by price, convenience or whim. Importantly, ethical consumers increasingly recognise that we are consuming too much at too great a rate and, thus, are more likely to question whether a product is needed in the first place (Rebouças and Soares, 2021).

Despite consumers' best intentions, there is a well-documented attitude-behaviour gap in ethical consumerism (Carrington et al., 2021). Consumers frequently say they support ethical motives but do not follow through in their purchasing decisions. One reason for this is that old habits die hard, and marketers, of course, have worked hard in the first place to build these habits. Our kitchen cupboards are likely to contain a variety of cleaning products – different ones for different rooms and purposes (bathrooms, showers, etc.) – that contain toxic materials. These are likely also to be familiar brand names – Jif, Mr Muscle, Ajax and so on – brands that we have come to rely on to clean our work surfaces and make the jobs easier. Such habits make it difficult for consumers to break out of existing routines and to find less harmful, natural substitutes, like baking soda, white vinegar or lemon. All of these will require a learning curve to use correctly and may not be nearly as easy or efficient as the brands on which consumers are dependent.

A further reason why it is so hard to be an ethical consumer is because what is viewed as ethical in any given circumstance is often subjective and depends from whose point of view the situation is being considered. A study carried out by Visconti et al. (2014) into how farmers markets contribute to sustainability identified key ethical trade-offs, highlighting how what seems ethical at a micro level may not be so ethical when a more macro picture is included. The number of farmers markets in the UK has been steadily growing, following their success in the US. Indeed, it is estimated that there are now over 800 farmers markets with sales of more than £250 million. Farmers markets sell food stuffs from farmers directly to consumers with participation in markets usually restricted by proximity of production to the site. For example, London Farmers' Markets is an organisation that manages a network of markets across London. Usually held once or twice a week in car parks, school playgrounds or local squares, produce must be grown (or made) within a 100-mile radius. Apart from being local (loosely defined in the case of LFM), produce must also be seasonal and middlemen are not permitted. Typical participants are farmers, nursery growers, fishermen, cooks, bakers, preserve makers and beekeepers, but various handicraft makers or local services may also be present, such as the Mobile Bike Workshop, a cycle-repair facility, which tours the London markets. Their commitment to local, seasonal production means farmers markets are hailed as a highly sustainable market form that also re-invigorates urban environments. Most cities have lost their traditional markets, and farmers markets help to regain a lost sense of community.

Assessing the contribution of farmers markets to sustainability is not as straightforward, however, as it first appears, and further analysis reveals inter-social, international and inter-gender trade-offs. In relation to inter-social trade-offs, farmers markets often operate in richer neighbourhoods, and consequently, there are implications for social inclusion. First, poorer people may not be able to afford the travel costs to access the market. Second, prices are often higher because of the limited economies of scale attainable, and sometimes, pricing policies aim at the tourists such markets attract, particularly when they have acquired a fashionable image. Similarly, if local enterprise is privileged over international trade – 'farmers markets are often represented as a form of local fair trade system' (Visconti et al., 2014, p. 14) – how does this reconcile with the idea of aiding developing countries through international (fair) trade? From this perspective, farmers markets may be more indicative of the entrepreneurialism encouraged by neoliberalist policies (i.e. allowing the 'free market' to dictate) rather than providing a resistance to globalization. Finally, there is the inter-gender trade-off as a result of the nostalgia that surrounds farmers markets and the idea they are a return to more pastoral ways of living. This pastoral idyll usually relies on prescribed gender roles that consign women to care of the home (and vegetable garden!). In addition, food shopping has traditionally been seen as a feminine role, and the extra time that it takes to attend and browse a farmers market is not conducive to changing this perception. Indeed, the statistics on the gender balance in farmers markets show a majority of women in most cases.

Similar trade-offs can be seen in many other areas of ethical and green consumption (Hiller and Woodall, 2019): palm oil is increasingly used in biofuels which are seen as an ethical alternative to burning fossil fuels, but as discussed earlier, palm plantations come at huge environmental costs; since smoking bans, pubs are now be free of indoor pollution, but the patio heaters provided for smokers to keep warm outside cause a different type of pollution. This then brings us back to the idea of more ecosocially holistic perspectives that look at the interconnectedness between humans and their natural world and call for an analysis of the interrelationships between each element of an ecosystem. Such perspectives mean challenging the premises of neoliberal capitalism and economic growth at any cost. Within marketing studies (Spry et al., 2021), this is also commonly referred to as the dominant social paradigm (DSP), a paradigm that prioritises economic growth and possessive individualism, together with the harnessing of the natural world to satisfy these ends (see Kilbourne, 2004).

From Ethically Consuming to Voting in the Marketplace

So far, we have used the terms ethical and political consumption interchangeably (Carrington et al., 2021). This is because, although there is certainly a difference between notions of ethics and politics, the way these terms are applied across fields in relation to consumption (e.g. psychology, politics, marketing studies) is not that different and mostly reflects distinct disciplinary traditions. The term 'political consumerism' and interrelated notions of 'voting' in the marketplace, for instance, are heavily used in political science. Therein, political consumerism is indicative of our era of 'individualised collective action', that is, 'the practice of responsibility-taking . . . on the part of citizens alone or together with others to deal with problems that they believe are affecting what they identify as the good life' (Micheletti, 2003, p. 26). Contrasting with the previous era of 'collectivist collective action', contemporary Western societies are witnessing a decrease in traditional forms of political participation, such as campaigning, voting in elections, protesting and joining political parties and an increase in more personal political actions and emotions that are disconnected from consolidated political structures and organisations.

It is worth clarifying here that although ethical and political consumerism may refer to similar phenomena, there are some key differences. First, political consumerism may not necessarily be viewed as 'ethical'. Beyond trading relationships with the Third World and environmental issues, it can be used as an expression of identity politics (as in the case of staging a same-sex kiss-in in anti-LGBT restaurant chains; Severson, 2012) and international politics (e.g. boycotting Israel products; www.waronwant.org/) and as a means to support rather less morally worthy aims, for example, in the case of supporting extreme-right corporations (Chatzidakis, 2013) and even the pro-colonial regime of the nineteenth century (Newholm and Newholm, 2016). In addition, political consumerism is more than just boycotting or 'buycotting' particular services and products on the basis of their social and environmental credentials (Copeland and Atkinson, 2016). It is also about campaigning through discursive and non-discursive means (e.g. writing letters to corporations, taking companies to court) and about endorsing lifestyle politics, in the sense of making 'the personal political' and trying to live one's life in line with their political ideals. (We will return to this later in this chapter.)

A common line of criticism against political (and ethical) consumerism, as a new individualised form of political participation, is that it substitutes for more traditional forms of political activism, that is, it 'crowds in' rather than 'crowds out' the political energies and impulses of everyday consumer-citizens. Various empirical studies, however, have consistently shown that political consumers are more likely than non-political consumers to be more engaged in a broader sense. For instance, they exhibit much higher partic-ipation rates in behaviours such as voting in elections, contacting politicians and working for political parties and organisations (see Copeland and Atkinson, 2016). This contradicts given critiques of political consumerism on the basis that it impedes people from engaging in more traditional forms of political action. Instead, it can be seen as an evolution of the ways in which contemporary consumer-citizens choose to exercise their political impulses and express their values.

Notwithstanding, political consumerism is still very much about individualised solutions to collective problems (and so is ethical consumerism of course). For many critics, as we discuss later in the chapter, it serves to remove responsibility from the traditional top-down institutions, such as the state and governmental institutions, and into the individual consumer-citizen. The consequences are often less obvious at the micro level of individual consumer choice and yet deeply profound at the level of macro-orientated structural change. For instance, individual consumers are called to bear the burden of equitable and environmentally sustainable trading with Third World producers, leaving little space for political action against the very institutions (e.g. WTO, IMF) that are responsible for uneven geographical development and unfair trading arrangements in the first place. Furthermore, the implicit emphasis on 'individualised' collective action tends to ignore the numerous modern-day exam-ples of 'collectivized' collective action across spaces and places, whereby alternative imaginaries of politicized consumption exist. For instance, Chatzidakis et al. (2012, 2021) talk about Exarcheia as an urban neighbourhood where new ways of doing consumer activ-ism are constantly tried out. These bear little resemblance with the model of 'individualised' collective action documented (mainly) in Northern European and American cities. More broadly, there is a wealth of anthropological and geographical research pointing to how politically-motivated consumption takes different forms and meanings outside the 'Global North' (e.g. Ariztia et al., 2016). Even within the Global North, there is a vast array of alternative economic activities and practices of political consumption that lies outside the conventional, if not restrictive, realm of marketplace exchange (Gibson-Graham, 2006).

Beyond Voting in the Marketplace? The Politics of Degrowth

An interrelated critique of political and ethical consumerism is that it is based less on challenging the dominant consumerist culture and more on maintaining it by casting votes firmly within (rather than outside) the conventional marketplace. In other words, it is a form of self-enlightened behaviour focused mostly on moderating some of the unintended consequences of consumer choice(s) as opposed to radically challenging Western consumer culture altogether. For proponents of 'degrowth', an increasingly influential tradition that places the insistence on economic 'growth' at the centre of contemporary social and environmental problems, this is a very limited model of civic-minded consumption. Degrowth 'does not only challenge the centrality of GDP as an overarching policy objective but proposes a framework for transformation to a lower and sustainable level of production and consumption, a shrinking of the economic system to leave more space for human cooperation and ecosystems' (www. degrowth.org/definition-2). Interestingly, for degrowth activists and scholars, the somewhat-religious preoccupation with economic expansion through the use of more natural resources, technological advances and the stimulation of consumption is not a characteristic of advanced capitalist markets only. It concerns all modern societies, including the planned economies of the Soviet Union. Contrasting the productivist orientation of these regimes, degrowth scholars advocate that societies of the Global North enter a 'virtuous circle of cultivated contraction' (Latouche, 2009). This would include re-assessment of societal values, re-distributing wealth between the North and the South and re-assessing the meaning of life altogether.

Everyday consumption plays a key role within the degrowth agenda, not least because it is at this level where everyday needs will have to be re-evaluated, re-localised and underpinned by an ethos of communality, care and sharing (e.g. Latouche, 2009). Unlike political consumerism, which is about boycotting and boycotting individual products in the way of expressing one's political values, the model of civic-minded consumption that is advocated by degrowth advocates and scholars is closer to what has been described in the consumer literature as voluntary simplicity or downshifting, that is, the foregoing of Western-style (over)consumption habits (e.g. Shaw and Newholm, 2002; Rebouças and Soares, 2021). It is also in line with what the political philosopher Kate Soper (2020) defines as 'alternative hedonism', urging us to reconsider materialism and, indeed, the extent to which the 'good life' is or should be associated with shopping an ever-expanding list of items. Interestingly, Soper emphatically argues that even if current Western consumer lifestyles were indefinitely sustainable and socially desirable, they would still be incapable of enhancing happiness and wellbeing or not beyond a point that has already passed. Numerous studies have documented the lack of correlation between material wealth and happiness after a certain level.

Chatzidakis et al. (2014) have contrasted more explicitly the model of consumption underpinned by the imperative for radical degrowth as opposed to more conventional campaigns in favour of social and environmental sustainability. As these authors explain, when business and other institutional actors urge us to consume more ethically or politically what they, in effect, espouse is a model of economic organisation that is still underpinned by an (over)productivist ethos, albeit of a more sustainable nature through the use of technological advancements and through minimizing harm wherever possible. According to many authors, the limits of this model have already become apparent given the inability of current societies to meet even modest sustainability targets as evident in the famous 1992 Kyoto protocol and/or the more recent 2015 Paris agreement. Accordingly, the associated model of consumption in societies of degrowth can be characterised as post- or de-consumerism in the sense that it rejects the idea of consumption as a central and meaningful act in and of itself. The primary focus is instead in collectivised forms of consumption, based around community participation, sharing and the re-imagining of local communities. The differences are summarised by the authors in the table in the next section.

Table 5.1 Logics of Growth in Consumption (Chatzidakis et al., 2014, p. 753)

Countervailing logic	Underpinning assumptions	Actors	Implications for consumption	Identity of the consumer
Cultivated growth	Economic rationality, Adam Smith's invisible hand, neoclassical theories of economics	Multinational, world-wide market elites. Concerned primarily with maximizing economic growth and profitability and with social order only in relationship to market threats.	Use up, use more (when possible) and throw away.	'Sovereign consumer', self-interested, position in society is defined by conspicuous consumption.
Sustainable growth	Market and society interact and impact upon one another	Governments and middle class – those concerned with maintaining social order within existing nation states.	Buy ethical and green; reduce, reuse, recycle	'Ethical consumer', socially aware, role and identity in society defined by consumption of ethical goods
Degrowth	Society resists the domination of market logics	Consumer-citizens, activists	Don't buy anything, produce what is needed within small communities, alternative hedonism	'Post- and de-consumerist', role in society defined by social participation rather than consumption

Getting Behind (and Working Against) the Veil of Commodity Fetishism

Whereas ethical and political consumerism are about managing and engaging with the consequences of particular consumption choices and 'de-consumerism' (and related notions of alternative hedonism and voluntary simplicity) about the consequences of Western consumption levels altogether, neo-Marxist and various other critical perspectives take a different point of departure. Here, the emphasis is on consumption objects themselves and the way in which affluent consumers of capitalist societies are entirely oblivious of their social nature. The notion of commodity fetishism is first presented in Karl Marx's first chapter of *Capital: Critique of Political Concept* (1867) as a means of explaining how in capitalist societies social relations between people are instead presented as 'an immense accumulation of commodities'. For Marx, this is because of the enigmatic or mystical nature of the commodities: 'A commodity appears at first sight an extremely obvious, trivial thing. But its analysis brings out that it is a very strange thing, abounding in metaphysical subtleties and theological niceties' (1976, p. 163). Marx clarifies that in pre-capitalist societies, there was nothing mystical about objects in so far as these were judged by their use-value. For instance, a table was the product of human labour (cutting and carving wood) aimed to provide some kind of utility (somewhere to dine, write and so on). Instead, the mysterious character of the table (and any other object) arises once it becomes a commodity because it is at this point – when the object acquires monetary value and is exchanged in the marketplace – that the social characteristics of human labour are presented as objective characteristics of the products themselves. What is a social relation between people now becomes 'the fantastic form of a relation between things' (p. 165).

Put differently, in capitalist societies, we perceive commodities as having some kind of autonomous value, expressed in monetary terms and understood solely in comparison to all other commodities. We tend be entirely oblivious to their social nature, as we hardly even wonder who makes them, under which conditions, how long it takes for them to be produced and so on. From this perspective then, understanding and engaging with the politics of consumption involves, first and foremost, understanding the politics of concealment: why and how capitalists' markets silence social information and relations and how, in turn, we can begin to imagine alternatives to current modes of production and consumption. As David Harvey (1990, p. 423) puts it, 'the grapes that sit upon the supermarket shelves are mute; we cannot see the fingers of exploitation upon them or tell immediately what part of the world they are from'. Accordingly, a substantial amount of academic and grassroots activism has been devoted in the development of cognitive maps that re-connect consumers with the producers and distributors of their commodities, aiming ultimately 'to get behind the veil, the fetishism of the market and the commodity, in order to tell the full story of social reproduction' (Ibid.).

Exemplary of this approach to consumption politics is Ian Cook's project titled 'follow-the-thing' (see, for example, Cook, 2004). Among others, Cook has been the main figure behind followthethings.com, a spoof website that looks like amazon.com but aims instead to tell the stories of the various commodities that we buy, using a variety of available resources – from news reports and documentaries to undergraduate student dissertation projects. Clicking on the grocery section, for instance, one comes across the story of avocados produced in Israel: Freddie Abrahams, an undergraduate student, 'is shocked to discover that the Israeli avocados he eats may be grown on illegally seized Palestinian land. There's a campaign going on in the UK to boycott these fruits. So he contacts the company that imports them into the UK and travels to Israel to find out more' (Abrahams, 2007). This approach to linking consumers with producers and re-imagining the relations between them (also discussed in the case study section) has in turn inspired a variety of other resources that inform consumers on the go through online tracking and barcode scanning such as the www.fair-tracing.com and www.buycott.com.

Another approach to redressing the 'veil of the markets' is through so-called 'de-commodification' projects that directly link consumers and producers and alter the ways in which commodities are traded. The de-commodification perspective (e.g. Lekakis, 2022) has inspired a vast array of alternative markets and economic practices. Examples include trading directly with Zapatistas, the revolutionary leftist group based in Chiapas, Mexico (Chatzidakis, 2013), community-supported agriculture and various eco-villages (e.g. Thompson and Coskuner-Balli, 2007) as well as more mainstream alternatives, such as Fairtrade consumerism. Such alternative economic arrangements clearly vary in the extent to which they pose a real challenge to capitalist markets. For instance, although perhaps the most widespread example of de-commodification, Fairtrade networks are typically viewed as very limited in terms of their ability to establish alternative economic relationships. They only pose (at best) a symbolic challenge to commodity fetishism, in so far as they employ practices that are largely mediated by conventional markets (e.g. supermarket chains, multinational retailers) and are fully confined by capitalist imperatives (Fridell, 2006). For harsher critics, Fairtrade products, like any other ethical product and/or examples of cause-related marketing, are, in effect, reflective of 'guilt fetishism' (Cremin, 2012). That is, they address a tendency by Western affluent consumers to look for ecological and ethical signifiers, ultimately assuaging themselves from the guilt they would otherwise experience, knowing the real politics behind the commodities they buy.

More generally, an often-cited approach to explaining what happens to countercultural and alternative consumer movements is co-optation theory (e.g. Holt, 2002). According to this perspective, in so far as consumer resistance functions from within the dominant symbolic order, it remains open to adaptation and commercialization by powerful marketplace actors. Somewhat ironically, through their everyday practices and resistance tactics, consumers provide creative resources that are ultimately converted into new counter-cultural and alternative commodities. For example, past the 1960s, many successful multinational brands, such as Volkswagen and Levi's, embraced the anti-authoritarian ethos of youth movements, adding to their brand image countercultural sensibilities that allowed them to attract what would otherwise remain an elusive market segment. Altogether then, co-optation theory suggests that rebelling against the (perceived as) conformist mainstream is impossible, and some-what ironically, it only serves to reinforce the dominant symbolic order that seamlessly absorbs countercultural tastes and sensibilities and converts into marketplace commodities. Although this may seem a likely outcome for a variety of market-mediated ethical and politi-cal projects, Thompson and Coskuner-Balli (2007) suggest that more intimate and human-scale initiatives, such as local food networks and solidarity trading arrangements, sufficiently diverge from the modal-ities of mainstream markets. Despite remaining a by-product of the global economic system, they allow their members to participate in infrastructures that are less alienating and further removed from unintended ecological and socio-economic consequences. In addi-tion, they provide space for experimenting with doing things differ-ently and for creating 'cracks' in current capitalist logics and practices (Holloway, 2010), a precondition for the formation of subjectivities other than that of the highly individualised and apolitical mainstream consumer (Carrington et al., 2021).

However, what if removing the fetish character of commodities proves all the more impossible? What if peeling off one mystical layer was to reveal another mystical layer, leaving nothing but layer upon layer upon layer? At least this seems to have been the case with Fairtrade (and other ethical) products, whereby otherwise genuine attempts to demystify forms of commodity production have led, as noted previously, to the creation of yet another kind of fetishism, described as 'guilt fetishism' (Cremin, 2012). Correspondingly, many authors now speak about the 'ethical spectacle' (akin to the moral-ised brandscape, Chapter 7), which has come to replace, or at least co-habit, the symbolic realm of many everyday commodities. Con-templating this state of affairs, Shukaitis (2013) argues that rather than trying to escape the mystical realm of commodities, a more politically progressive approach may be to dispel it. In fact, that was exactly the logic of 1920s Russian constructivists who had to con-template the role of objects in the building of a communist society. Their purpose, in many ways, became 'confronting the phantasmic power of the community object and reclaiming it for socialism' (Kiaer, 2005 in Shukaitis, 2013, p. 440). Accordingly, some of the products of the Constructivist era were designed not only with utility in mind but also the more socio-political role they could play in harnessing col-lective living. A prime example, here, has been Soviet clothing with two famous designers, Varvara Stepanova and Liubov Popova, taking somewhat different approaches (Kravets, 2013). Stepanova designed patterns such that their dynamism came from the chromatic vibrating effect in the fabric design, an effect that multiplied when seen on many dresses at once, hence, enhancing the dress's sociality. Popova, on the other hand, focused on constructing versatile designs that could be transformed through use rather than tailoring. In both cases, the dresses were meant to be more 'honest' and social. Although such logics seem miles apart from the highly individualised, fast-fashioned and sweatshop-fuelled garments of our day, Chatzidakis (2013) reminds us that there are still many commodities that are politically invested in a decidedly phantasmatic manner, such as 'fascist rice', a rice that was removed from Athenian solidarity trading networks due to its producers' affiliation with neo-Nazi parties, and 'anarchist drinks' consumed in various squats and social centres in support of political causes. The question whether and how such objects can be effectively implicated in political struggles remains open.

Being a Consumer in a Neoliberal World

A different entrée to understanding the intersection of politics with consumption is through questioning the very role that consumption and consumerism plays in our everyday lives, as a discourse and as an identity that we are increasingly asked to adopt in spheres other than our traditional seller-customer encounters. For instance, in spaces such as hospitals and universities, we are increasingly treated as 'consumers' or 'customers' rather than patients or students. Importantly, we are often complicit in this, foregrounding the language of consumer rights and demanding procedures and services that up until recently would have been viewed as incompatible with the provision of public goods. For many philosophers and social thinkers of our time, this is exemplary of the particular era of late capitalism, aka neoliberalism, that we live in. According to Zygmunt Bauman (2009), for instance, consumerism as we understand it is the product of 'liquid modernity', a distinct period that started in the latter part of the twentieth century. Under liquid modernity, we transitioned from a society of producers to a society of consumers and grown accustomed to be recognised mostly and primarily on the basis of our buying power. This has very profound implications in terms of how we understand the world and engage with it. Our contemporary vocabulary is one that favours words such as customer and consumer over citizen, choice and markets over community ties, self-interest over solidarity, individual over collective. More than just describing a reality, these words directly feed into our everyday dreams and fantasies, constructing and reinforcing our subjectivities (Massey, 2013).

But what is neoliberalism and how is consumption so heavily implicated in it? Neoliberalism, as David Harvey (2007) explains, is, in the first instance, 'a theory of political economic practices that proposes that human well-being can best be advanced by promoting individual entrepreneurial freedoms and skills within an institutional framework characterised by strong private property rights, free markets, and free trade'. To do so, the role of the state must be restricted. Firstly, it has to guarantee that this framework is effectively implemented, for example, by ensuring the integrity of the financial system and by providing services, such as policing and enforcing the implementation of laws and regulations. Other than that, state interventions must be kept to a minimum and called to task only if there are opportunities for creating markets that do not yet exist, such as those around the use of land, water, healthcare, education and environmental protection. The underlying assumption is that compared to the private sector, state investments provide a far less efficient means to dynamic entrepreneurship and innovation (despite compelling evidence suggesting the contrary, for example, Mazzucato, 2013).

Neoliberalism is distinct from classical or traditional liberalism. To begin with, critics highlight that the former serves more particular class interests in so far as, at least in practice, financial capital is protected at any cost. Many liberal economists, for instance, would advocate letting a big bank pay for the risks it has undertaken, even if that translates into bankruptcy or institutional collapse. Instead, as the 2008 crisis has rather vividly illustrated, neoliberalism supports the privatisation of financial risk-related profits and the collectivisation of risk-related losses (in the form of governmental bail-outs that use taxpayer money). Perhaps more importantly and certainly more profoundly, classical liberalism and neoliberalism differ in their implicit assumptions about human nature. Whereas the former has traditionally assumed that humans are innately individualistic, competitive and acquisitive, neoliberalism assumes that these values cannot be taken-for-granted and, thus, need to be cultivated by the state and other institutional actors (Gilbert, 2013). Accordingly, neoliberalism is invested in promoting particular modes of thinking and being, ones that celebrate entrepreneurial virtues, marketplace freedoms, personal accountability for successes and failures (as opposed to any structural constraints or systemic injustices, such as class exclusions) and, at best, forms of 'individualistic' as opposed to collectivist egalitarianism (e.g. via widening access to private property ownership).

It is the convergence of neoliberal values with the rationalities and the promises of Western-style consumerism that have foregrounded the latter as the key arena of everyday action. As Noam Chomsky, the famous public intellectual, puts it, neoliberalism is invested in the production of consumers, instead of citizens, of shopping malls, instead of communities. Accordingly, the emphasis on consumer choice as basic to individual freedom and personal wellbeing – as opposed to any form of collective investment in and/or dependency upon common or social goods – is paramount to neoliberal forms of governance. To be sure, this is not to say that prior to neoliberalism, people did not enjoy shopping or that they did not develop passionate attachments to things. There is a vast amount of anthropological and historical research on 'consumer cultures' that vividly illustrates the contrary (e.g. Trentmann, 2016). Likewise, various studies have heavily criticised traditional critiques of consumers as passive and easily manipulated, portraying instead a far more active and subversive role of consumers and consumer subcultures. However, such counter-crit-icisms are often based on oversimplifying traditional Marxist critiques of consumerism and/or ignoring their more recent reformulations and adaptations (Schor, 2007). In the era of full-fledged privatisation and marketization of pretty much everything (from public transport to social housing and hospitals), it is hard to argue there is a lack of connection between neoliberalism and the focus on consumer choice and entrepreneurial individualism.

Furthermore, as the feminist scholar Lynne Segal (2017) puts it, nowadays, Marx's notion of commodity fetishism has been given a rather more dystopian twist, with not only products obscuring the social relations behind their production but also with consumers, too, becoming commodities, competing to improve their 'brand value' and impact in social media (see *Facebook*) and beyond. Wendy Brown, another famous social theorist, acknowledges that such new technol-ogies of consumption can be indeed much fun and seductive, render-ing them all the more dangerous:

> It's exciting and delicious in many ways to think about how to enhance the value of various bits of your self, how to brand your-self, how to attract investors, how to get more likes on *Facebook*, how to get re-tweeted, how to self-invest and get others to invest in you.
>
> (Cruz and Brown, 2016, p. 84)

For critics such as Segal and Brown, what is problematic with these otherwise pleasurable and seemingly benign activities is the intensification of particular modes of thinking about one's selfhood, their lives and their way of relating to their surrounding world. That is, they normalise a certain kind of atomised individualism and forms of self-branding and 'human capital' that are akin to the neoliberalisa-tion of all spheres of social life. Rather inevitably, any form of depend-ency or insistence in more collectivised forms of consumption and alternative socialisation are viewed as lefty side projects that are irrel-evant to the population at large. The perils of such new technologies of consumption and (ultimately) selfhood, however, are increasingly felt across the world, with many individuals deciding to break away from social media – even if only temporarily (e.g. whilst on holidays). Popular TV series such as *Black Mirror* portray zombie-like people that are too busy looking at their smartphones and trying to improve their personal ratings, and political parties such as Podemos publish their political programmes in the form of IKEA-like catalogues – even if only to subvert their brand-savvy electorate.

What is to be done? More than three decades ago, before new technologies of consumption and self-branding were conceived, Michel Foucault put it rather eloquently:

> The political, ethical, social, philosophical problem of our day is not to try to liberate the individual from the economy . . . but to

liberate us both from the economy and from the type of individu-
alization that is linked to the economy. We have to promote new
forms of subjectivity through the refusal of this kind of individuality which has been imposed on us.

(Foucault, 1983 in Gibson-Graham, 2006, pp. xvi–xvii)

For many political activists and scholars, new politics of collective
action (and anti-consumption) are urgently needed, ones that not
only address people's everyday needs – from solidarity economies
to gifting bazaars and community gardens – but also ones that help
them cultivate new ways of thinking about themselves, their desires
and their social relations and ones that are devoid of (socially and environmentally) damaging market logics and neoliberal vocabularies.

Summary

There are multiple ways of understanding the intersection of ethics and
politics with everyday consumerism. This chapter has outlined three
key perspectives. The first one focuses on the consequences of everyday consumption and the extent to which more ethical and politicised
consumer choices can achieve desirable outcomes, such as the promotion of certain environmental and labour standards. A related stream of
research focuses on the need to reduce consumption levels altogether
rather than carrying on consuming, albeit more conscientiously. A second perspective to understanding the ethics and (mostly the) politics of
consumption centres on Marx's notion of commodity fetishism and the
extent to which people are oblivious of the social nature of the goods
(and services) they consume. Accordingly, what becomes imperative is
the advancement of new politics of 'de-commodification' that inform
consumers of the actors and politics involved in commodity supply
chains, as well as attempts to narrow the distance between consumers and producers through alternative and solidarity-based economies. Finally, a different stream of scholarly thought has focused on
the role of consumption within neoliberal regimes. At stake here is the
ways through which we as 'consumers' unknowingly reproduce modes
of thinking and feeling that are aligned with the increased commodification of everyday life, ultimately leading to the normalisation of a
socially and environmentally unjust economic system.

Case Study: De-commodifying Jamaican Papayas

Attempts to re-connect consumers with the producers and distributors of their commodities often draw on Professor Ian Cook's follow-the-thing approach. Cook (2004) provides an example of this
approach by identifying seven key 'stakeholders' in the produc-
tion-consumption nexus of Jamaican papayas (imported to the UK) –
that is, the papaya fruit, the papaya farmer, the farm workers, the
Jamaican economy, the UK buyer, the UK importer and the UK consumer. Each of these stakeholders is implicated in the fetishisation of
papayas, albeit in different ways. Specifically:

The UK Buyer

Mina has been a speciality fruit and vegetable buyer for major UK supermarket chains for over eight years. Her main role involves assessing the demand and supply for speciality fruits and vegetables, a task that is far more complex and challenging than it may seem. It involves, among others, monitoring the quality and quantity of their production across an international range of suppliers whilst also assessing consumer trends and attitudes. In the case of papayas, for instance, the two main supply routes are from Brazil and Jamaica. Either way, papayas have to be the right look and size, right taste and sold under the psychological £1 barrier (per item) whilst also allowing for a profit margin of at least 16%. Mina once visited one of the production sites of pineapple in Ivory Coast and got rather depressed with the amount of poverty she witnessed. Yet such memories have little space in her everyday work rhythm of constantly checking spreadsheets and computer screens, writing reports and making phonecalls.

The Political Economy of Jamaica

Jamaica remains a relatively impoverished economy with a big national debt. It has long moved away from relying on sugar production, not least because of the colonial references, the tough working conditions and more importantly, the various 'free-trade' agreements imposed by organisations such as the EU and WTO and which have made Jamaican sugar uncompetitive. Jamaica's economy is now far more diversified and focused on niche, higher-value tropical fruits, such as papayas.

The UK Importer

Tony is a supplier of fruits based in a small suite of offices in central London. He is, in effect, a broker between international suppliers and (UK-based) buyers and has known Jim, the Jamaican papaya farm owner for quite some time. In general, much of Tony's work involves visiting suppliers with a view to establish trust and confidence in their business. Such visits often prove rather unpleasant, as they involve direct exposure to the exploitation entailed in the production of global commodities. However, at the end of the day, Tony cares more about feeding his own family back in London. His focus is on getting the supplier to sell at the right price (usually lower rather than higher) and to exploit circumstantial factors such as currency fluctuations.

The Papaya Plant

Papayas come in different shapes, and they are susceptible to various climatic changes and plant viruses. Among others, their size fluctuates depending on tree height and gender, with the hermaphrodite variety being the one that is actually sold in supermarket shelves. Yet according to the FAO/WHO/WTO (1993) Codex Alimentarius volume

5B, there is only one shape, colour and look for papayas, not least for the sake of 'consumer safety'.

The Papaya Farmer

Jim is a second-generation white Jamaican, who, back in 1990, took the risk of setting up one of the first papaya farms and now enjoys considerable demand and reputation for his products. However, he still has to be on top of things, including protecting the farm from the very real risk of viral diseases, weather fluctuations and a constant expectation to meet the quality and quantity standards set in each order.

The Workers

Phillips is the *farm foreman*, dealing with day-to-day decisions, such as illness, time off, discipline and so on. His main task is to be authoritative without ever losing his temper. Pru is one of the papaya *packers*. Like the rest of her colleagues, she has to work really hard, often staying at work until the late evening hours. Her standards of living deteriorated massively due to the Jamaican currency devaluation, making most of the commodities that she buys significantly more expensive. Papaya packers such as Pru would often get blistered fingertips and thumbs from the latex-like skin of unripe papayas. Other workers included packing house *supervisor(s)*, papaya *pickers, weighters, washers* and *wrappers*.

The UK Consumer

Emma is a 25-year-old, AB young professional who enjoys cooking and travelling in exotic destinations. She likes experimenting with various ingredients in her cooking, although she does not buy papayas. Why is she here? Because she still consumes, rather unknowingly, the white latex found in unripe papaya peduncle, aka 'papain'. Because of its unique protein-digesting enzymes, papain is found in a remarkably diverse range of products, from chewing gum and toothpaste to canned meats, leather goods and vegetarian cheese. The politics of papaya consumption are, therefore, rather trickier to untangle and so are the politics of de-commodification more broadly.

Seminar Exercises

Discussion Topics

1   Discuss critiques of ethical and political consumerism. What are the key arguments in favour of and against the idea of casting our votes in the marketplace? What is your opinion?
2   Over the last decade, there have been various calls for boycotting retailers that have been supporting specific politicians (e.g. www.businessinsider.com/trump-related-businesses-boycotted-2016-11/#belk-3). Is this an effective form of political activism? Discuss by presenting arguments and counter-arguments.

3   Go to www.theguardian.com/world/2016/jun/09/podemos-mani-festo-ikea-catalogue-flat-pack-policies. How can you explain this advert from a 'politics of consumption' perspective? Or is this more about the 'consumption of politics'?

4   What is wrong with the idea of 'branding' ourselves through social media, such as *Instagram* and *Facebook*? Discuss with reference to neoliberalism and neoliberal subjectivities.

Group Exercises

1   Read the article by Cook (2004) in the key readings section.

i   Assume your group represents one of these stakeholders. From your perspective, can you make a case for buying or not buying papayas?

ii   Compose the whole supply chain and identify the ethical dilemmas involved in each stage.

iii Would you, as an individual consumer, cast your consumption vote in favour for or against papayas?

2   Go to www.*youtube*.com/watch?v=z8fAmiomHgA and watch the film *Skoros: Anti-consumption in Crisis*.

i   How is this form of collective anti-consumption different to casting our votes in the markeplace?

ii   How and why did the economic crisis challenge the original ideas of the collective?

iii In the last part of the film, it becomes clear that the members of the collective disagree about the extent to which Skoros still represents an anti-consumerist initiative. What is your view?

Notes

1 www.theguardian.com/environment/2022/nov/07/cop27-climate-summit-un-secretary-general-antonio-guterres

2 www.newscientist.com/article/2323175-the-worlds-1-5c-climate-goal-is-slipping-out-of-reach-so-now-what/

Key Readings

Bradshaw, A., Campbell, N., & Dunne, S. (2013). The politics of consumption. *Ephemera*, *13*(2), 203–216.

Carrington, M., Chatzidakis, A., Goworek, H., & Shaw, D. (2021). Consumption ethics: A review and analysis of future directions for interdisciplinary research. *Journal of Business Ethics*, *168*(2), 215–238.

Chatzidakis, A., Larsen, G., & Bishop, S. (2014). Farewell to consumerism: Countervailing logics of growth in consumption. *Ephemera*, *14*(4), 753.

Cook, I. (2004). Follow the thing: Papaya. *Antipode*, *36*(4), 642–664.

Gilbert, J. (2013). What kind of thing is 'neoliberalism'? *New Formations*, *80*(1), 7–22.

References

Abrahams, F. (2007). *The Fruits of Our Labour: An Avocado's Story*. 2007 BA Geography Dissertation, University of Birmingham, UK.

Ariztia, T., Kleine, D., Bartholo, R., Brightwell, G., Agloni, N., & Afonso, R. (2016). Beyond the "deficit discourse": Mapping ethical consumption discourses in Chile and Brazil. *Environment and Planning A*, 0308518X16632757.

Bauman, Z. (2009). *Does Ethics Have a Chance in a World of Consumers?* Harvard University Press.

Bradshaw, A., Campbell, N., & Dunne, S. (2013). The politics of consumption. *Ephemera*, *13*(2), 203–216.

Carrington, M., Chatzidakis, A., Goworek, H., & Shaw, D. (2021). Consumption ethics: A review and analysis of future directions for interdisciplinary research. *Journal of Business Ethics*, *168*(2), 215–238.

Chatzidakis, A. (2013). Commodity fights in Post-2008 Athens: Zapatistas coffee, Kropotkinian drinks and Fascist rice. *Ephemera*, *13*(2), 459.

Chatzidakis, A., Larsen, G., & Bishop, S. (2014). Farewell to consumerism: Countervailing logics of growth in consumption. *Ephemera*, *14*(4), 753.

Chatzidakis, A., Maclaran, P., & Bradshaw, A. (2012). Heterotopian space and the utopics of ethical and green consumption. *Journal of Marketing Management*, *28*(3–4), 494–515.

Chatzidakis, A., Maclaran, P., & Varman, R. (2021). The regeneration of consumer movement solidarity. *Journal of Consumer Research*, *48*(2), 289–308.

Cook, I. (2004). Follow the thing: Papaya. *Antipode*, *36*(4), 642–664.

Copeland, L., & Atkinson, L. (2016). Political consumption: Ethics, participation and civic engagement. In D. Shaw, M. Carrington & A. Chatzidakis (Eds), *Ethics and Morality in Consumption: Interdisciplinary Perspectives*. Routledge, pp. 171–188.

Crane, A., & Matten, D. (2004). *Business Ethics: A European Perspective: Managing Corporate Citizenship and Sustainability in the Age of Globalization*. Oxford University Press, p. 224.

Cremin, C. (2012). The social logic of late capitalism: guilt fetishism and the culture of crisis industry. *Cultural Sociology*, *6*(1), 45–60.

Cruz, K., & Brown, W. (2016). Feminism, law, and neoliberalism: An interview and discussion with Wendy Brown. *Feminist Legal Studies*, *24*(1), 69–89.

Fridell, G. (2006). Fair trade and neoliberalism assessing emerging perspectives. *Latin American Perspectives*, *33*(6), 8–28.

Gibson-Graham, G.J. (2006). *The End of Capitalism (As We Knew It): A Feminist Critique of Political Economy*. University of Minnesota Press.

Gilbert, J. (2013). What kind of thing is 'neoliberalism'? *New Formations*, *80*(1), 7–22.

Harvey, D. (1990). Between space and time: Reflections on the geographical imagination. *Annals of the Association of American Geographers*, *80*(3), 418–434.

Harvey, D. (2007). *A Brief History of Neoliberalism*. Oxford University Press.

Hiller, A., & Woodall, T. (2019). Everything flows: A pragmatist perspective of trade-offs and value in ethical consumption. *Journal of Business Ethics*, *157*(4), 893–912.

Hilton, M. (2007). Consumers and the state since the Second World War. *The Annals of the American Academy of Political and Social Science*, *611*(1), 66–81.

Holloway, J. (2010). *Crack Capitalism*. Pluto Press.

Holt, D.B. (2002). Why do brands cause trouble? A dialectical theory of consumer culture and branding. *Journal of Consumer Research*, *29*(1), 70–90.

Kilbourne, W.E. (2004). Sustainable communication and the dominant social paradigm: Can they be integrated? *Marketing Theory*, 4(3), 187–208.

Kravets, O. (2013). On things and comrades. *Ephemera: Theory and Politics in Organization*, 12(2), 421–436.

Latouche, S. (2009). *Farewell to Growth*. Polity.

Lekakis, E.J. (2022). *Consumer Activism: Promotional Culture and Resistance*. Thousand Oaks: SAGE.

Marx, K. (1976). *Capital, Volume One* (trans. Ben Fowkes). Penguin.

Massey, D. (2013). Vocabularies of the economy. *Soundings*, 54(54), 9–22.

Mazzucato, M. (2013). *The Entrepreneurial State: Debunking Private vs. Public Sector Myths*. Anthem.

Micheletti, M. (2003). *Political Virtue and Shopping: Individuals, Consumerism, and Collective Action*. Palgrave.

Micheletti, M., & Stolle, D. (Eds.). (2004). *Politics, Products, and Markets: Exploring Political Consumerism Past and Present*. Transaction Publishers.

Newholm, T., & Newholm, S. (2016). Consumer ethics in history. In D. Shaw, M. Carrington & A. Chatzidakis (Eds), *Ethics and Morality in Consumption: Interdisciplinary Perspectives*. Routledge, pp. 97–115.

Newholm, T., Newholm, S., & Shaw, D. (2015). A history for consumption ethics. *Business History*, 57(2), 290–310.

Rebouças, R., & Soares, A.M. (2021). Voluntary simplicity: A literature review and research agenda. *International Journal of Consumer Studies*, 45(3), 303–319.

Schor, J.B. (2007). In defense of consumer critique: Revisiting the consumption debates of the twentieth century. *The Annals of the American Academy of Political and Social Science*, 611(1), 16–30.

Segal, L. (2017). *Radical Happiness*. Verso.

Severson, K. (2012, July 25). Chick-fil-A thrust back into spotlight on gay rights, *The New York Times*. Retrieved from www.nytimes.com/2012/07/26/us/gay-rights-uproar-over-chick-fil-a-widens.html

Shaw, D., & Newholm, T. (2002). Voluntary simplicity and the ethics of consumption. *Psychology & Marketing*, 19(2), 167–185.

Shukaitis, S. (2013). Can the object be a comrade? *Ephemera: Theory & Politics in Organization*, 13(2), 437–444.

Soper, K. (2020). *Post Growth Living: For an Alternative Hedonism*. Verso.

Spry, A., Figueiredo, B., Gurrieri, L., Kemper, J.A., & Vredenburg, J. (2021). Transformative branding: A dynamic capability to challenge the dominant social paradigm. *Journal of Macromarketing*, 41(4), 531–546.

Thompson, C.J., & Coskuner-Balli, G. (2007). Countervailing market responses to corporate co-optation and the ideological recruitment of consumption communities. *Journal of Consumer Research*, 34(2), 135–152.

Trentmann, F. (2016). *Empire of Things: How We Became a World of Consumers, from the Fifteenth Century to the Twenty-First*. Penguin.

Visconti, L.M., Minowa, Y., & Maclaran, P. (2014). Public markets: An ecological perspective on sustainability as a megatrend. *Journal of Macromarketing*, 34(3), 349–368.

6

MARKETING INEQUALITIES

Feminisms and Intersectionalities

Introduction

Societies around the globe have recently been experiencing a series of crises which have highlighted more than ever the structural inequalities that exist in our world. These inequalities cut across a range of protected characteristics to include (amongst others) race, disability, gender and sexual orientation. Consider, for example, the unlawful killing of George Floyd in May 2020 at the hands of police in Minneapolis, USA. This event spurred the multiracial Black Lives Matter protests which reverberated around the world, gaining media attention and spurring transnational participation. More recently in the UK, the rights of transgender people have been the subject of the political and media spotlight. In April 2022, the UK government was forced to cancel a conference that was intended to promote LGBTQ+ rights around the world. This was because their decision to ban conversion therapy for gay or bisexual people in England and Wales but not transgender people prompted a backlash which meant they had to cancel the event. While data is lacking, a study of suicide risk in transgender people in Canada found that 22% to 43% of transgender people had attempted suicide in their lifetime (Bauer et al., 2015). Inequalities have very real consequences in the mental and physical wellbeing of people.

As marketers, there is potential to rethink the role of branding, marketing and advertising in society at the current time. There is a pressing need to address marketing theory and practice to embrace inclusion, diversity and equality and to reflect on the ways in which marketing contributes to structures of oppression (Parsons et al., 2022). When we consider how marketing might contribute to inequality, we might think first of the role of advertising in perpetuating stereotypes, whether linked to gender, sexuality, race or disability. In addition, marketing messages in a range of guises serve to act as standards against which we may measure ourselves. Messages such as what constitutes the 'ideal family' or standards of 'attractiveness, body shape and beauty'

DOI: 10.4324/9781003201151-6

have potential to marginalise some groups and prompt feelings of anxiety and inadequacy in others.

This chapter explores the mechanisms through which marketing theory and practice can serve to perpetuate inequality and oppression. We start by looking at recent feminist views on, and critiques of, the market. This is followed by a consideration of marketing research studies on queer theory, critical race theory and theories of intersectionality. While these theories (and the underlying oppressions they address) have long scholarly histories, they have only more recently achieved sustained visibility within marketing. We then turn our attention to advertising to explore how inequality can be reproduced through visual representations of gender, sexual orientation and disability and their intersections. Finally, we explore how marketing creates norms and expectations surrounding roles and responsibilities connected to mothering, fathering and the family more generally. This can be oppressive to some groups who may measure their own lives via these expectations. For other groups, their own experiences may be so far from those represented in marketing messages that they may just be left out of the conversation altogether.

Feminisms and Gender in the Marketplace

There exists a long history of feminist work which explores the ways in which the market and marketing practices might serve to reproduce gender inequalities (Bristor and Fischer, 1993). It is important to recognise the existence of multiple feminisms, the idea that there isn't only one way to be a feminist. While historically, marketing scholarship has tended to focus on a white Anglo-American view of feminism, this has begun to change with the increasing visibility of research that is based on Black, decolonial and intersectional feminisms. Marketing scholars have charted the historical emergence of feminism in the US and UK contexts through a framework of successive waves of feminism (i.e. Maclaran, 2015). Here, scholars note that early waves of feminism were concerned with the more practical and pressing issues of gaining equality for women in the eyes of the law in the workplace and in the public and political sphere. Earlier feminists were concerned with securing the vote for women and the activities of the suffragettes, and the suffragists, in campaigning for the vote for women, gained particular media attention. While they began a campaign of activism at the turn of the century in the UK, women weren't granted equal rights as men to vote in the UK until 1928. Feminist activism continued to revolve around changing legislation notably in the areas of equal pay and access to credit but also in marital rights, abortion and childcare. Fast forward to the 1970s and a book that encapsulates the spirit of the times is Germaine Greer's (1970) *The Female Eunuch*. Greer's target was the issue of female oppression. She argues that, historically, the norms that women use to measure their perception of self and their role in society were shaped by male expectations. She calls on women to challenge these norms, reject their traditional roles, question the power of authority figures and explore their own sexuality.

However, two more recent forms of feminism have very direct implications for marketing, these are: choice feminism (or postfeminism) and digital feminism (or fourth-wave feminism).

Choice Feminism (or Postfeminism)

In recent decades, companies have appealed more and more to the consumer as an 'individual' that would buy their products to construct and maintain their identity. They have achieved this through increasingly fine-grained and sophisticated market segmentation which not only embraced categories such as gender, age and class but also identified segments on the basis of 'lifestyle'. This mode of lifestyle marketing sought out groups whose aim might have been to resist or counteract mainstream culture in order to sell to them – or perhaps harness their countercultural values and sell them to a wider audience. Feminism ultimately became the target, and feminist values and dispositions were repackaged (and watered down) for mainstream consumption. This version of feminism has been called 'choice feminism'. Choice feminism is perhaps the version of feminism which has the closest links with neoliberal, or marketized, thinking. This is because choice feminism has 'individual choice' at its heart – the idea that women have the option to choose and that this choice is a source of empowerment. Key examples of this are the idea of 'girl power' promoted by groups such as the UK pop group Spice Girls and the 'pink pound' which touted female empowerment as their key selling point.

While this idea sounds very positive, this version of feminism has been widely criticised for disregarding the social context women live in. In particular, it has little conception of the ways in which women may be located in relation to race, sexual orientation, ability or class. These locations may mean that women have different ability and opportunity to access choice. The concept of postfeminism has also been linked to choice feminism. The foremost scholar in this field is Rosalind Gill, who helpfully talks about a 'postfeminist sensibility', which, rather than trying to describe postfeminism as a movement, sees it as a general orientation to the world. She describes a series of elements of a postfeminist sensibility:

> including the emphasis upon choice and autonomy, the focus on women's bodies as their source of value, and the centrality of ideas of 'makeover', including the requirement to 'upgrade' one's psychic life to be positive, confident and glowing.
>
> (Banet-Weiser et al., 2020, p. 5)

In Gill's description, we can see elements of postfeminism which run distinctly counter to the project of emancipating women. Instead, we see a set of elements which seem to reproduce the objectification of women's bodies and the commodification of their emotions (and psychic life). This marketisation of feminism is also problematic because, as feminists argued, the market only ever appeals to the individual in its efforts to persuade them to consume. This has the potential effect of dispersing the collective power and solidarity so central to feminism and other collective movements. The feminist project also faltered with the idea that women (Western ones anyway) had all the choices available to men and, thus, that feminism was no longer relevant to society.

Digital (Fourth-Wave) Feminism

A more recent incarnation of feminism (sometimes called fourth-wave feminism, or digital feminism) that emerged around 2008 represents a backlash against the idea of 'choice feminism' in making attempts to reclaim female bodies from the marketplace (Cochrane, 2013; Stevens and Houston, 2016; Matich et al., 2019, 2022a). It harnesses the power of the internet and social media to create a new space in which to re-order gendered inequalities, critique and question dominant representations of women (such as those in the media and advertising) and take back power in setting the agenda for the way in which women choose to present themselves. In this sense, the internet facilitates a globalised 'call-out' culture in which instances of racism and sexism can be 'called out' and challenged. Indeed, it can be argued that digital communication has also facilitated a rise in a more intersectionally focused understanding of inequality and oppression. There has been an explosion of feminist blogs, social media campaigns and online organising which has given form and voice to a range of thought leaders and grassroots activists. The number of women using digital spaces is on the rise. And, according to a report, women aged between 18–29 are the 'power users of social networking' (Martin and Valenti, 2012). However, globally, in relation to economic opportunity, it is important to remember there remains a big digital divide by gender. A report by the Organisation for Economic Co-operation and Development (OECD) in 2018 found that 'worldwide some 327 million fewer women than men have a smartphone and can access the mobile internet. Women are under-represented in ICT jobs, top management and academic careers and, men are four times more likely than women to be ICT specialists' (OECD, 2018).

However, grassroots initiatives are important in acting as a form of consciousness raising, building on existing debates and exposing those debates to a wider range of global participants. One good example is the Doula Project which is an organisation that provides care and support for women across the spectrum of pregnancy to include birth, miscarriage, stillbirth, fetal anomaly or abortion. They use the online environment as a vital platform for their activities. The sites Women in Media and News and The Women's Room are education and advocacy groups which work to create a space for women in the media. Another example is *gal-dem*, started in 2015 as an online zine which platformed the work of non-binary women of colour (Matich et al., 2022a, 2022b). Since then, it has grown and extended its remit, describing itself as 'an award-winning media company committed to sharing the perspectives of people of colour from marginalised genders' (*gal-dem* website, Oct 2022). The F Word is an online magazine which includes debate and discussion about contemporary feminism. Very often, there is a symbiosis between online and offline activity with many campaigns, such as Free the Nipple (a campaign which opposes sexual objectification of women – see Matich et al., 2019), The Everyday Sexism Project (which catalogues experiences of sexism in everyday life) and No More Page 3 (a campaign opposing *The Sun* newspapers' publication of topless women), creating a seamless relation between online blogs, *Twitter* feeds and video material and offline events, such as seminars, rallies and support groups. With hundreds of new sites popping up every month, it is impossible even to capture the variety of issues covered and the array of creative interventions feminists are using on this platform. Important from a marketing perspective, though, is the power of these groupings in calling out the big brands on their activities. *Facebook* was forced to deal with the hundreds of instances of gender-based hate speech and shut down offensive pages as a result of the #Fbrape campaign. Critiques of Dove's Real Beauty campaign appeared all over the pages of feminist blogs and *Twitter* feeds as 'peddling the same old beauty standards'. However, this communication format is not without its challenges. For example, the limited *Twitter* feed allowance of 280 characters and the *Facebook* 'like' facilities encourage a shallow and binary (yes/no) engagement with debates. Also, the format encourages individualistic judgements as opposed to collective solidarity.

Recently, the big brands have started to get in on the act themselves, perhaps another example of the way in which consumer capitalism has modified itself to subsume countercultural ideas in the pursuit of profit (Wechie, 2016; Sobande, 2019). It seems that elements of fourth-wave feminism have become marketplace fodder in the guise of femvertising. Brands have begun to use hashtag feminism to sell products by launching feminist-orientated social media campaigns. For example, the energy company, EDF, have launched #prettycurious, a campaign to encourage young women into jobs where they have traditionally been under-represented such as science, technology, engineering and maths. Cosmetics brand CoverGirl's #GirlsCan campaign, fronted by Pink, Ellen DeGeneres and Janelle Monae, is aimed at breaking down barriers for girls. Pantene's #ShineStrong included a short film titled *Sorry, Not Sorry* which highlighted how women constantly apologise in a range of situations at home and at work. The video went viral. These are just some examples of brands' use of the idea of female empowerment to sell products and services. The question remains as to whether they do in fact empower individuals. Rather, ideals of empowerment of marginalised groups are used to build their brand image, acting as a form of brand virtue signaling. As we discuss in the next section, the use of race and racial empowerment messages by brands operate as an insidious form of 'woke-washing' (Sobande, 2019).

Race in the Marketplace

Race and its practical and ideological impacts in marketing have, to date, received scant attention within marketing academia. While race did begin to trickle into thinking in marketing in the 1980s and 1990s, a lengthy history of Black and racial justice scholarship has yet to gain any sustained visibility in the pages of academic marketing and consumer research journals and textbooks. As we explor in Chapter 8, existing hierarchies of knowledge, both in academia and industry, privilege some ways of being and thinking, while holding others on the margins. As such, the lack of scholarship on race goes hand in hand with histories of colonialism and an Anglo-American and Eurocentric dominance in marketing thought and scholarship (see Chapter 8 for a detailed discussion).

It is important to recognise that the construct of 'race' is used as a classification that acts as a powerful organising principle in society. The race construct itself is steeped in a colonial legacy: 'Forged historically through oppression, slavery, and conquest, the race construct has persisted over time because false notions of racial difference have become embedded in the beliefs and behaviours of societies' this embedding 'is also known as racism' (Poole et al., 2021, p. 127).

The lack of marketing attention to race is also particularly stark given the ways in which marketplace structures and even very recent marketing activity continue to perpetuate racial oppression and inequality – from the whiteness that is historically enfolded into consumer research scholarship and thinking about markets (Burton, 2009) to the relative lack of people of colour in marketing and advertising roles in industry and the under-representation and misrepresentation and commodification of Blackness and Black experiences in advertising (Crockett, 2008) and in digital media more generally (Sobande et al., 2020). While there have been some small inroads made, there is still much to do to understand both how racialised power dynamics operate in the marketplace but, more significantly, to recognise and attend to the historical structural oppression of Black people (Grier et al., 2019).

One worrying trend is the practice of 'woke-washing' in the branding sphere. This practice has undoubtedly been sparked by the increased media attention to Black social justice activism. Structural oppression and violence against Black people have resulted in the killing of Black adults and children for centuries. However, one recent example, the unlawful killing of George Floyd in May 2020 at the hands of police in Minneapolis, USA, gained a particularly large amount of global media attention and along with it the Black Lives Matter social movement. Some brands have been accused of using this as an 'opportunity' to capitalise on, and profit from, what they (inappropriately) view as a cultural trend. Francesca Sobande (2019) refers to this as 'woke-washing'. In her study of ten marketing campaigns by Gatorade, H&M, Nike, Pepsi, Ram Trucks and Smirnoff, she explores how individuals from different racial backgrounds and with different gender identities are presented. She identifies a series of themes which characterise these representations to include 'White Saviour, Black Excellence, Strong Black Woman (and Mother), and "Woke" Change Agent' (Sobande, 2019, p. 2723). She observes that these representations draw on wider discourses (and themes) within media and culture about gender equality and Black social justice activism, such as the Black Lives Matter social movement. But because these discourses are used to build brands, as part of a commercial venture, they reinforce a market-based view of individual power and achievement rather than the collective politics and solidarity that underpin social justice activism, a solidarity that is needed to effect any real change. In this way, she argues that they undermine the activism that they reference in their campaigns.

Queering the Marketplace

Queer theory has roots in gay, lesbian and feminist thinking and has the objective of questioning hierarchies of power within marketing thought. In this vein, Pirani and Daskalopoulou (2021) put forward a 'queer manifesto' which unpacks the potential of queer theory and queer thinking to interrogate 'the inequality produced by the normative alignment of gender, sex and desire' (Butler, 1990, cited in Pirani and Daskalopoulou, 2022). A helpful contribution by Coffin et al. (2019) gives an overview of work within marketing and consumer research on LGBTQ+ studies (see also Shepherd and Hamilton, 2022, on transgender studies). These overviews find a lack of work which attempts to explore the lifeworlds and experiences of this group (albeit very diverse). Much existing research has tended to spectacularise the experiences of LGBTQ+ people, focusing on identity and viewing their consumption behaviour as making a symbolic point rather than merely being the mundane provisioning of everyday life. In addition, and as with work on other marginal groups, existing work has tended to focus on white middle-class Anglo-American views. There is also a pressing need for more intersectional studies to help us to understand how sexual orientation intersects with other protected characteristics to reproduce inequality. Understandings also too easily fall into unhelpful binaries. In particular, LGBTQ+ has largely only been understood in relation to heterosexuality. In this way, the complexity of gender identity, gender expression, sexual orientation and sex assignment are collapsed into one another and only understood in terms of what they are not (i.e. 'not heterosexual'). They are also only understood in relation to a heterosexual way of being and experiencing the world. As such, there is much work to do to capture the variations in experience and complexity of the lifeworlds of individuals identifying as LGBTQ+.

Again, we need to be wary of merely pointing to isolated examples, although this can be helpful if we see them as visible instances of a deeper-seated functioning of systemic inequality. A recent study that both captures the systemic functioning of inequality and manages to work with the complexity of LGBTQ+ identification is by Bettany et al. (2022). They use the example of the emergence of HIV PreExposure

Prophylaxis (PrEP), a drug used to prevent transmission of the human immunodeficiency virus (HIV) to explore how stigma is generated and disseminated across a range of different media. Rather than only researching the individuals using the drug or the companies supplying it, they examine a diverse range of sources to include NHS published documents, activist published commentary, and films and documentaries, along with individual and group interviews and observations in online groups and at GBM and LGTBQ+ events. In this way, they were able to explore how stigma develops and travels (is diffused) through a complex system, in their words:

> It might be argued that PrEP is more central to the milieu of sexual health than PrEP-consuming subjects, given that consumers are just one of many actants involved in ideas of healthy sexuality. Also relevant are sexual-health clinics (private and state-funded), media outlets, creative outputs, religious authorities, condom producers, sauna owners, NHS and other governmental regulatory bodies, online pharmacies, activists, marketing scholars, the HIV virus, other STIs, condoms, competing supply-chains, even seemingly disconnected diseases like Covid-19.
>
> (Bettany et al., 2022, p. 5)

In exploring both the contexts in which stigma is experienced, what they term 'gazing across' but also at the same time looking at how stigma is produced, by whom and for what ends, what they term 'gazing up'. Then they are able to explore a 'systemic' view of the way in which inequality is perpetuated. In other words, rather than looking at individuals and isolated instances, they can connect individual experience with larger institutions (such as the NHS, pharmacies and other government bodies). They find that stigma is managed by the consumer but also through the market (through sourcing, purchasing and supply). Importantly, their study methods also allow us to explore how stigma operates intersectionally, both via the intersections of protected person or group identity characteristics (i.e. by race, gender, sexuality, etc.) and via other stigma effects (e.g. age, HIV status and partner status) (Bettany et al., 2022).

In the previous discussion, the need for more work within marketing that takes an intersectional approach to understanding inequality is very clear. As yet, there is a limited number of studies that explore intersections, but this is changing, see, for example, Morris's (2017) study of fashion consumption by Black middle-class women or Matich et al.'s (2022b) work on *gal-dem*, a media company that platforms the work of people of colour from marginalised genders. But there are fewer still that embrace intersectionality as a paradigm (as a way of thinking about research and of doing research). To fully embrace intersectionality is to rethink entrenched theory and long-established practices in marketing that perpetuate oppressions and inequalities.

Developing an Intersectional Understanding of Markets and Consumers

Understanding inequality by looking at intersections, or crossroads of differing sources of oppression, has long been at the heart of work by Black and racial justice activists and scholars. The Black feminist scholar Kimberlé Crenshaw argued in 1991 that to fully understand the experiences of Black women in relation to male violence, it is necessary to examine how race and gender intersect and that looking at either one or the other alone does not adequately capture their experience, in her words:

> Women of color are differently situated in the economic, social and political worlds. When reform efforts undertaken on behalf of women neglect this fact, women of color are less likely to have their needs met than women who are racially privileged.
>
> (Crenshaw, 1991, p. 1250)

In her paper, she refers to a series of interventions that were made on the basis of the needs of women who were largely white and middle class. For example, rape crisis counsellors reported that they spent time addressing needs other than rape itself that took a higher priority for women of colour. Therefore, a uniform approach based on the needs of white middle-class women doesn't adequately meet the needs of women of colour because these women require different prioritising of resources. It is important to note that Crenshaw's work, while landmark, merely gave voice to decades of work by Black feminist scholars and activists.

> intersecting oppressions are mutually constituted by each other. There is no meaning to the notion of 'black', for instance, which is not gendered and classed, no meaning for the notion of 'woman' which is not ethnocized and classed, etc.
>
> (Yuval-Davis, 2007. P. 565)

However, intersectionality is a way of working as well as of understanding. At its heart is the need to understand power relations and social inequalities so that they might be acted upon (Collins, 2015). Steinfield et al. (2019) develop a framework for applying an intersectional approach in the business and marketing context in order to transform practice. This objective of change also motivates Poole et al. (2021), who draw on critical race theory (CRT) in a similar way. While it would be beyond the scope of this chapter to give a full description of CRT here, Poole et al. highlight its main contribution as follows:

> Critical race theory moves the focus beyond the representational level (of who is depicted in marketing, who is targeted, etc.) and involves a historical contextualization (reflection on racist and

colonial histories, etc.) that shifts the focus from diversity and inclusion to equity and liberation.

(2021, p. 137)

In practical terms, this would mean rather than just analysing advertisements to explore how individuals from different racial backgrounds are represented, it would acknowledge and excavate the racist and colonial histories they are embedded within. This would involve asking questions, such as why they are represented in this way, which images and ideas are presented, which historical legacies they originate from, which institutions support these representations and who benefits from them. Poole et al. (2021) also offer some practical advice on approaches that may foster critical reflection on the systems we are embedded within and, therefore, challenge white supremacy and racial power. They suggest placing experiential knowledge at the heart of studies to acknowledge the diversity of experience focusing in particular on people of colour. They also suggest collaborating across disciplines to bring together different viewpoints with those from within marketing, including, for example, critical race studies, sociology, history, media and communications and feminist and queer studies. Bringing together differing bodies of knowledge and their methodologies and theories facilitates an exploration of interdependencies between systems of oppression, such as the patriarchy, racism and capitalism. Further, this helps to embrace intersections, for example, exploring how race intersects with capitalism or with gender or class to reproduce inequality.

Reproducing Inequality in Advertising

There has been a continued focus on the way in which marketing practices reproduce inequality through advertising. Advertising can reinforce norms of appearance and behaviour of specific groups via stereotyping and exaggeration. Advertising can also marginalise groups through a lack of visible representation. Much earlier research focused on visual representations of men and women and of masculinity and femininity. These representations are complex, but importantly, they gain their meaning through being juxtaposed against each other.

> Within this system, iconic masculine activities such as shaving the face, driving fast cars, having a hearty appetite, smoking cigars, and drinking liquor are juxtaposed to feminine visions of applying makeup, driving a minivan, eating 'light', doing the laundry, and decorating houses.
>
> (Schroeder and Zwick, 2004, p. 21)

As this quotation suggests, these images are not just flat two-dimensional representations. They suggest appropriate modes of dress and appearance, but also, more significantly, they suggest appropriate *activities*, ways of doing, living and being masculine and feminine. Further, as the author previously argues, advertising does not act on its own. Rather, it is part of a *system* of meaning which involves both advertising and consumption – responding to and acting out these representations through our consumption activities reinforce them and give them meaning.

The problem with this is that most often, these images remain largely elusive to us. They are exaggerated stereotypes and perfected images which bear little resemblance to everyday reality. Consider the heavily made-up, translucent-skinned images of femininity in cosmetics adverts or the chiselled and muscled images of masculinity in aftershave adverts. These images are a long way from lived reality for most of us. The clothing retailer H&M recently tried to slim down images of the singer Beyoncé in one of their swimwear campaigns. After significant pressure from the celebrity herself, they ended up running the original advert. The skincare brands L'Oreal and Olay have also been forced to withdraw adverts due to the over-use of airbrushing to remove wrinkles and make skin appear flawless. However, some brands are making real attempts to change things. Marketers have begun to address women in all of their various lumps, bumps, shapes and sizes in order to better reflect the reality of everyday life. The Dove Campaign for Real Beauty, launched in 2004, used regular women in place of models. This campaign was accompanied by a whole series of associated initiatives, including an online discussion forum, fundraising to help girls with low self-esteem, self-esteem workshops and the establishment of the Program for Aesthetics and Well-Being at Harvard University. The campaign was also followed up by a series of others involving real women. Unilever defined this approach using the mission strategy: 'To make women feel comfortable in the skin they are in, to create a world where beauty is a source of confidence and not anxiety' (Unilever). This approach has had mixed responses with some women finding it empowering, showing that beauty comes in many guises. Other women, however, argued that this was just another clever attempt at manipulation and that because Dove is a beauty brand, it still reinforces the message that beauty defines women.

The Dove campaign is just one example of a recent trend in advertising which has been called femvertising, or pro-female advertising. These adverts have taken up the feminist mantra of female empowerment and used it to sell a range of products from energy (EDF) to yoghurt drinks (Organic Valley), clothes (JCPenney), beer (Budweiser), software (Microsoft) and shampoo (Pantene). These adverts tackle a range of issues, including the objectification of women – in particular, combatting stereotypical negative portrayals of women in terms of body shape, sexuality, strength and intelligence. The women's media company Sheknows Media has instituted an annual #femvertising award in order to 'honor brands that are challenging gender norms by building stereotype-busting, pro-female messages and images into ads that target women' (Sheknows Media website).

Back in 1999, Steven Kates (1999) observed that representations of gay men in advertising were significantly undergirded by heteronormative values. Similarly, in a more recent study of explicit portrayals of LGBTQ+ people in mainstream advertising from 2009–2015, Nölke (2018) found that there was very little intersectional diversity within the sample of LGBTQ+ people portrayed with nearly a third being middle-aged (35–50), middle-class, white gay men. She observes:

> advertising perpetuates certain types of sexualities and gender representations, while others are symbolically annihilated, thus reinforcing a hierarchy of respectability in which only a certain type of heteronormative gayness is accepted.

There is still a long way to go though in representing diversity in advertising. Kearney et al. (2019) observe that even though disability is one of the largest minority groups worldwide (with one in five people having a disability), images of disabled people and disability have historically been largely excluded from mainstream media and advertising. Where disability is visible, it has often been criticised as not accurately representing the lived realities of disabled people and also individualising disability through a focus on overcoming impairment rather than taking a societal view which prioritises the need for social accommodation and change rather than individual effort and triumph over adversity. In their study of the 'We're the Super Humans' advertisement developed for the Rio 2016 Paralympic Games, they find the following:

> when drawing from stereotypical, fantasy narratives to construe representations – whether in relation to gender, age, disability or other body characteristics – advertising can (re)create existing or new mythologies of norms for the ideal types more generally and 'able disability' in particular, thus maintaining or increasing barriers to marketplace inclusion.
>
> (Kearney et al., 2019, p. 559)

However, as Higgins (2020) carefully conceptualises, the market can also marginalise and oppress disabled people at the psychological and emotional (psycho-emotional) levels. Her study of people living with an impairment and their family members and carers finds that structural barriers in consumption settings and social interactions with other consumers and service providers are the cause of significant psycho-emotional stress. Further, she finds that disabled people and their carers can internalise these experiences, becoming emotionally disabled, most often by fear, for example, of reprisal or exclusion if they complain or fear of the unknown in marketplace settings. Overall, Higgin's study underscores how 'marketplace practices, interactions and services' continue to "internally oppress and psycho-emotionally disable consumers living with impairment"' (2020, p. 2692).

Marketing Roles and Relationships

As we suggested earlier, a key criticism of advertising concerns its promotion of stereotypes, significantly impacting on the way we think about roles within society. Think about the happy Oxo family of the 1980s and 1990s, with Mum serving up dinner, or the Fairy Liquid mum, who is always at the kitchen sink. Adverts have started to embrace some of the diversity that exists in family roles and household makeup, but these adverts still tend to reproduce a heteronormative view of the world. For example, a recent Oxo advert includes Dad giving cooking advice to his son as he tries to make a stir-fry for his girlfriend or a McDonald's advert in which a single mum asks her boyfriend to move in with her and her two children. In the next section, we explore the way in which the market promotes two particularly dominant and largely heteronormatively inflected roles: motherhood and fatherhood.

Markets and Motherhood

Pregnancy, motherhood and consumption are inextricably intertwined in contemporary Western cultures. This relationship between mothers and markets is two way – with women's experiences of mothering being significantly shaped by the marketplace but equally with women using the marketplace to shape and make sense of these experiences. Thus, we might consider the making of mothers *by* the marketplace but also what mothers make *out of* the marketplace (O'Donohoe et al., 2014).

Thinking first about the ways in which mothers are made by the marketplace, we might consider the role that advertising plays in shaping our conceptions and expectations of mothering (Hogg et al., 2011). A study which explored the way in which motherhood has been depicted in food advertising in *Good Housekeeping* magazine found a series of ideal archetypes that were promoted across the period 1950–2010 (Marshall et al., 2014). In the 1950s, mothers were depicted in the role of nurturers very much tied to the home. In the 1960s and 1970s, mothers were still tied to the domestic sphere, but alongside their role of nurturers, they were increasingly presented as experts – encapsulated in the phrase 'mother knows best'. In the 1980s, narratives of mothering in the magazine moved away from the domestic sphere. They also shifted towards health and wellbeing – particularly in relation to childrearing. So advertising serves to shape mothering by depicting specific modes of mothering and ideal motherly types. However, it also acts in a more direct manner by appealing to the anxieties that surround mothering. A study of the advertising used by Danonino (a children's dairy brand) in five European countries found that the adverts dealt with five kinds of anxieties (Coutant et al., 2011). These anxieties were linked to children's growth, intellectual development, exclusion from peer groups, family bonding relationships and lack of parental presence. The study found that once they had presented the risk, the adverts then offered a resolution in the form of their own products to maintain mothers' peace of mind. This is just one example of the way in which brands routinely play on existing motherly anxieties and indeed create new ones in order to sell products. As such, advertising significantly shapes motherly experiences and expectations.

Turning to think about what mothers make *out of* the marketplace, mothers have increasingly been encouraged to use consumer goods to buy their way into their identity as mothers (Thomson et al., 2011). In this sense, motherhood is seen as something that can be achieved or accomplished through consumption. Good, or successful, mothering is intertwined with a series of consumption projects. At the domestic level, this may be as simple as creating a family meal (Cappellini and Parsons, 2012). At the public level, objects themselves and the ways in which they are used, styled together and displayed may play a significant role in mothering. Here, we can find examples of objects and brands which have come to stand as models of classed mothering: 'What the stigmatized dummy (or "dirty-did") is to some model of compromised working-class motherhood, the Bugaboo pram is to "achieved middle class" motherhood' (Clarke, 2014, p. 50). These examples highlight that choosing and using products within the practice of mothering is not as straightforward as it may first seem. The assumptions that mothering should be second nature and that knowing how to mother is something that women should already know put significant pressure on choices of what to buy, where to buy and how to use these products and brands. This is even more the case considering that practices of mothering are often very public and open to scrutiny. There is a premium attached to getting it right and a risk of failure in getting it wrong. Miller (2014, p. 161) observes:

> The contours of successful motherhood can be seen as a socially constructed performance, which is increasingly managed and 'read' through the consumer goods and consumption patterns which signal and facilitate its successful accomplishment.

Therefore, products and brands don't always help in the project of motherhood. While sometimes they may act as props to the doing of mothering, at other times, the array of products and brands available and their promoted uses may be bewildering and may even jeopardize attempts at managing impressions as a new mother (Miller, 2014).

Markets and Fatherhood

Arguably, contemporary fatherhood is not as deeply intertwined with the marketplace and consumption as motherhood. This may well be because as yet, the market of fathers for many child-focused products is simply not as big as the market of mothers. Put simply, in Western contexts at least, mothers are still doing most of the shopping for child-focused (and family) products. They are, therefore, still the main target for marketing activity (Coffey et al., 2006). In addition, we know much less about fatherhood per se from a marketing and consumption perspective because it has been the focus of fewer studies. This is largely due to the privileging of men in society through the operation of masculine hegemony. Studies have, therefore, tended to focus on the ways in which women have been marginalised and oppressed through the operation of the marketplace, and studies into men and masculinity have been seen as a less pressing concern.

The relationship between men and their role as fathers may well be more complex and conflictual than between women and their role as mothers. This might be because of the deeply entrenched social and cultural link between women and mothering in many cultures. This link is weaker for men who seem to have a wider range of roles open to them, and the norms surrounding fathering that do exist often conflict with those surrounding masculinity (Gentry and Harrison, 2010). Men also feel detached and isolated from what is seen as a very woman-centred process of parenting. So while in the discussion previously about mothering we found that the marketplace tended to give mothers a series of relatively clear signals about what constitutes 'good mothering', it seems that for fathers, things are more blurred. Rather than giving clear signals about fathering, the marketplace offers men a tapestry of resources that they use to cope with some of the role conflicts they experience in becoming fathers. Navigating the marketplace is not that easy for fathers, though. A study which explored the role of mundane caring technological objects (such as baby monitors and baby rockers) in the transition to new fatherhood found them to be largely ambivalent (Bettany et al., 2014). These technologies smoothed but also exacerbated fatherhood-role conflict and gender struggles in the home.

It is still largely the case that fatherhood is linked to the public arena of paid employment, whereas motherhood is still wedded to the domestic sphere. This means that stay-at-home fathers find that they occupy a marginalised-role status in society that contradicts the traditional breadwinner role. A study of at-home fathers who previously were breadwinners in their homes finds that they use consumption to legitimize this marginalised status (Coskuner-Balli and Thompson, 2013). To regain some status, they create a distinctive gender identity which is neither masculine breadwinner nor feminine carer and nurturer but which draws on elements of both of these positions. Thus, fathers seem to engage in a form of productive domestic consumption which reproduces their socialisation into the world of work and which contrasts with the typical depiction of mothers as consuming as part of the wider project of care and nurture. A study of men and DIY in the home nicely illustrates this (Moisio et al., 2013). The study finds that men with low levels of cultural capital view their domestic DIY as a form of work likening the home to a workplace, whereas men with existing high levels of cultural capital see DIY as a leisure activity. A Finnish study examined a range of materials that offer advice surrounding fathering, including a parenting manual, a textbook, a guide for professionals and government sources on fatherhood and parenting (Eraranta and Moisander, 2011). They found that there was a wide chasm between advice and depiction of fathering in these texts and the sorts of behaviours that were required in the workplace. Depictions of good fathering included involved fathering, with ideals of caring, family-orientated parenting. However, this does not readily match with the ideals surrounding the committed employee who is available and able to work long hours. In sum, this results in conflicts for men surrounding their identities as workers and as fathers.

Just as advertising shapes conceptions of mothering in direct ways, it also shapes conceptions of fathering. Advertising studies have shown that male portrayals still reflect a very traditional masculine perspective (Gentry and Harrison, 2010). These hyper-masculine portrayals can be problematic because they often clash with the more caring and nurturing roles required of fatherhood. This portrayal, therefore, is the cause of male confusion concerning what masculine roles are expected of them. However, things do seem to be changing. Interestingly, in 2016, a new category was added to the #femvertising competition mentioned earlier titled 'Dadvertising' to encompass adverts that directly target and counteract stereotypical portrayals of fatherhood.

In summary then, it seems – from the limited studies to date on the links between fatherhood and the market – that (in Western contexts at least) fathers are not a target for marketers to the same extent as mothers are. Equally, it seems that the market has nowhere near as pervasive a role in shaping expectations of fathering and indeed shaping the notion of what it is to be a good father. Undoubtedly, as society changes and fathers continue to take on a more central role in relation to parenting, the market will morph and reflect these changes. In the future, it is likely that we will see fathers as a target market emerging much more clearly.

Summary

Marketing is a powerful force in society. It influences how we see the world and how we view the others around us. In this respect, it has the capacity to (re)produce inequality, but it also has the capacity to effect real change in society. In this chapter, we have explored some of the mechanisms that can serve to reproduce inequality, including the stereotyping and misrepresentation of some (marginalised) groups and the promotion and dominance of values associated with groups who hold more power in society. We have explored some of the challenges posed by different theories and ways of thinking to include queer theory, critical race theory and feminist theory. What all of these theories have in common is a drive towards an intersectional understanding of consumers so that we can begin to grasp the ways in which consumers can be located within differing and multiple systems of oppression at the same time. We need more studies which cut across marginal groupings. But giving isolated examples is not enough to address what are much more deeply ingrained systemic issues. What this means is that rather than pointing to, and calling out, individual instances of oppression and inequality in marketing activity, we need to look underneath at the structures and systems that perpetuate them.

Case Study: Femvertising: Selling Empowerment

Feminist Theory: Throwing Like a Girl

In 1980, the political philosopher and feminist Iris Marion Young wrote an essay which she titled *Throwing Like a Girl*. In the essay, Young explores the issue of embodiment (i.e. how we live in our bodies, how we move them, understand them and experience them and how this differs between the sexes). She describes the way in which women (and girls) tend to be overcautious and self-conscious about their bodies, leading to feelings within themselves that they are incapable. She argues that this is a socially conditioned mind-set, though, that women are conditioned to limit their bodily abilities. Vitally, she argues that this is because their bodies are often seen by others as mere objects (they are objectified) and that women sometimes internalise this and are, therefore, very self-conscious of their body, worrying about how they look to others. Thus, when engaging in activities like sports, women, instead of focusing on what they aim to do (i.e. hit a target), they self-consciously focus on what their body needs to do.

> We often experience our bodies as a fragile encumbrance, rather than the media for the enactment of our aims. We feel as though we must have our attention directed upon our bodies to make sure they are doing what we wish them to do, rather than paying attention to what we want to do through our bodies.
>
> (Young, 1980, pp. 146–147)

'Throwing like a girl' is also a phrase that has passed into common usage with negative connotations of inadequacy and lack of power and direction. In fact, to do anything 'like a girl' is generally seen to be both ineffective and not be taken seriously.

Femvertising: Always #LikeAGirl Campaign

Fast forward 34 years to 2014 and the sanitary product brand Always released their advertising campaign, #LikeAGirl. The campaign builds significantly on the ideas in Young's (1980) essay. It is a good example of a growing trend that has been called 'femvertising' which is said to draw on feminist values of female empowerment to target women and encourage them to consume (Iqbal, 2015).

The creatives at the advertising agency Leo Burnett designed what they called a 'social experiment', where they asked people of both sexes, both young and old, to show them what it was like to do things 'like a girl'. So in an individual interview, they asked them to 'throw like a girl', 'fight like a girl' and 'run like a girl'. What they found was that many of the older participants (male and female) ran, threw and fought in half-hearted and ineffective ways, appearing 'sissy' and putting in little effort. But when they asked the younger girls the same question, they ran, threw and fought in uninhibited, energetic and determined ways. In essence, the young girls gave it their best shot. The interviews were captured on film. The final cut included sequences of the older participants' half-hearted activities set against the young girls uninhibited and determined activities. Sequences also included interview material where they asked participants to reflect on their depictions, asking them what 'like a girl' meant for them. Towards the end of the advert, the text 'Let's make #LikeAGirl mean amazing things' appears on the screen.

The campaign quickly went viral and, in the year that followed, notched up more than 50 million *YouTube* views. The advert was aired at the 2015 Super Bowl and was named by CBS as one of the top three Super Bowl commercials of all time. It has won a plethora of industry awards, including the 2015 Emmy Award for Outstanding Commercial, the Grand Clio Award, a Cannes Grand Prix, a Black Pencil and a White Pencil at D&AD and 11 Webby Awards. The campaign was designed at Leo Burnett, with the London, Chicago and Toronto offices collaborating on the advert. The lead creative was Judy John (CEO in Canada and Chief Creative Officer in North America at Leo Burnett). John has an impressive CV with over 25 years' experience in copywriting and creative directing in advertising. She was ranked number one Chief Creative Officer in the world in Advertising Age's Awards Report 2015 and number eight in Business Insiders' 30 Most Creative People in Advertising. Hopefully in the future, John won't be an anomaly as a woman in the upper echelons of the advertising industry. As we discussed earlier in the chapter, to tip the balance, more women are still needed in advertising creative departments.

The parent company of the Always brand (Procter & Gamble – P&G) augments the advertising campaign through a series of other initiatives. In the developed country context, P&G is focusing on providing puberty education resources for girls. Their schools program has developed kits containing information on puberty for parents and lesson plans and materials for teachers. They have developed a similar set of resources to build confidence and help keep girls in sports. They launched the Always Confidence Teaching Curriculum in 2015 with conferences in ten cities around the globe, featuring thought leaders, educators and inspiring young girls. The curriculum was created in partnership with confidence and education experts.

In developing countries, P&G works with partners such as local ministries of education and NGOs such as Save the Children and organisations like Girlology to deliver puberty education. The program has been endorsed by UNESCO and is active in more than 65 countries. Due to a lack of sanitary products, girls in underprivileged areas are often forced to skip school. P&G has partnered with the Department of Basic Education, UNICEF, the Small Projects Foundation and other stakeholders to initiate a program which delivers sanitary towels and health education to girls in these areas to help keep them in school. P&G has also teamed up with UNESCO to offer a literacy education program in Africa. In 2016, the program had reached around 60,000 girls in Nigeria and Senegal, mainly through information and communication technologies. P&G intends to extend the program to reach a further 50,000 girls and women in Northern Nigeria by the end of 2019. P&G also contributed to the UN Women's 'One Win Leads to Another' program in 2016. The program began in Brazil, offering 10–18-year-old girls free sports facilities in the Olympic Villas, with experts providing workshops on health, preventing violence and leadership. There are plans to expand the program globally.

Femvertising: Is It Really Empowering?

Questions have been asked as to whether femvertising is truly empowering, as Nosheen Iqbal from *The Guardian* noted recently, 'Behind the hype, who is really benefitting?' Most of these campaigns use the power of the internet to reach their target audience. They rely on creating such a resonance with women's core values and beliefs that they willingly share these adverts through their social media sites, such as their *Facebook* pages and *Twitter* accounts. This online presence might make this trend a possible example of fourth-wave feminism with companies cashing in on riding this wave. Is the marketing of feminist values O.K. if it does genuinely challenge gender norms and battle inequality? The problem lies – as other commentators have observed (i.e. Sobande, 2019) – in tensions between the ideologies underlying the feminist movement and the market. These ideologies are at odds with one another. This is because the market is predicated on individual choice and agency, and the feminist movement relies wholly on collectivity and solidarity, a coming together rather than a separation of individuals. As such paradoxically, advertising like #LikeAGirl ultimately undermines the very collective action needed to make a difference to gender equality, as *The Guardian*'s Iqbal somewhat cynically comments:

> The idea that confidence and self-belief is what the debate and struggle is missing is seductive: it encourages sisterly encouragement – likes, shares and stories told in 140 characters are easily digestible, and a soft way to get adolescents, in particular, hooked on the movement – and, of course, your brand.

A series of key issues emerge here. First, clearly, this kind of questioning of existing gendered norms and stereotypes is needed within society, but are commercial organisations in the best position to do this in a fair and balanced way? Might it be possible that they are merely just selling a different brand of femininity back to us? Second, is social media the best medium to use to engage in this struggle? It allows for short, snappy and ultimately, easily sharable stories to be told, but are these always the most helpful ones? In summary, though, perhaps the popularity and resonance of these campaigns is a little depressing, merely evidence of how little distance we have travelled in achieving true gender equality. A comment from Laura Bates, the founder of Everyday Sexism Project, sums it up nicely:

> while I applaud progress, wouldn't it be nice to live in a world where we didn't have to celebrate ad campaigns that give children equal access to toys or don't present women in a sexist way because [those things were] just the norm?
>
> (Davidson, 2015)

Seminar Exercises

Discussion Topics

1 Discuss the range of ways that the marketplace has shaped our conceptions of either race, gender or sexual orientation.
2 Choose a brand or product which specifically targets male, female or non-binary consumers and discuss the values it promotes and how it achieves this (think about advertising, packaging, price, etc.).
3 Discuss the range of ways that social justice activists are making use of the internet to support their cause. (This could relate to any axis of inequality.) Which ones do you think are most effective and why?
4 Having read the case study previously, consider whether you think femvertising might be seen as successful. What are its drawbacks?

Group Exercises

1 Ask each group member to bring in an example of an advert that they particularly like or dislike that draws on racial and/or ableist and/or gendered norms or stereotypes (think about role portrayals as well as representations of masculinity and femininity).

   i   Discuss why you particularly like or dislike the advert.
   ii Explore which particular stereotype the advert is drawing on.
   iii Discuss how you think the advert promotes the wider values of the brand.
   iv Discuss whether you think the advert is likely to be successful and why.

2 Read the chapter by Ourahmoune and El Jurdi (2022), 'Marketing and the Missing Feminisms: Decolonial Feminisms and the Arab Spring'. Focus in particular on the sections titled 'Arab feminisms, marketing and the Arab Spring'. See the reference list for the full reference.

   i   Using the section 'Arab feminisms, marketing and the Arab Spring' for inspiration, research one feminist activist campaign or social movement in a MENA country of your choice.

   ii Discuss your example with the group.

      a Identify the key challenges the campaign or movement is addressing.

      b Offer an assessment about whether you think it will have an impact and, if so, how.

Internet Resources

Gal-dem, https://gal-dem.com/

The Everyday Sexism project an online platform which encourages people to post their experiences of sexism, http://everydaysexism.com/

Women's lifestyle digital media company: Sheknows Media, www.sheknowsmedia.com/

Key Readings

Arsel, Z., Eräranta, K., & Moisander, J. (2015). Theorising gender and gendering theory in marketing and consumer research. Special issue of *Journal of Marketing Management*, 31(15–16)

Maclaran, P, Stevens, L., & Kravets, O. (2022) (eds). *The Routledge Companion to Marketing and Feminism*. London, UK: Routledge.

Poole, S.M., Grier, S.A., Thomas, K.D., Sobande, F., Ekpo, A.E., Torres, L.T., Addington, L. A., Weekes-Laidlow, M., & Henderson, G.R. (2021). Operationalizing Critical Race Theory in the Marketplace. *Journal of Public Policy & Marketing*, 40(2), 126–142.

References

Banet-Weiser, S., Gill, R., & Rottenberg, C. (2020). Postfeminism, popular feminism and neoliberal feminism? Sarah Banet-Weiser, Rosalind Gill and Catherine Rottenberg in conversation. *Feminist Theory*, 21(1), 3–24.

Bauer, G., Schiem, A., Travers, R., & Hammond, R. (2015). Intervenable factors associated with suicide risk in transgender persons: A respondent driven suicide risk sampling study in Ontario, Canada. *BMC Public Health*, 15, 525. https://doi.org/10.1186/s12889-015-1867-2

Bettany, S., Coffin, J., Eichert, C., & Rowe, D. (2022). Stigmas that matter: Diffracting marketing stigma theoretics. *Marketing Theory*, 22(4), 501–518.

Bettany, S.M., Kerrane, B., & Hogg, M.K. (2014). The material-semiotics of fatherhood: The co-emergence of technology and contemporary fatherhood. *Journal of Business Research*, 67(7), 1544–1551.

Bristor, J.M., & Fischer, E. (1993). Feminist thought: Implications for consumer research. *Journal of Consumer Research*, 19(4), 518–536.

Burton, D. (2009). 'Reading' whiteness in consumer research. *Consumption Markets & Culture*, 12(2), 171–201.

Butler, J. (1990). *Gender Trouble and the Subversion of Identity*. New York: Routledge.

Cappellini, B., & Parsons, E. (2012). (Re) enacting motherhood: Self-sacrifice and abnegation in the kitchen. In R. Belk & A. Ruvio (Eds), *Identity and Consumption*. London: Routledge, pp. 119–128.

Clarke, A.J. (2014). Designing mothers and the market: Social class and material culture. In S. O'Donohoe, M. Hogg, P. Maclaran, L. Martens, & L. Stevens (Eds), *Motherhoods, Markets and Consumption: The Making of Mothers in Contemporary Western Cultures*. London: Routledge, pp. 43–55.

Cochrane, K. (2013). *All the Rebel Women: The Rise of the Fourth Wave of Feminism*. London: Guardian Shorts.

Coffey, T., Siegel, D., & Livingstone, G. (2006). *Marketing to the New Super Consumer: Mom and Kid*. Ithaca: Paramount Market Publishers.

Coffin, J., Eichert, C.A., & Nölke, A.I. (2019). Towards (and beyond) LGBTQ+ studies in marketing and consumer research. In S. Dobscha (Ed), *Handbook of Research on Gender and Marketing*. Cheltenham: Edward Elgar Publishing, pp. 273–293.

Collins, P.H. (2015). Intersectionality's definitional dilemmas. *Annual Review of Sociology*, 41, 1–20.

Coskuner-Balli, G., & Thompson, C.J. (2013). The status costs of subordinate cultural capital: At-home fathers' collective pursuit of cultural legitimacy through capitalizing consumption practices. *Journal of Consumer Research*, 40(1), 19–41.

Coutant, A., de La Ville, V. I., Gram, M., & Boireau, N. (2011). Motherhood, advertising, and anxiety: A cross-cultural perspective on Danonino commercials. *Advertising & Society Review*, 12(2) (Advertising Educational Foundation. Retrieved September 26, 2016, from Project MUSE database).

Crenshaw, K.W. (1991). Mapping the margins: Intersectionality, identity politics, and violence against women of color. *Stanford Law Review*, 43(6), 1241–1299.

Crockett, D. (2008). Marketing blackness: How advertisers use race to sell products. *Journal of Consumer Culture*, 8(2), 245–268.

Davidson, L. (2015). Femvertising: Advertisers cash in on #feminism, *The Telegraph*, 12 January, www.telegraph.co.uk/women/womens-life/11312629/Femvertising-Advertisers-cash-in-on-feminism.html

Eraranta, K., & Moisander, J. (2011). Psychological regimes of truth and father identity: Challenges for work/life integration. *Organization Studies*, 32(4), 509–526.

Gentry, R., & Harrison, R. (2010). Is advertising a barrier to male movement toward gender change? *Marketing Theory*, 10(1), 74–96

Greer, G. (1970). *The Female Eunuch*. London: Harper Perennial.

Grier, S.A., Thomas, K.D., & Johnson, G.D. (2019). Re-Imagining the marketplace: Addressing race in academic marketing research. *Consumption Markets & Culture*, 22(1), 91–100.

Higgins, L. (2020). Psycho-emotional disability in the marketplace. *European Journal of Marketing*, 54(11), 2675–2695.

Hogg, M., Maclaran, P., Martens, L., O'Donohoe, S., & Stevens, L. (2011). Special issue: (Re)creating cultural models of motherhoods in contemporary advertising. *Advertising & Society Review*, 12(2) (Advertising Educational Foundation. Retrieved September 26, 2016, from Project MUSE database).

Iqbal, N. (2015). Femvertising: How brands are selling #empowerment to women, *The Guardian*, 12 October, www.theguardian.com/lifeandstyle/2015/oct/12/femvertising-branded-feminism

Kates, S.M. (1999). Making the ad perfectly queer: Marketing "normality" to the gay men's community? *Journal of Advertising*, 28(1), 25–37.

Kearney, S., Brittain, I., & Kipnis, E. (2019). "Superdisabilities" vs "disabilities"? Theorizing the role of ableism in (mis) representational mythology of disability in the marketplace. *Consumption Markets & Culture*, 22(5–6), 545–567.

Maclaran, P. (2015). Feminism's fourth wave: A research agenda for marketing and consumer research. *Journal of Marketing Management*, 31(15–16), 1732–1738.

Marshall, D., Hogg, M., Davis, T., Schneider, T., & Peterson, A. (2014). Images of motherhood: food advertising in good housekeeping magazine 1950–2010. In S. O'Donohoe, M. Hogg, P. Maclaran, L. Martens & L. Stevens (Eds), *Motherhoods, Markets and Consumption: The Making of Mothers in Contemporary Western Cultures*. London: Routledge, pp. 116–128.

Martin, C., & Valenti, V. (2012). *New Feminist Solutions Volume 8. #FemFuture: Online Feminism*. New York: Barnard Center for Research on Women, Columbia University.

Matich, M., Ashman, R., & Parsons, E. (2019). #Freethenipple – Digital activism and embodiment in the contemporary feminist movement. *Consumption Markets & Culture*, 22(4), 337–362.

Matich, M., Ashman, R., & Parsons, E. (2022a). Seeking safety and solidarity through Self-documentation: Debating the power of the self(ie) in contemporary feminist culture. In P. Maclaran, L. Stevens & O. Kravets (Eds), *The Routledge Companion to Marketing and Feminism*. London: Routledge.

Matich, M., Ashman, R., & Parsons, E. (2022b). Zine Infrastructures as forms of organizing Within feminist Social movements, *Gender, Work and Organization*, early view https://doi-org.liverpool.idm.oclc.org/10.1111/gwao.12970

Miller, T. (2014). Engaging with the maternal: Tentative mothering acts, props and discourses. In S. O'Donohoe, M. Hogg, P. Maclaran, L. Martens & L. Stevens (Eds), *Motherhoods, Markets and Consumption: The Making of Mothers in Contemporary Western Cultures*. London: Routledge, pp. 159–170.

Moisio, R., Arnould, E. J., & Gentry, J.W. (2013). Productive consumption in the class-mediated construction of domestic masculinity: Do-it-yourself (DIY) home improvement in men's identity work. *Journal of Consumer Research*, 40(2), 298–316.

Morris, A.N. (2017). *Fashion, Social Media, and Identity Expression: An Intersectional Approach to Understanding the Fashion Consumption Patterns of Black Middle-Class Women*, Doctoral dissertation, The University of Texas.

Nölke, A. (2018). Making diversity conform? An intersectional, longitudinal analysis of LGBT-specific mainstream media advertisements. *Journal of Homosexuality*, 65(2), 224–255.

O'Donohoe, S., Hogg, M., Maclaran, P., Martens, L., & Stevens, L. (2014). *Motherhoods, Markets and Consumption: The Making of Mothers in Contemporary Western Cultures*. London: Routledge.

Organisation for Economic Co-operation and Development (OECD). (2018). *Bridging the Digital Gender Divide: Include, Upskill, Innovate*. Paris: OECD.

Ourahmoune, N., & El Jurdi, H. (2022). 'Marketing and the missing feminisms: Decolonial feminisms and the Arab Spring. In P. Maclaran, L. Stevens & O. Kravets (Eds), *The Routledge Companion to Marketing and Feminism*. London: Routledge. pp. 257–267.

Parsons, E., Pirani, D., Ashman, R., Daskalopoulou, A., Kerrane, K., & McGouran, K (Feminist Collective) (2022). Manifesting feminist marketing futures: Undertaking a 'visionary' inventory. In P. Maclaran, L. Stevens & O. Kravets (Eds), *The Routledge Companion to Marketing and Feminism*. London: Routledge, pp. 460–476.

Pirani, D., & Daskalopoulou, A. (2022). The Queer Manifesto: Imagining new possibilities and futures for marketing and consumer research. *Marketing Theory*, 22(2), 293–308.

Poole, S.M., Grier, S.A., Thomas, K.D., Sobande, F., Ekpo, A.E., Torres, L.T., Addington, L.A., Weekes-Laidlow, M., & Henderson, G.R. (2021).

Operationalizing critical race theory in the marketplace. *Journal of Public Policy & Marketing*, 40(2), 126–142.

Schroeder, J.E., & Zwick, D. (2004). Mirrors of masculinity: Representation and identity in advertising images. *Consumption Markets & Culture*, 7(1), 21–52.

Shepherd, S.D., & Hamilton, K. (2022). Consumption beyond the binary: Feminism in transgender lives. In P. Maclaran, L. Stevens & O. Kravets (Eds), *The Routledge Companion to Marketing and Feminism*. London: Routledge, pp. 296–307.

Sobande, F. (2019). Woke-washing: "Intersectional" femvertising and branding "woke" bravery. *European Journal of Marketing*, 54(11), 2723–2745.

Sobande, F., Fearfull, A., & Brownlie, D. (2020). Resisting media marginalisation: Black women's digital content and collectivity. *Consumption, Markets & Culture*, 23(5), 413–428.

Steinfield, L., Minita S., Tuncay Zayer, L., Coleman, C.A., Ourahmoune, N., & Harrison, R.L. (2019). "Transformative intersectionality: Moving business towards a critical Praxis. *Journal of Business Research*, 100, 366–375

Stevens, L., & Houston, S. (2016). Dazed magazine, fourth wave feminism, and the return of the politicised female body, *Paper Presented at the 13th Conference on Gender, Marketing and Consumer Behaviour*, 4–6 July, ESCP Europe, Paris.

Thomson, R., Kehily, M.J., Hadfield, L., & Sharpe, S. (2011). *Making Modern Mothers*. Bristol: The Polity Press.

Wechie, T. (2016). A 'post' post feminism: The utopian possibilities of a fourth wave of feminism and its intersections with the continued dominance of a tyrannical consumer capitalism, *Paper Presented at the 13th Conference on Gender, Marketing and Consumer Behaviour*, 4–6 July, ESCP Europe, Paris.

Young, I.M. (1980). Throwing like a girl: A phenomenology of feminine body comportment motility and spatiality. *Human studies*, 3(1), 137–156.

Yuval-Davis, N. (2007). Intersectionality, citizenship, and contemporary politics of belonging. *Critical Review of International Social and Political Philosophy*, 10(4), 561–574.

7

PSYCHOANALYSIS
IN MARKETING

Introduction

Psychoanalysis is a 'form of inquiry, a theory of mind and a mode of treatment concerned, above all, with the unconscious mind' (Pick, 2015, p. 19). Many of the key concepts of psychoanalysis were developed by Sigmund Freud (1856–1939), the 'father of psychoanalysis', but have since been redeveloped and substantially revised by many key figures, including Melanie Klein, Jacques Lacan, Wilfred Bion, Donald Winnicott and Carl Jung among others. As a consequence, contemporary psychoanalysis offers a very large repertoire of tools and concepts that have inspired both therapeutic work and the broader realms of arts, humanities and social sciences.

Psychoanalysis has a long and rather fluid relationship with marketing theory and practice. It begins with Sigmund Freud's nephew, Edward Bernays (1891–1995), the pioneer of public relations, propaganda and for some, of Western consumer culture. Bernays employed many of his uncle's ideas for the benefit of promoting commodities as diverse as cigarettes, soap and the bacon-and-egg breakfast. In his autobiography, he claims to be the agent behind the first psychoanalytic application to advertising: that is a longstanding campaign for American Tobacco, starting in 1929, that successfully repositioned cigarettes as 'torches of freedom' in women's battle for socio-economic liberation. As a result, cigarettes became a far more popular consumption habit for women in America and beyond. No wonder then that during his visit to the US, Freud was somewhat amused by his nephew's aggressive marketing campaigns, including, for instance, an undertaker's advert saying, 'Why live when you can be buried for only $10?' (Freud and Freud, 1960).

In this chapter, we introduce some key psychoanalytic ideas and explain their relevance to marketing and consumer behaviour. We begin with a short discussion of three key figures of psychoanalysis, that is, Sigmund Freud, Melanie Klein and Jacques Lacan. Subsequently, we discuss applications of psychoanalysis in marketing, focusing on three distinct areas: advertising, marketing research and consumer behaviour.

DOI: 10.4324/9781003201151-7

The Return of the "Repressed" in Marketing

Psychoanalysis originally entered the field of marketing under the guise of 'motivational research' and most famously through Ernest Dichter's promotion of new methods of understanding and influencing the increasingly affluent consumers of post–World War II. Also known as 'the Freud of Maddison Avenue' and 'Mr. Mass Motivations' (Fullerton, 2007), Dichter has been credited with the rise of various famous household brand names, such as Chrysler and General Mills. He introduced many innovative approaches to marketing research, including 'focus groups', 'depth interviews' and projective techniques. At times, he had a rather outlandish take on the symbolic meaning of everyday consumption acts: smoking was 'comparable to sucking at the nipples of a gigantic world breast', whereas cake mixes that did not involve adding eggs were a threat to women's fertility. For critics of motivational research, Dichter's research programme had unprecedented moral implications:

> All this probing and manipulation has its constructive and its amusing aspects; but also, I think it fair to say, it has seriously anti-humanistic implications. Much of it seems to represent regress rather than progress for man in his long struggle to become a rational and self-guiding being.
>
> (Packard, 1957, p. 34)

Ironically, however, such criticisms made Dichter even more influential, not least because of the numerous TV and radio invites to talk about his research to the general population.

Despite the early affair of psychoanalysis with marketing communications and consumer research, subsequent decades experienced what Cluley and Desmond (2015) describe as the 'repression' of psychoanalysis, whereby psychoanalytic understandings of the consumer, to some extent, continued to take place outside the marketing discipline but firmly not within it. This mirrored the evolution of the fields of psychology and psychiatry more broadly (e.g. Pick, 2015), with more sanitised and less speculative forms of inquiry as exemplified in the emergence of Cognitive Behavioural Therapy and the consolidation of biological (as opposed to psychoanalytic) psychiatry (O'Shaughnessy, 2015), earning a significantly higher status. Past the 1970s, psychoanalysis began to be viewed as outdated, largely reliant on reductivist ideas, empirically unsubstantiated and sexist among others.

Over the last decade, however, the 'repressed' psychoanalysis has returned, according to Cluley and Desmond (2015). For some, this is not surprising. In one sense, the return to psychoanalysis reflects the relative failure of other disciplines to account for human and social behaviour on the basis of what is commonly understood as 'scientific proof'. There is increasing awareness that human behaviour is far less rational and 'measurable' in the sense that experimental psychologists and quantitative marketers wish it would have been. Psychoanalysis, with its focus on the unconscious and inherent critique of outcome testing (Pick, 2015), is in a very good place to explicitly confront more conventional and tried understandings of consumer behaviour. Beyond questions of empirical validity, it provides a rich vocabulary, a series of sensitising concepts that can prove very useful in developing alternative accounts of marketing and consumption. As we will illustrate in the next section, psychoanalytic applications can be particularly creative and counter-intuitive. Psychoanalysis has also played a key role in so-called psycho-social studies, that is, an emerging stream of research that attempts to overcome dualisms of inner versus outer and individual (consumer) versus society and to develop more nuanced accounts of how individuals' inner and outer realities are mutually constitutive (Frosh, 2010; for an application in consumer behaviour, see Chatzidakis et al., 2021). For example, rather than pathologising and individualising notions such as narcissism and autism, psychosocial approaches would attempt to view them instead as products of the socio-cultural, discursive and material environments that we inhabit.

Key figures: Freud, Klein, Lacan

Sigmund Freud

Freud is the founder psychoanalysis, coining the term in 1896. Attempting to understand 'hysteria', a common mental illness at the time that Freud witnessed being treated with hypnosis, he developed a new technique called 'free association'. That involves asking patients to talk freely about their thoughts and emotions without any self-censorship or prohibition. His belief was that patients with symptoms of hysteria suffered from repressed memories and thoughts and by bringing them to consciousness in a safe environment, effective treatment was possible. As his technique begun to bring positive outcomes, Freud developed a series of terms and concepts that have since become part of the psychoanalytic vocabulary, embraced by specialists and laymen alike.

In accounting for how repression operates, Freud originally developed the so-called topographical model of the mind, comprising the unconscious (thoughts that are completely repressed and cannot be recalled), the preconscious (thoughts that can be recalled) and the conscious (thoughts that are recalled). Later on, he significantly revised his observations in what was now called the structural model (Freud, 1923), comprising the id, the ego and the superego. The id is the completely unconscious part of the brain that contains instinctual sexual urges and aggressive drives. But equally far from conscious awareness may lay the superego, an internalised authority that watches and judges often in extremely punitive and sadistic ways. For Freud, the superego is constituted through the internalisation of parental prohibitions and demands. Finally, the ego is what is more commonly associated with common sense, what perceives and mediates internal and external reality and which, for Freud, has to strive a very fine balance in fighting 'three dangers', the external world, the superego and the id. Accordingly, a key purpose of psychoanalysis is 'to strengthen the ego, to make it more independent of the super-ego, to widen its field of perception and enlarge its organisation, so that it can appropriate fresh portions of the id' (Freud in Pick, 2015, p. 46).

The Freudian vocabulary still informs everyday understandings of people's personalities and psychological states. Terms such as the Oedipal complex, Freudian slip, the unconscious, narcissism, repression, fetishism, neurotic obsession and displacement remain in regular use across various parts of the world.

Melanie Klein

Melanie Klein (1882–1960) is relatively less well known but very influential, especially in the UK and other countries where 'object-relations theory' has become a popular alternative to traditional Freudian psychoanalysis. Klein viewed herself as the ultimate successor of Freud, leading to an infamous conflict with Freud's daughter, Anna, who also claimed the same in a series of meetings called the 'controversial discussions' (1942–1944). Despite considering herself a faithful adherent to Freud's ideas, she significantly departed from him, not least by locating the emergence of unconscious conflict way before the formation of the Oedipal complex (around 6 months as opposed to 3–5 years old). Klein was the first to use traditional psychoanalytic theory and practise with children, often as young as 2 years old, and in doing so, she developed various innovative techniques, such as play therapy.

Klein is mostly known for her formulation of the *paranoid-schizoid* and *depressive* positions. The paranoid-schizoid position represents a primitive mode of mental organisation, located during the infant's early developmental stage (from birth to 6 months old) and characterised by their inability to experience the mother (or caregiver) as a whole object. Instead, the caregiver is split into a 'good breast' and a 'bad breast', with corresponding feelings of love and hate (Klein, 1946, 1948). These early affective states are *schizoid* because bad and good objects are split. They are *paranoid* because of the threat entailed in realising that the good object associated with satisfaction (the feeding breast) is also a frustrating object (non-feeding breast) that cannot be relied upon, hence, why infants often attack the mother's breast. The *depressive* position reflects a later developmental stage in which the infant moves from a part-object to a whole-object relation and becomes capable of recognising good and bad aspects in the loved and loving object (first of all, the mother or caregiver). For Klein, these positions persist into adulthood: for example, we are often able to see both the good and bad in other objects (be it people, institutions or actual consumption items), whereas at other stages, we may be overwhelmed by irrational feelings and thoughts of excessive love or hate.

Jacques Lacan

Jacques Lacan (1901–1981) has become very popular within a small milieu more recently, especially through his influence on celebrated contemporary social theory scholars, most notably Slavoj Žižek. He is associated with the application of psychoanalysis to the realm of language and, by implication, broader socio-cultural processes. Lacan's mantra has been that the 'unconscious is structured like a language', at least since his famous essay titled *The Instance of the Letter in the Unconscious, or Reason Since Freud* (Lacan, 2010; originally written in 1957). Central to his thinking is the development of the 'mirror stage', the time in which a baby progressively moves away from the fantasy of a fragmented and disorderly body to recognising its image in the mirror. It is important to recall here that, like Klein, Lacan recognises that prior to this stage (around 6 months old), the baby does not experience its body as whole and complete. Seeing its image as a whole and the synthesis of this image threatens the child with fragmentation; in other words, the distance between the subject and its image is profoundly traumatising until the ego is formed. But what constitutes the ego is a misunderstanding, as the 'me' becomes alienated from itself through an *imaginary* dimension. In Lacan's thinking, the imaginary contrasts with the *symbolic*, the realm of law and language, and *the real*, what is left outside language and resists symbolisation.

Another key and strongly interrelated concept in Lacan's writings is the idea of desire, here always viewed as lack and forever unsatisfied, as it is expressed through language that always leaves a leftover or surplus. Accordingly, for Lacan, the aim of psychoanalysis is to make the analysand (a term used for someone who is undergoing psychoanalytic treatment) realise and uncover the truth about his/her desire:

> what is important is to teach the subject to name, to articulate, to bring desire into existence. The subject should come to recognize and to name his/her desire. But it isn't a question of recognizing something that could be entirely given. In naming it, the subject creates, brings forth, a new presence in the world.
>
> (Lacan, 1988, pp. 228–229)

Psychoanalysis Outside the Clinic and into Marketing

There has been ongoing controversy as to whether psychoanalysis can be applied beyond the clinic, let alone outside the particular historical and spatial context in which it was developed and practiced. Indeed, the links between modernity and the specific notion of the inner self that psychoanalysis offered have been extensively documented (Zaretsky, 2005) as has psychoanalysis's specific geographical-cultural context. Even for Freud (1916, p. 431), psychoanalysis was the product of a very particular European city:

> psychoanalysis, especially the assertion that the neuroses can be traced back to disturbances in the sexual life, could only have

originated in a city like Vienna, in an atmosphere of sensuality and immorality not to be found in other cities.

Likewise, the therapeutic method is always undertaken within a specific spatial context (including the analyst and the analysand) and within particular time intervals, aiming altogether for a 'consistent frame' (Pick, 2015). With this in mind, it is remarkable how readily and often unreflectively psychoanalytic concepts have been applied to arts, humanities and social sciences.

Psychoanalysis, therefore, still holds a rather precarious status within social sciences more generally and the field of marketing in particular. On the one hand, psychoanalytic applications rely on 'evidence' that is the product of subjective interpretation and, thus, are too questionable for the type of logical empiricism that predominates in disciplines such as marketing and consumer research. On the other hand, interpretivist and social constructivist researchers often reject psychoanalysis because of the 'innerness' it involves, the employment of a totalising, 'expert' discourse that is inherently reductionist. That is, to say, it imposes frameworks and ways of thinking that are self-fulfilling. Between these two positions lie more sympathetic views that see something in the ability of psychoanalysis – or at least in some versions of it – to fill the 'gaps' left in the language and methodologies employed by other research paradigms. According to Michael Rustin (2010; see also Frosh, 2010), for example, psychoanalysis, with its focus on the unconscious and seemingly irrational, has the capacity to 'disrupt' or 'unsettle' more normalised and taken-for-granted understandings: 'The assertion is that, where psychoanalysis has something valuable to say . . . it will mostly be where its contribution is counter-intuitive or even paradoxical' (p. 472).

Accordingly, in the remainder of this chapter, we review some psychoanalytic applications with a twofold aim. First, we address questions around empirical validity as well as the moral debates that followed some of the more prominent examples of psychoanalytically-inspired marketing. Second, we attempt to illustrate psychoanalysis's broader ability to inspire more disruptive and creative modes of thinking. We begin with some psychoanalytic premises on 'how to sell sex' before moving on to discuss Dichter's ambitious programme to uncover consumers' hidden motivations. Last, we discuss some psychoanalytic understandings of contemporary consumption and consumer culture.

Selling Sex (and Other Primal Instincts)

The idea that much communication passes below our conscious radar and that aspects of our mind will always remain obscure was bound to have a major influence on those interested in manipulating them, not least marketers and advertisers. As vividly explained in the award-wining documentary series by Adam Curtis, *The Century of the Self* (also mentioned in Chapter 7), psychoanalytical techniques have been widely and systematically employed at least since the end of

World War II, when the consumerist way of living was, for the first time, promoted to a mass audience. According to this account, previously insignificant and mundane objects, such as cigarettes, cars and power detergents, were now psychically and sexually charged, unconsciously linked with 'phallic symbols', narcissistic objects or alleviators of women's 'penis envy' among others. As critics saw it, consumers were duped by an extremely sophisticated and professionalised body of marketers and advertisers that, having mastered major Freudian works such as *The Interpretation of Dreams*, were able to manipulate the symbolic imagery of consumer objects and, via them, to arouse sexual fantasies in socially acceptable ways. This was often accompanied with a 'knowing wink' to those in the know (i.e. other advertisers and communication experts) and quickly became the paradigm for the communication of all kinds of otherwise controversial messages (Desmond, 2012).

Meanwhile, the unconscious approach to advertising and promotional communication was most notoriously exposed in Packard's (1957) *The Hidden Persuaders* (also mentioned in Chapter 7). By 'hidden', Packard meant 'beneath our level of awareness', also known as subliminal, that is, stimuli that are below the individual's absolute threshold of awareness and cannot be experienced at a conscious level. The same year, exploiting the popularity of Packard's book, James Vicary, owner of a marketing research firm invested in motivation research, published the famous Coca-Cola experiment. According to this hoax, the messages 'Drink Coca-Cola' and 'Hungry? Eat Popcorn' were flashed at 1/3,000 of a second every five minutes to over 45,000 people in a New Jersey cinema, resulting in a sales increase of 18% and 58% of Coca-Cola and popcorn respectively. However, a series of subsequent experiments refuted his claim, showing that persuasion at the subthreshold or subliminal level is not possible (e.g. Moore, 1982; Beatty and Hawkins, 1989). This echoed the views of advertisers, with the vast majority of them claiming strong disbelief in the potential effectiveness of subliminal advertising (Rogers and Seiler, 1994). Altogether, further consumer research on subliminal advertising effects stagnated despite the fact that the possibility of subliminal persuasion continued to capture the general public's imagination (Bargh, 2002).

Part of the reason why the notion of unconscious advertising went out of fashion throughout the 1980s and the 1990s was because the very idea of a less rational and non-agentic consumer was in direct contrast to the models of deliberate consumer decision making promoted in positivistic marketing research (Desmond, 2012). However, more intense experimentations with the unconscious processing information continued elsewhere, including the fields of clinical and cognitive psychology and neuroscience (Albanese, 2015; Elgendi et al., 2018). Therein, numerous studies have consistently shown subliminal effects on consumption and product evaluation (Bargh, 2002). Unlike earlier consumer research, this stream of literature concludes that consumers' goals (e.g. to satisfy one's hunger) can be activated unconsciously but only when they are pre-existing (that is, only if one is indeed hungry in the first place). Meanwhile, studies relating more directly to advertising effect have consistently shown that unconscious manipulation is possible, especially when focused on more realistic outcome measures, such as brand-name recall and brand-name liking, as opposed to hard measures, such as changes in actual behaviour or intention (Albanese, 2015).

As John Bargh (2002) observes, this makes uncomfortable reading for contemporary consumer and advertising researchers, who are still largely ignorant of recent advances in knowledge of non-conscious processes, not to mention the very real possibility that these are already exploited by marketplace and governmental actors. Furthermore, he points to the additional influence of supraliminal effects, that is, cues or primes that consumers may be aware of but grossly underestimate their influence. For instance, we may watch an advert that is obviously 'dirty' or manipulative by using negative stereotypes, and although consciously, we will reject it, we may still be influenced at an unconscious level. For Bargh, this form of persuasion is far more pervasive in contemporary advertising. His observation is even more pertinent today, where the dream-like qualities of advertising are often downplayed by empowered and confident consumers whilst, at the same time, everyday life is increasingly commoditised in ways that would have perhaps been unimaginable in Freud's era.

Indeed, it is arguably within the realm of what experimental scientists call supraliminal effects, rather than subliminal ones, that psychoanalysis can showcase greater explanatory power. After all, what is often cited as research on unconscious or subliminal processing is primarily concerned with 'non-conscious' processing. The latter assumes that thoughts remain non-conscious only until a need or want is activated and then they become conscious. In contrast, psychoanalysis assumes that unconscious thoughts are goal directed and can influence behaviour without ever becoming conscious. In this sense, Freud's (and his followers') observations on how unconscious will fulfilments can be projected into (consumer) objects, feed into narcissistic anxieties and self-destructive instincts, not to mention broader insights on the intersection of psychic and external reality(es), are not fully compatible with the experimental studies on non-conscious effects.

Elsewhere, however, such as in the fields of cultural and visual studies, psychoanalytic concepts have been frequently employed with a view to account of what happens in relation to an image and how we may be influenced by it. For instance, drawing on Lacan, Judith Williamson (1978) focuses on the mirror-like qualities of advertising and their ubiquity, forcing us to engage intimately with 'a sort of independent reality that links them to our own lives' (Williamson, 1978, p. 11). For Williamson, advertising is a signifying system within the symbolic and is also able to represent to the subject his place in the imaginary:

> Ads set up, in your active relationship towards them, the fictional creation of an impossibly unified self: an 'Ego-Ideal'. They show you a symbol of yourself aimed to attract your desire; they suggest that you can become the person in the picture before you.
>
> (p. 65)

Lacan's imaginary is not, of course, the only psychoanalytic concept that can explain the visual rhetoric of advertising. For instance, Freud's ideas around psychic displacements and Melanie Klein's understanding of projective identification can be readily employed in advertising images with a view to account for their production of meaning and symbolism (cf. Oswald, 2010) and, more broadly, for the creation of the fantasy space(s) of contemporary consumerism.

Researching the Unconscious with Dr. Dichter

As mentioned in the introduction, psychoanalysis also implies a particular method of understanding the mind, one that goes beneath the surface with a view to uncover the hidden (unconscious) motivations of human thoughts and actions. Likewise, when applied outside the clinic, psychoanalytic methods share in common a more 'penetrative' outlook, the belief that by somehow researching beneath the surface (e.g. Clarke and Hoggett, 2011), there is scope for uncovering psychodynamic processes and mechanisms that are inaccessible in other research methods.

Within marketing and consumer research, psychoanalytically-inspired methods are highly interconnected with so-called depth or motivational research, pioneered in the 1930s by Paul Lazarsfeld but more commonly associated with Ernest Dichter (see Schwarzkopf and Gries, 2010). Born in Vienna to a working-class Jewish family, Dichter fled to the US to escape Nazi persecution. His rather flamboyant, if not narcissistic, personality helped him cause widespread sensation by fiercely criticising what he considered largely outmoded and blunt methods of consumer research, such as conventional interviews and surveys. He began his career by sending a simple (and rather overconfident) letter to six big corporations of his choice, stating that 'I am a young psychologist from Vienna and I have some interesting new ideas which can help you be more successful, effective, sell more and communicate better with your potential clients'. (Dichter, 1979, p. 33). Amongst them, *Esquire* was the first one to reply positively. From then on, he moved from strength to strength, developing a programme of motivational research that sought to understand three distinct categories of motives in their entirety: 1) those that consumers are consciously aware of, 2) those consumers are aware of but unwilling to reveal and 3) those motives that consumers are unaware of (Tadajewski, 2006).

Despite common misunderstandings, the purpose of motivational research was neither to apply psychoanalytic tools comprehensively on the consumer nor in any sense to 'cure' them. Rather, the relationship between psychoanalysis and motivation research could be summarised in their common insistence on 'psycho-detective work' (Tadajewski, 2006), what is also described previously as penetrative. His observational techniques and 'depth interviews' identified consumer motivations beyond the ones revealed in classical survey or interview-based questions. For instance, he found that men, when directly asked, would state that women did not influence their car-buying habits. In standard surveys, they would also cite additional rational buying criteria, such as reliability and price. For Dichter, however, in reality, men preferred convertibles over sedans and that is why they purchased them far more frequently before getting married rather than after and once again after they passed 45 or 50. Dichter's psycho-detective explanation was that the sedan represented the wife:

> comfortable and safe. The convertible, the 'mistress', youthful, was the dreamer . . . . the wind blows through your hair, you feel much closer to the road and the landscape. Many men have a secret wish for a mistress. This wish becomes stronger as they get older. Buying a convertible represented the realization of this wish, without the expense and the guilt feeling of having a live mistress.
>
> (Dichter, 1979, p. 38)

Although Dichter was personally in favour of individual rather than group interviews, his consulting company also trained a large number of first-generation 'focus group' researchers, developing the so-called 'depth group interview' (Stewart and Shamdasani, 2014). Dichter was rather more instrumental in introducing a variety of projective techniques to marketing research. Drawing on Freud's idea of projection as a defence mechanism by which individuals unconsciously attribute their own negative personality traits to others, his 'non-directive interview technique' (Dichter, 1960) allowed interviewees to project themselves onto another person (e.g. by asking them to comment on other consumers' behaviour) and, by doing so, reveal some of their own thoughts, feelings and fears. Although projective techniques have since played a central role in the marketing research industry (e.g. Boddy, 2005), the extent to which Dichter directly contributed to their development and dissemination remains questionable. For Fullerton (2007), other motivational researchers, including Lazarsfeld, had much more meaningfully and extensively engaged with projective techniques and in fact with motivational research more broadly. However, no one was a master mythmaker in the way that Dichter proved to be: 'The very hyperbole and imaginative verve expressed in his "discoveries" transcend those of any other marketing figure of the 20th century'. (p. 380).

In a similar vein, Schwarzkopf (2015, p. 41) notes the far wider-reaching, socio-cultural consequences of Dichter's work in so far as 'he helped bring about in the public imagination of what consumer

desire was and what significance "libidinal drives" had for the political economy of consumer capitalism'. In other words, Schwarzkopf
(2015) argues, Dichter's pro-hedonistic outlook was very much in line
with the promotion of the 'consumer' as the central form of human
existence; Freud's 'pleasure principle', aiming for immediate, libidinal
gratification, was, for the first time, pushed ahead the 'reality principle', aiming for self-control and delayed gratification for the purpose
of longer-term individual and collective wellbeing. In Dichter's words
at the Institute for Motivational Research (Packard, 1957, p. 74): 'One
of the main jobs of the advertiser in this conflict between pleasure
and guilt is not so much to sell the product as to give moral permission
to have fun without guilt'.

Consumers in the Clinic

Beyond potential commercial applications and their ethical implications, psychoanalysis remains a body of knowledge vested in understanding human subjectivity, conceptualising it as fundamentally
ambivalent: both loving and hating, altruistic and selfish, rational
and irrational. It invites us to reconsider taken-for-granted ideas that
individuals are rational, have stable identities and are free to exercise
their 'choice', be it in the marketplace and/or other spheres of social
life. This section reviews some illustrative attempts to psychoanalyse
the 'consumer', acknowledging that the possibilities are as rich as the
history of psychoanalysis with its variety of different traditions and
therapeutic outcomes.

   One of the key Freudian concepts that have been applied to
understand contemporary consumers and consumerism is that of a
narcissist personality. This is no coincidence given the well-explored
link between consumer culture and the emergence of more hedonistic and self-absorbed lifestyles. Most famously, Christopher Lasch's
(1979) bestselling book, *The Culture of Narcissism*, illustrates how
the creation of what can be called narcissistic consumption was a
necessary turn in the evolution of capitalism, circa post–World War
I, as the increasingly expanding domain of production had to meet
corresponding levels of consumer demand for conspicuous and
experiential goods. Freud (1991) theorised narcissism as a tendency
to withdraw from one's external world and redirect desire into oneself, in other words, excessive re-directing of one's sexual libido from
external objects (here understood more broadly as other people and/
or material objects) into herself. For Lasch (1979), such tendencies
are pervasive in modern societies the more paternal (or authority)
figures lose their credibility. Therefore, 'the superego in individuals
increasingly derives from the child's primitive fantasies about his parents, fantasies charged with sadistic rage – rather than from internalised ego ideals formed by later experience with loved and respected
models of social conduct' (p. 12). Lasch, therefore, does not use narcissism as a metaphor or synonym for selfishness, a common assumption in lay accounts of our narcissistic culture. Rather, he insists on a

psychoanalytic understanding of narcissism, viewing it as a common pathology that is produced by the socio-cultural conditions of our times.

Interestingly, Freud himself rarely spoke directly about notions such as 'consumption' and 'identity'. One notable exception was in relation to narcissism and, in particular, parents' consumption practices. He argued that seemingly affectionate parental actions towards their children may instead be a revival and reproduction of their own narcissism, for example, when buying one's child the most exclusive shoes. For Freud (1991, p. 91), such examples of consumption show us that 'parental love, which is so moving and at bottom so childish, is nothing but the parents' narcissism born again, which, transformed into object-love, unmistakably reveals its former nature'. Through consumption, let alone purchasing for others, narcissistic behaviours that would otherwise be viewed as socially unacceptable become acceptable. Cluley and Dunne (2012) extend this argument to account for the darker and more sadistic instances of consumer behaviour, such as ignoring the exploitative social relations that underline commodity production. Arguing against conventional accounts of unethical and unsustainable consumption that draw on Marx's notion of commodity fetishism, they point to the repressed narcissistic pleasure in knowing that one is better than others, the idea that the only good neighbour may indeed be the dead neighbour.

Consumption, of course, serves more than just a narcissistic function. For Gabriel (2015), the idea of consumers' freedom to choose and construct their own identities also serves a disciplining/controlling function and a therapeutic function. The former becomes clear when considering how, in contemporary societies, those who fail to enjoy the pleasures of consumerism (due to lower incomes) are considered as largely responsible for their choices and, thus, examples for others to avoid. Consumption also serves a therapeutic function in so far as it can compensate us when things go wrong and reward us when things go well. From a Freudian point of view, consumers' identities and choices can, therefore, be viewed as wish fulfilments or fantasies. They are unconscious defences to the challenges that contemporary civilisations place on individuals.

Psychoanalysis also provides ideas and concepts that can help explain our preoccupation with particular commodities. Most commonly, Freudian readings emphasise how consumers displace their desires (mostly of a sexual nature) into material goods, ultimately defending themselves against deeper anxieties and contradictions. Somewhat-alternative readings of the relationship between people and material artefacts can be provided by object-relations traditions. Melanie Klein, for instance, began her work by studying the interaction of infants with their toys. Although she moved on to consider images of people as the most significant psychic 'objects', her work enabled a reconsideration of the relationship between subjects and (some of their) material objects. Drawing on Melanie Klein, Chatzidakis, Shaw and Allen (2021) develop an account of how particular consumption objects (from sushi to leather sofas) are 'taken in' (introjected) their psychic realities as 'good objects', whereas others are 'put out' (projected) as 'bad objects'. Another key contribution is Donald Winnicott's (1971) notion of the 'transitional object', which accounts for the relationship children develop with their first comfort objects, such as a toy or a blanket. These objects mediate children's relationship with external reality and become part of the processes of separating the 'me' from the 'not-me'. Such transitional objects have often been considered in consumer research. Further, later work on anthropology and material culture has reconsidered the significance of object-relations theorist, arguing that processes of projection, introjection and projective identification provide the basis for the development of a more sophisticated understanding of the subject-object relationship (e.g. Miller, 1997).

Psychoanalysis, particularly in its Lacanian guises, also provides powerful concepts for understanding our contemporary culture's obsession with the screen and self-representation. For example, focusing on mobile phone usage, Reyes et al. (2015) argue that Lacanian concepts not only help us understand the pleasures of looking (see section xx) but also the underlying anxieties that are a precondition for such pleasure. In doing so, the authors draw on Lacan's distinction between the 'look' and the 'gaze'. Whereas the former is more in line with the notion of commodity fetishism (in line with Cluley and Dunne, 2012) and the pleasures of seeing and constructing identities via the mediation of (consumer) objects, the latter addresses the more disruptive and anxiety-inducing aspects associated with Lacan's symbolic. Ultimately, the authors argue that beyond commonplace understandings of contemporary culture's obsession with the 'screen', there is something more profound and anxiety-inducing, associated with Lacan's real – that is, our inescapable existential dilemmas associated with a lack of being and being gazed by the 'other'. Drawing on Lacan and related works of Dufour, Lambert (2019) has more recently addressed the extent to which neoliberal consumer culture promotes the cultivation of psychotic and acritical subjects, not least through perpetuating precarity while lacking a stable symbolic field that once characterized the modern subject. Ultimately, Lambert's empirical exploration of two case studies of young consumers paints a more complicated 'yes-and-no' picture.

Evident of the field's (increasing) maturity in dealing with psychoanalytically inspired applications are more recent attempts to both challenge and move beyond the more established psychoanalytic schools. Drawing on Deleuze and Guattari, for instance, Coffin (2021) makes a case for a more proto-machinic rather than linguistic understanding of the (consumer) unconscious, that is, understood as comprised of free-floating and colliding forces rather than as a meaningful structure based on symbolic and/or linguistic associations. Concurrently, diverse psychoanalytic perspectives are employed to revisit the ontological and epistemological assumptions underpinning conventional understandings of marketing and consumption altogether.

Building on the notion of 'terminal marketing', Ahlberg, Coffin and Hietanen (2022) challenge deeply rooted ontological assumptions of a coherent, agentic consumer or the idea that meaning-making (versus more unconscious processes) drive consumption. In a similarly critical vein, Hietanen, Ahlberg and Botez (2022) discuss how semio-capitalism is a system that closely aligns unconscious forces of desire with the desiring forces of capitalism, marking the creation of consumer individuals 'without an essence'.

Summary

Psychoanalysis has a long and rather contentious relationship with marketing theory and practice. Despite the early enthusiasm of post–World War II marketers, interest in understanding and influencing the consumers' unconscious waned throughout the 1970s–2000s. More recently, however, we have been witnessing some kind of a return to psychoanalysis, not least because of its renewed infusion into contemporary social theory, and, from there, to more specific applications to marketing and consumption. Key figures of psychoanalysis that continue to be highly influential are Sigmund Freud, Melanie Klein and Jacques Lacan. Their theories and concepts have been applied in one way or another to all areas of marketing, from advertising and marketing research to consumer behaviour and consumer culture.

Psychoanalytic approaches continue to be controversial, not least because of their incompatibility with the (still) dominant project of logical empiricism. However, there is increasing recognition of the ability of psychoanalysis to provide a rich vocabulary and a series of sensitising concepts that are particularly useful for multi-perspective and multi-method approaches to understanding consumers (e.g. O'Shaughnessy, 2015). Besides, we should also note that psychoanalytically inspired ideas have always been in heavy use, albeit under different labels, in various fields of research, from social anthropology to neuroscience. Notwithstanding, for some advocates of psychoanalysis, it does not necessarily matter if some of the underlying premises prove to be 'true' or 'false'. Rather, as Stuart Hall, one of the foremost social theorists used to say, what matters is that they remain 'good ideas to think with'.

Case Study: Unethical and Self-Harming Consumers

Chapter 5 discussed the emergence of ethical consumption and the adjoining observation of the so-called 'attitude-behaviour gap', that is, the tendency of most consumers to behave in ways that are in apparent contradiction to their expressed ethical and environmental concerns. Psychoanalysis, with its focus on the unconscious, offers an entirely different explanation for why we may behave in ways that are far removed from our moral ideals (Chatzidakis, 2015).

For Freud, the key explanatory concept when it comes to ethical and moral wrongdoing is the presence of unconscious guilt. Distinguishing it from conscious feelings of guilt (the ones commonly experienced when we do something wrong), unconscious guilt arises as part of the Oedipal configuration (see section xx). It is a 'reaction to the two great criminal intentions of killing the father and having sexual relations with the mother' (Freud, 1916, p. 333). Subsequently, through the establishment of the superego, the fear of the father (and later of any kind of authority) becomes internalised and regulates our everyday behaviour. Sometimes, however, the superego can be so punitive and torturing that unconscious guilt becomes unbearable. In these instances, one may commit actual misdeeds with a view to release some of these feelings into more conscious or 'real manifestations', as Freud (1916) wrote in *Criminals from a Sense of Guilt:*

> various wrongdoings were done principally because they were forbidden, and because their execution was accompanied by mental relief for their doer. He was suffering from an oppressive feeling of guilt, of which he did not know the origin, and after he had committed a misdeed this oppression was mitigated. His sense of guilt was at least attached to something.
>
> (p. 332)

Therefore, the underlying presence of guilt may not only be unconscious but also so extreme that individuals may harm themselves or others with a view to release some of its otherwise unbearable presence.

With Freud's development of the superego, guilt took centre stage in psychoanalytic accounts of morality. However, for many subsequent psychoanalysts (see Hughes, 2008), it was Melanie Klein that provided a more comprehensive understanding of everyday morality. For Hughes (2008), Melanie Klein significantly extended Freud by locating the emergence of unconscious guilt in earlier developmental stages, that is, during the child's dyadic relationship with its mother (or caregiver). Klein's paranoid-schizoid position (see section xx) resembles Freud's understanding of unconscious guilt in so far as the splitting of the self into good and bad objects (first, being the mother's breast) results into persecutory anxiety and fear of revenge in the same way that the formation of the superego does. However, Klein's understanding of unconscious guilt significantly departs from Freud in her conceptualisation of the depressive position. Here, the child moves from a part-object to a whole-object relation and becomes capable of recognising good and bad aspects in the loved and loving object (first, being its mother) that it has previously inflicted harm upon. Subsequently, it experiences anxiety and a different kind of guilt that Klein calls 'depressive guilt'. This guilt primarily aims at reparation and is qualitatively different from the 'persecutory' guilt that characterises the paranoid-schizoid position. For Klein and her followers, it signifies entry into a more advanced model of morality, during which we can see the good and the bad as co-existing in many aspects of our lives. More importantly still, we can constructively engage with it, perhaps try to do our bit in 'repairing' the various social and environmental injustices underlying contemporary life.

Psychoanalytic readings of morality contrast significantly with the dominant tradition of understanding consumer (and marketing) ethics as a largely instrumental and cognitive process (see Chapter 7). Likewise, the widespread observation of 'attitude-behaviour' gaps is less surprising from a psychoanalytic point of view. The presence of unconscious guilt may mean that a certain amount of inconsistency between moral beliefs and actions is necessary in order to release conscious guilt and, therefore, serves an important adaptive function. In other words, 'a certain amount of conscious consumer guilt, as an outcome of moral attitude-behaviour inconsistency, is necessary so that unconscious guilt finds both periodic relief and a more rationalised, cognitive explanation' (Chatzidakis, 2015, p. 86). What are the practical implications of this? For instance, the presence of unconscious guilt may be the reason why some people consistently do harm to their bodies (through excessive alcohol consumption, smoking, etc.), feel guilty about it and still fail to change their behaviour. Others may avoid harming themselves but may still experience guilt for harming others, for example, through socially and environmentally harmful behaviour. Here, Chatzidakis (2015) also notes the relevance of 'depressive guilt' which is more explicitly linked with a capacity to care for rather than harm oneself or others. Many altruistic and solidaristic behaviours, from a Kleinian point of view, may be viewed in the light of a profound need for 'reparation', at first towards important others, but once extended, it could be a broader will to make the world a better place after realising all the harm we have inflicted upon it.

Seminar Exercises

Discussion Topics

1 Discuss the controversy around the application of psychoanalytic techniques to marketing. What are the key arguments in favour of and against psychoanalysis? What is your opinion?
2 Select one advertisement and try to apply a psychoanalytic reading. What are your insights?
3 Think of a particular object that is very important to you. Can you provide a psychoanalytic interpretation?
4 How does narcissism play out in contemporary consumer culture? Give examples where you can.

Group Exercises

1 Read the article by Chatzidakis (2015) in the key readings section.

    i In what ways is unconscious guilt different from conscious guilt? Explain the key difference between psychoanalytic models and more conventional understandings of (consumer) guilt.
    ii Consider the attitude-behaviour gap discussed in Chapter 7. How (if at all) can it be reduced from a psychoanalytic point of view?

iii Consider other examples of 'virtuous' and morally degrading consumption. How could you reinterpret them on the basis of Freud and Klein?

2 Projective techniques are widely employed in contemporary marketing research. In surveys, one common example includes asking participants to fill incomplete sentences (e.g. 'Mary bought a new iPhone because ____'), whereas in depth interviews, participants are often asked to project their thoughts and feelings to a third party (e.g. 'What would your friends think of people who are driving SUVs?').

i Ask two members from your group to respond to these questions. How are their responses different?
ii To what extent do these questions make participants reveal more about themselves rather than others?
iii Can you apply a psychoanalytic interpretation to their responses? What are your key insights? To what extent can you consider these to be 'valid'?

Key Readings

Chatzidakis, A. (2015). Guilt and Ethical Choice in Consumption: A Psychoanalytic Perspective. *Marketing Theory*, 15(1), 79–93.

Cluley, R., & Desmond, J. (2015). Why Psychoanalysis Now? *Marketing Theory*, 15(1), 3–8.

Cluley, R., & Dunne, S. (2012). From commodity fetishism to commodity narcissism. *Marketing Theory*, 12(3), 251–265.

Pick, D. (2015). *Psychoanalysis: A Very Short Introduction*. Oxford: Oxford University Press.

Schwarzkopf, S., & Gries, R. (Eds) (2010). *Ernest Dichter and Motivation Research*. London: Palgrave Macmillan.

References

Ahlberg, O., Coffin, J., & Hietanen, J. (2022). Bleak signs of our times: Descent into 'Terminal Marketing'. *Marketing Theory*, 22(4), 667–688.

Albanese, P.J. (2015). The unconscious processing information. *Marketing Theory*, 15(1), 59–78.

Bargh, J.A. (2002). Losing consciousness: Automatic influences on consumer judgment, behavior, and motivation. *Journal of Consumer Research*, 29(2), 280–285.

Beatty, S.E. and Hawkins, D.I. (1989), Subliminal stimulation: Some new data and interpretation. *Journal of Advertising*, 18(3), 4–8.

Boddy, C. (2005), Projective techniques in market research: valueless subjectivity or insightful reality, *International Journal of Market Research*, 47(3), 239–254.

Chatzidakis, A. (2015). Guilt and ethical choice in consumption: A psychoanalytic perspective. *Marketing Theory*, 15(1), 79–93.

Chatzidakis, A., Shaw, D., & Allen, M. (2021). A psycho-social approach to consumer ethics. *Journal of Consumer Culture*, 21(2), 123–145.

Clarke, S., & Hoggett, P. (Eds.) (2011). *Researching Beneath the Surface: Psycho-social Research Methods in Practice*. London: Karnac Books.

Cluley, R., & Desmond, J. (2015). Why psychoanalysis now? *Marketing Theory*, 15(1), 3–8.

Cluley, R., & Dunne, S. (2012). From commodity fetishism to commodity narcissism. *Marketing Theory*, 12(3), 251–265.

Coffin, J. (2021). Machines driving machines: Deleuze and Guattari's asignifying unconscious. *Marketing Theory*, 21(4), 501–516.

Desmond, J. (2012). *Psychoanalytic Accounts of CONSUMING Desire: Hearts of Darkness*. London: Palgrave Macmillan.

Dichter, E. (1960) *The Strategy of Desire*. New York: Doubleday and Company, Inc.

Dichter, E. (1979). *Getting Motivated by Ernest Dichter: The Secret Behind Individual Motivations by the Man Who Was Not Afraid to Ask Why?* Amsterdm: Elsevier.

Elgendi, M., Kumar, P., Barbic, S., Howard, N., Abbott, D., & Cichocki, A. (2018). Subliminal priming – State of the art and future perspectives. *Behavioral Sciences*, 8(6), 54.

Freud, S. (1916). The history of the psychoanalytic movement. *Psychoanalytic Review*, 3, 406–454.

Freud, S. (1923). The Ego and the Id. *The Standard Edition of the Complete Psychological Works of Sigmund Freud, Volume XIX (1923–1925): The Ego and the Id and Other Works*, 1–66.

Freud, S. (1991). 'On Narcissism', in J. Strachey (Ed.), On *Metapsychology: The Theory of Psychoanalysis*, pp. 59–99. London: Penguin.

Freud, S., & Freud, E.L. (1960). *Letters of Sigmund Freud*. North Chelmsford: Courier Corporation.

Frosh, S. (2010). *Psychoanalysis Outside the Clinic: Interventions in Psychosocial Studies*. London: Palgrave Macmillan.

Fullerton, R.A. (2007). 'Mr. MASS motivations himself': Explaining Dr. Ernest Dichter. *Journal of Consumer Behaviour*, 6(6), 369–382.

Gabriel, Y. (2015). Identity, choice and consumer freedom – The new opiates? A psychoanalytic interrogation. *Marketing Theory*, 15(1), 25–30.

Hietanen, J., Ahlberg, O., & Botez, A. (2022). The 'dividual'is semiocapitalist consumer culture. *Journal of Marketing Management*, 38(1–2), 165–181.

Hughes, J.M. (2008). *Guilt and Its Vicissitudes: Psychoanalytic Reflections on Morality*. New York: Routledge.

Klein, M. (1946). Notes on some schizoid mechanisms. *The International Journal of Psychoanalysis*, 27, 99–110.

Klein, M. (1948). A contribution to the theory of Anxiety and Guilt. *The International Journal of Psychoanalysis*, 29, 114–123.

Lacan, J. (1988). *The Seminar. Book II. The Ego in Freud's Theory and in the Technique of Psychoanalysis, 1954–55*. Cambridge: Cambridge Unviersity Press.

Lacan, J. (2010). The instance of the letter in the unconscious, or reason since Freud (1957). *Cultural Theory: An Anthology*, 432.

Lambert, A. (2019). Psychotic, acritical and precarious? A Lacanian exploration of the neoliberal consumer subject. *Marketing Theory*, 19(3), 329–346.

Lasch, C. (1979). *The Culture of Narcissism: American Life in an Age of Diminishing Returns*. New York: Norton.

Miller, D. (1997). How infants grow mothers in North London. *Theory, Culture and Society*, 14(4), 67–88.

Moore, T.E. (1982). Subliminal advertising: What you see is what you get. *Journal of Marketing*, 46, 38–47.

O'Shaughnessy, J. (2015). Note on the marginalizing of psychoanalysis in marketing. *Marketing Theory*, 15(1), 17–19.

Oswald, L.R. (2010). Marketing hedonics: Toward a psychoanalysis of advertising response. *Journal of Marketing Communications*, 16(3), 107–131.

Packard, V. (1957). *The Hidden Persuaders*. New York: Pocket Books.

Pick, D. (2015). *Psychoanalysis: A Very Short Introduction*. Oxford: Oxford University Press.

Reyes, I., Dholakia, N., & Bonoff, J.K. (2015). Disconnected/connected On the "look" and the "gaze" of cell phones. *Marketing Theory*, 15(1), 113–127.

Rogers, M., & Seiler, C.A. (1994). The answer is no: A national survey of advertising industry practitioners and their clients about whether they use subliminal advertising. *Journal of Advertising Research*, 34(2), 36–45.

Rustin, M. (2010). Looking for the unexpected: Psychoanalytic understanding and politics. *British Journal of Psychotherapy*, 26(4), 472–479.

Schwarzkopf, S. (2015). Mobilizing the depths of the market motivation research and the making of the disembedded consumer. *Marketing Theory*, 15(1), 39–57.

Schwarzkopf, S., & Gries, R. (Eds) (2010). *Ernest Dichter and Motivation Research*. London: Palgrave Macmillan.

Stewart, D.W., & Shamdasani, P.N. (2014). *Focus Groups: Theory and Practice* (Vol. 20). Thousand Oaks: Sage Publications.

Sutherland, R. (2013). Tips from the Marlboro Man. *Campaign*, 4, 15.

Tadajewski, M. (2006). Remembering motivation research: Toward an alternative genealogy of interpretive consumer research. *Marketing Theory*, 6(4), 429–466.

Williamson, J.E. (1978). *Decoding Advertisements: Ideology and Meaning in Advertising*. London: Marion Boyars.

Winnicott, D. (1971). *Playing and Reality*. London: Tavistock Press.

Zaretsky, E. (2005). *Secrets of the Soul: A Social and Cultural History of Psychoanalysis*. New York: Vintage Books.

8

HIERARCHIES OF KNOWLEDGE IN MARKETING

Introduction

Knowledge is systemically hierarchical. The institutions, cultures and value systems underpinning the work of individuals make it so. Individuals naturally are caught within the apparatus; there are those who grow up in rich territories which offer greater access to opportunities, while others do not. Knowledge is also hierarchical because much of the theory that has been spun in marketing journals hails from institutions at the top of the Global MBA Rankings (*Financial Times*, 2022), such as *Wharton, Columbia* and *INSEAD*. In addition, there are other centres of theoretical marketing excellence, for example, the *Nordic school* is known as a powerhouse of sophisticated critical marketing thought (Gummerus, 2015; Askegaard and Östberg, 2019). The commonality between these institutions is that they have Western outlooks and values. These hierarchies do a disservice to theory which originates from elsewhere by privileging ways of knowing and experiencing the world, working to make some ideas more visible than others. Existing publishing structures and practices mean that there are hierarchies of knowledge distributing only a small portion of thinking, creating missed opportunities to recognise the wealth of diverse theory in the world – written in various languages and from non-Western perspectives. Understanding the scope of knowledge hierarchies and how they operate within marketing theory and practice is the purpose of this chapter.

Knowledge refers to the accumulation of theoretical or practical subject-based information built up over time. Knowledge comprises facts, information, statistics and learned skill sets. The development of knowledge is highly valorised in society, with innovation and change typically based on what is thought to be the 'best' knowledge, often evaluated and monetised by a homogenous minority of hyper-individualist authors (Gurrieri et al., 2022) – for example, the highest-quality marketing research produced at the world's 'elite' universities, 'evidence-based' policy created in leading think tanks or 'gold-standard' practices adopted by blue-chip companies.

Knowledge also tends to be evaluated through accepted systems. Patients seek rigorously studied interventions, academics readily promote research based on the highest journal ranking and venture capitalists invest in business practices with optimal key performance

DOI: 10.4324/9781003201151-8

indicators. This might sound pedestrian, but the story which is largely untold is that the creation of knowledge itself is not without its own issues and inequalities and, consequently, should be scrutinised.

Privileged and tacitly accepted knowledge in society is typically supervised and controlled by an elite group of individuals. Within these knowledge hierarchies, processes and practices of evaluation and control have perpetuated over time, resulting in the emergence of a particular form of geopolitics, which tends to favour those habiting within Eurocentric countries. It is difficult for individuals living in these countries and being part of the university system to see and accept our own privilege, but this is becoming increasingly important in producing a fairer, happier society, where multiple voices are heard and accepted and where 'knowledge' is not based on a myopic point of view.

Within the subject of knowledge hierarchies, there are significant complexities and multiple viewpoints. Within the scope of this chapter, it is not possible to cover all of these. In this chapter, a simplistic overview is offered as a starting point to the subject of hierarchies of knowledge. It is also important for us to acknowledge that the authors write from a position of privilege as academics living and working in the UK.

Chapter Outline

This chapter critically examines some of the issues surrounding entrenched hierarchies of knowledge in marketing theory and practice. Firstly, a broad outline of knowledge creation in marketing and its competitive dynamics are described, defining hierarchies of knowledge. Secondly, a contextual outline of the geopolitics of knowledge is provided, focusing on the differences between the Northern and Southern hemispheres and how this produces over-recognised and under-recognised perspectives within knowledge hierarchies. The over-recognised perspectives include a pro-business lean towards systems of capitalism and the over-valued perspectives in the Eurocentric and Global North regions of the world. Thirdly, in terms of the under-represented perspectives, this chapter profiles how researchers from the Global South are marginalised in marketing academia and are historically and colonially influenced. This leads into a discussion of how academics are taking an active role in decolonizing marketing curricula in business schools to make classrooms more inclusive spaces and places for multiple voices to be heard and for difficult topics to be interrogated. Following this, the next section considers how access to education can be exclusionary, through providing an example of how MBA qualifications can replicate problematic assumptions and hierarchical thinking. Within the conclusion, practical recommendations are made, whereby students can enact small changes in their studies which incrementally break down knowledge hierarchies.

Knowledge Creation in Marketing

All disciplines are craven to the production of knowledge and marketing is no exception. One only needs to consult the monthly output of marketing academia to see how knowledge exponentially grows each year. As a student in the system, it is easy to drown in a sea of the latest textbooks and journal papers, all promising that they have *the* answer or the latest expertise. Amongst this plethora of resources, staying abreast of the latest trends in marketing feels impossible. Certain theorists have written about this predicament. For example, E.O. Wilson, a world leading biologist, famously said that 'we are drowning in information, while starving for wisdom. The world henceforth will be run by synthesizers, people able to put together the right information at the right time, think critically about it, and make important choices wisely', his point being that simply having information is not tantamount to being knowledgeable. It is how you use information critically and analytically which is a distinguishing factor in the production of quality knowledge.

Marketing knowledge is created in a similar vein to other social science disciplines. Academics, who are typically hired by universities after obtaining a PhD qualification, write books, journal articles, white papers and research grants (based on their research) which are assessed through a peer-reviewed blind system, whereby publications are cyclically revised and reviewed until the journal editors (typically being senior academics) deem the work ready to publish. Publishing is a lengthy process. A piece of research is typically in review for over a year and for the top journals, could stretch to multiple years. The findings of the research are then fed back, via business school teachings, to students, hopefully eventually trickling into organisations when students begin their professional careers. Knowledge is also shared with businesses through consultancy projects, impact projects or through creating a policy change in government. Research projects range from being highly theoretical to deeply practical, with marketing scholarship employing a broad church of methodological approaches ranging from interpretive ethnographies to quantitative experimental designs and everything in between.

Within marketing academia, groups of scholars periodically interrogate how those involved in the discipline are creating knowledge. These evaluative, critical exercises are usually undertaken via the publishing of special-issue sections in journal outlets. A special-issue section is a collection of around eight to ten research papers which collectively consider a specific topic based on a call for papers, written by the editors. In this chapter, special issues are introduced about knowledge production and hierarchies of knowledge (Brownlie and Saren, 1995; Kravets and Varman, 2022).

The Competitive Landscape of Marketing Knowledge

One such special issue in the *Journal of Marketing Management*, published in 1995 and edited by highly regarded professors, Douglas Brownlie and Michael Saren, is entitled 'On the Commodification of Marketing Knowledge'. This special issue promotes the wealth and variety of marketing knowledge being developed. It describes the acceleration of the 'cognitive currency' of marketing knowledge, contextualised by the post-industrial information culture which was emerging at the turn of the century (Brownlie and Saren, 1995). In this issue, the editors describe the increasingly competitive nature of the knowledge creation industry and how the publishing landscape has changed through rapid technological innovation. New technologies have enabled academics to communicate with greater speed via rich media (e.g. infographics, visuals and video) (Joonas et al., 2018) and through social media (Veletsianos, 2016). These changes have caused a shortening of the life cycles of ideas and in turn an escalation in the difficulty of producing something truly novel. Marketing academics have responded by recycling new ideas in different forms, as E.O. Wilson predicted in the quote previously, becoming *synthesisers* of information. As a result, competition in the marketing discipline is intense, which is an important point in understanding why some knowledge and ways of knowing are tacitly prioritised over others.

Defining Hierarchies of Knowledge

Hierarchies of knowledge are concerned with the epistemic structures of marketing and how these are historically and socially grounded (Kravets and Varman, 2022). The previous sections of this chapter explained how knowledge production is structured within the marketing discipline, largely via a traditional university academy, which privileges elite institutions (in the UK, this would include the *Russell Group* institutions) and employs the privileged few. However, this is not the full scope of understanding hierarchies of knowledge. Hierarchies of knowledge are also related to the relationship between 'the production of knowledge *and* the histories of empire, race and capitalism' (Kravets and Varman, 2022, p. 127). This quote demonstrates that hierarchies of knowledge do not exist in isolation. While they hold significant power within academic institutions, they are also externally facing and their effects are further reaching, feeding knowledge into society via published outputs and anointed graduates; they are also historically and culturally connected within the roots of capitalism and colonialism. Capitalism is the economic and political system which controls a country's trade and industry to make private owners a profit. Capitalism is connected to colonialism, which is when one country controls another through conquering its population of people and exploits it for their own benefit. This connection is not superficial, as capitalism has been cited 'in its different forms – colonial, slave, mercantile, financial, market – has used racist logic to demarcate whiteness from others and to distribute wealth and privileges along racial lines' (Eckhardt et al., 2022). There are many instances where capitalism and colonialism intersect within the marketplace. For example, in the wake of the 2020 *Black Lives Matter* movement, a plethora of racist branding embroiled in colonialism was highlighted, involving companies producing *Aunt Jemima*, *Uncle Ben's Rice* and many more (Francis, 2022). Certainly, themes of conquest, monopoly and extraction are familiar branding logics in the capitalist marketplace. As marketing takes the role of reproducing the zeitgeist of society, it naturally follows that it would reflect and perpetuate structurally rooted issues of capitalism and colonialism within everyday sociality (Bonsu, 2009).

Since capitalism and colonialism are interconnected, the fabric of society has inherent structural biases. For example, research in the USA has found that wages are lower for Black American consumers and that fast-food outlets are overrepresented in Black communities, even when controlling for their income levels (Grier et al., 2019). Within the context of educational settings, such as business schools in the Global North (referring to regions such as North American, Europe and Australia), knowledge hierarchies are also structurally biased. Their pro-business and pro-capitalist outlooks perpetuate and replicate unequal power relations between countries who are 'colonially rich' (for example, Eurocentric countries) and those countries and cultures which have been historically colonially exploited (for example, countries within the Global South). To create change, in terms of producing greater equity and re-imagining hierarchies of knowledge, it is important to intentionally oppose these epistemic knowledge structures and proactively create new systems and ways of being which are for the *many* and not for the *few*.

Entrenched Knowledge Hierarchies in Marketing

Another recent special issue is entitled 'Hierarchies of Knowledge in Marketing Theory', published in 2022 in the journal *Marketing Theory*. The references in this section will largely be drawn from this forward-thinking issue which advocates for a 'critical examination of epistemic structures of marketing' (Kravet's and Varman, 2022, p. 127). In doing this, the special issue editors aim to advance under-recognised or under-advanced scholarship within domains such as gender studies, decoloniality and postcolonial theory. Within this, many nuanced issues are illuminated and non-Western focused research contexts are profiled. Within this special issue, it is important to note that the guest editors worked consciously to include scholars working in and from Global Majority countries.

Geopolitics of Knowledge in Marketing Theory and Scholarship

Anglo-American and Eurocentric dominance in theory is the theme of Özlem Sandikci's paper, in which she problematizes how consumption and marketing are studied outside the West. This is a radical charge, considering the prominence of Western theory present in the marketing literature (Kravets and Varman, 2022). Within her essay, Sandikci (2022) conducts a narrative review of the research on consumption and marketing outside the West. In doing this, three terms to describe regions of the world are identified, including *Third World*, non-Western and emerging markets. Sandikci suggests (2022) that these designations bring about an imagined distance between those in the Western world and others. Further, they conjure up negative connotations, such as 'underdevelopment', 'poverty' and 'dependency'. Consequently, a complex and unequal relationship is developed between the production of knowledge and the histories of empire, race and capitalism. This relationship is interrogated, along with the discipline's theoretical canon which works to reproduce dominant Eurocentric perspectives.

In the case of research focusing on the Third World, Sandikci (2022) describes how this labelling has contributed to a lower 'scaled' position within entrenched hierarchies of marketing knowledge. Within existing hierarchies of marketing knowledge, the Western world is 'scaled' as the First World – with this label comes connotations of these societies being highly modernised, pro-capitalist, with a flourishing marketplace and a thriving economy in consumer goods. In contrast, the term Third World has been imagined to label countries which have lagged behind in their technological development and societal modernization. Scholars have conceived the Third World as standing between First World capitalist and Second World communist communities (Iqani, 2016). Within Third World countries, marketing and consumer culture is not conceived as well-established. Instead, it lags, a poor relation of their First World counterparts. For example, many may perceive that the consumer in First World Western economies would own a car, whereas in a Third World economy, there is a lack of basic services, such as water and sanitation. Consequently, non-Western countries have been labelled as lacking in management know-how and in desperate need of modernization. Marketing scholars have sought to solve these problems via promoting the positive effects of marketing on a country's development and, in doing so, applying knowledges created in the Global North to promote greater efficiency in distribution systems, improve category management of products by encouraging Third World countries to emulate First World consumer culture (Belk, 1988; Kaynak and Hudanah, 1987; Steenkamp et al., 2003). An outcome of this scholarship is the positioning of Western scholars as models of superiority and power, and tangentially, the West has accumulated knowledge-based capital in their theoretical ideas and their methodologies. This has ignited discourses of inferiority about Third World countries. In contrast, First World countries are heralded as saving bastions of modernity. Over time, these discourses create identities and become difficult to overcome.

In her work, Sandikci (2022) problematizes neoliberal global capitalist systems and the hierarchies of knowledge produced within them. In doing this, she conceives knowledge creation as a *collective* outcome of global power struggles and demonstrates how a privileged subject/object line of inquiry within a discipline is created. The notion that different areas of the world have been 'scaled' according to their level of development produces a view that being lower in the scale is poor. This problematizes differences between worlds and shuts down opportunities to embrace diversity. Instead, promoting a contextual understanding of why a country has developed in a certain way over time would be valuable. Sandikci (2022) suggests letting go of subjective scaling, labelling and name-calling. Further, through scholars embracing a greater degree of reflexivity and understanding, geopolitical hierarchies of knowledge could be better understood and dissolved. This would create greater global equity. One of the first tasks in doing this is through re-framing the notion that modernity is superior and letting go of the ideal that capitalism must be replicated at all costs.

Over-Recognised Perspectives in Marketing

Within marketing academia, assumptions are made which support the development of knowledge within the discipline. Within marketing theory, the most widely circulated academic journals and their outputs are underpinned by these assumptions. This means that knowledge produced in these journals replicate and over-recognise (publish more) studies which conform to these assumptions. Within this section, over-recognised perspectives, including those which are pro-business and aligned with capitalism and those which are overwhelmingly originating from the Global North, are described. It is important to note that these perspectives are also reflective of the entrenched privileges at play within consumer society. This chapter highlights some of the assumptions at play within the marketing publishing apparatus, of which there are many more.

Pro-business Perspectives in Marketing Research

The mainstay of marketing literature is written under the assumption that business and marketing are a positive force within society. This is in tandem with longstanding neoclassical economic paradigms which encourage competition and exchange within a free market (Agenjo-Calderón and Gálvez-Muñoz, 2019). The economic, free market paradigm assumes that business and wealth should be pursued at all costs. Within this mind-set, marketing is productive and increases the level of modernity within a country, which in turn increases its overall wealth and standing within the world. If individuals strive hard enough, marketing prowess will level our society upwards. And as such, marketers should do everything they can to maintain flourishing economies. Further, within businesses themselves, employees are seen as units of economic capital. They should strive to be ideal workers and offer as much as possible to an organization within the lifetimes of their career, prioritising their work above the rest of their life. Growth is key, and continual innovation must be sought to keep abreast of other competitors. Stagnation or position maintenance within the eyes of business is failure. These assumptions have had a significant influence on Global North marketing academia (including both research and teaching), global politics and even on consumers' everyday life choices.

When considering these assumptions, it is important to question whether this position can and should be maintained, especially given many societies are waking up to realise the effects of the pro-business agenda, manifesting within the climate crisis. Should a society pursue growth at all costs (see Chatzidakis et al., 2014) when we are within a global climate crisis amidst diminishing resources? Can academics maintain a pro-business stance despite being overwhelmed with debt created by spurious spending and an overcommitment to consumer sociality? Should workers be viewed as units of economic capital, whereby organisations' sole purpose is to advance the business agenda? These are critical considerations for those working within the marketing field, whose publishing trajectory will be shaped by these overarching assumptions and who has the power to reshape them in their actions.

The outlook of marketing scholarship is not all dystopian doom and gloom. There are alternatives to the pro-business outlook. These alternative outlooks are creating new paradigms and assumptions by which society could be re-ordered. One such paradigm has been developed via the lens of feminist economics and care. Academics from disciplines, including marketing, have pooled together to create 'The Care Manifesto' (Chatzidakis et al., 2020), which places care in the centre of the seemingly unsolvable problems which our society faces in order to re-orientate the way the natural world is viewed and understood. Within this purview, care, rather than pro-business economic growth, is prioritised. People are encouraged to work collectively to achieve joy in the world, rather than privileging their own interests at the expense of others. If marketing's purpose was to create a greater level of care and collectivism in society, it can be imagined how different our society might be.

An example of a company taking strides in this area is *Patagonia*, whose founder, Yvon Choinard, has, in 2022, given the company away, transferring their ownership to a trust and non-profit organization who will spend all the companies' profits in fighting climate change and to protect undeveloped land around the world. This example is an instance whereby an ethic of care has been applied within the marketing industry to repair the world, rather than to remove its resources in order to exploit them for profit and capital generation. This innovation demonstrates how an alternative to the pro-business agenda could reimagine our world.

Eurocentricity and the Global North

Another over-recognised perspective in marketing theory is Eurocentricity and emphasising the theoretical canon of the Global North. A theoretical canon is a set of work within a discipline which is deemed as essential to read and is in itself a problematic term. It includes the major thinkers, and everyone wishing to study or work within this discipline is expected to know them. For the most part, the canon within marketing research is dominated by Global North authors. Authors who fall outside this categorisation tend to be seen as 'others' and are often not fully understood from their perspective (Westwood, 2006). Canon knowledge dominates marketing research. It serves as the foundation from which new research is built and how students are taught. It is easy to see how this creates a hierarchy of knowledge which privileges the few.

Under-Recognised Perspectives in Marketing

Within marketing theory and practice, there are under-recognised perspectives which reside in the margins of the marketing discipline. Publications such as the ones published in the special issue on the hierarchies of knowledge are rare. They sit at the periphery of the discipline, and with an increasingly conservative swing in the charge of many Global North business schools, it is feared that within the next decade, critical perspectives will be pushed further to the periphery. Within this section, a light is shined on these under-recognised perspectives to push these streams of knowledge from the margins more firmly into the centre.

Perspectives from the Global South

Perspectives from the Global South remain mostly at the bottom of knowledge hierarchies and are largely absent from the theoretical canon of consumer behaviour (Iqani, 2016). The phrase Global South relates to the regions which are outside of Europe and North America, largely referring to Latin America, Asia, Africa and Oceania. Alongside the term Third World, Global South also implies people living on the periphery, on a low income and has connotations of people with little agency living chaotic lives (Iqani, 2016). Due to this characterization, films depicting life in the Global South are often dark and violent, pointing to the inequalities present between capitalist, colonial agendas and the wider world. The South Korean blockbuster, *Parasite*, is an excellent recent example of a film which exemplifies these qualities.

Within marketing practice, the Global South has been shaped by 'imported' marketing practices which influence the practices of local business, trickling into the cultural fabric of nations (Denegri-Knott et al., 2013). For example, in Peru, marketing education is taught from texts written by American authors yet simultaneously tailored to the needs and unique infrastructures of the country (Denegri-Knott et al., 2013). In doing this, the scope, definition and application of global marketing is reinvented.

In terms of marketing theory, scholars from the Global South are subject to the colonial forces of academic knowledge hierarchies, whereby the normative languages and cultural values in publishing pervade any tendency to approach the publishing system with a new or different perspective. Kravets and Varman (2022) write about this issue in their special issue, citing that these problems do not only exist in the instance of an author from the Global South trying to publish in a publication in the Global North but more perniciously that the institutional structures in the Global South are often marred by the history of colonial power so much so that this has influenced the development of knowledge within a social science discipline, such as marketing. Jafari (2022, p. 212) demonstrates how the colonial past of a country, whereby 'the coupling of the institutions of the state and religion has historically influenced social theory development'. Social theory development relates to academic work about how societies develop and change and how social structures and power relations are described, for example, in relation to how gender dynamics are experienced. If there is a discord between a researcher's reflexiveness and their approach to research, this can create a situation, whereby individual researchers are less likely to be able to speak to the reality of a context. Reflexivity is crucial in marketing and consumer research because it refers to the examination of the individual researchers' beliefs and judgements and, in addition, how these may have influenced how the research process was carried out and the quality of its findings (Flick, 2018). If a researcher does not examine their own beliefs and value systems in the construction of a research design, there is a lack of understanding of where one sits within the ecosystem of knowledge production and why. Due to this, within their research, Jafari (2022) found that researchers can end up perpetuating a West-centric viewpoint which may not be a culturally or socially proximate reflection of their lived experiences or belief systems. This is problematic because if research is not imbued with a quality of reflexivity and truth, there is a lost opportunity in raising consciousness around areas of society which may need to be understood further, developed or rethought. Unfortunately, this creates a risk of leaving the voices of the many unheard (non-Western), with the voices of the few (Western) being reinforced within knowledge hierarchies.

Decolonising the Curriculum

Decolonising the curriculum is an increasingly commonplace agenda within business schools, being adopted as a way of re-ordering how marketing is taught within academic institutions and, more broadly, a way to increase inclusivity in the classroom. A starting point in decolonising the curriculum is via reading lists, which are handed out by academics to guide students' studies. Reading lists are important representational devices (Schucan and Pitman, 2020) which reflect the perspectives and underpinning knowledge of an individual, module or programme. Diversifying these resources is a helpful start, although doing this in isolation is somewhat superficial. Within the classroom, marketing students and teachers need to be critical and reflexive when reading academic sources and highlighting where colonialism has had an impact in the creation of knowledge. Critical questions might include the following: Where have the sources given in the reading list come from geographically? Historically? And how has this impacted the practice which is being shared (i.e. who is being profiled?)? But who might be hidden? Are any ideas being perpetuated because of this?

A deeper engagement with decolonising the curriculum involves a 'critical analysis of how colonial forms of knowledge, pedagogical strategies and research methodologies . . . have shaped what we know, what we recognise and how we reward such knowledge accordingly' (Arshad, 2020). To do this, marketing academics, alongside their students, need to proactively acknowledge the effects of capitalism

and colonialism within a subject area and seek to remove those influences. One way of doing this could be leading the discussion on 'the
dark side' of a particular topic to interrogate ways of knowing and to
consider which aspects of a topic have been validated but also which
voices have become marginalised and hidden as a result (Eckhardt
et al., 2022). This can be as simple as academics and students working
together recognising where colonialism has had an impact and being
critical about the sources being used in the classroom, by considering
their geography, history and what this means in practice.

Moreover, decolonising the curriculum can be more holistic when
marketing academics take the perspective that the curriculum not
only encompasses taught content or assigned reading but also the
entire way that learning happens, for example, the multiplicity of
micro-interactions taking place in class between student-student,
academic-student and the micro-political interface between students
and the practices of the institution. For example, making sure that
everyone interacts with all the other members of the group within a
seminar and do not avoid each other based on the idea that they do
not have an affinity or share the same culture or, for example, making sure that multiple students' perspectives are platformed within
discussions. Particularly, if some students, who may naturally tend
towards needing more encouragement to share their thoughts, are
proactively offered the opportunities to share their ideas and experiences. The techniques described previously are simple but can be very
impactful in generating benefits from sharing diverse viewpoints and
creating an inclusive learning environment.

Access to Education and Widening Participation

Access to education, which is often described as 'widening participation', is a common way that universities encourage diversity in
marketing cohorts and indirectly into marketing university teaching
staff. Encouraging diversity within a learning environment, fostered
through a critical collaboration between students and academics, can
increase the potential for building inclusive worldviews for everyone
in the classroom.

Within the education system, hierarchies of knowledge and participation exist. The university academy is a system, whereby those who
can afford fees for education, accommodation and living costs are the
ones who will receive the teaching. Particularly in the wake of esca-
lating fees and living costs, this is not a possible route for the underprivileged, whose families simply cannot overcome financial barriers
to entry. Sponsorships and scholarships are few and far between
and tend to be reserved for the academically gifted. One solution to
this could be to encourage marketing companies to think reflexively
about supporting young people from diverse backgrounds who would
be highly valuable in an inclusive boardroom.

An example of how marketing education can conceive participation hierarchies through their design is with MBA courses, which are
qualifications with high visibility and a high price tag. MBA stands for

Master's in Business Administration. It is a highly prestigious qualification which business schools promote as a premium offering to commercial organisations charging significantly more than their other postgraduate programmes, focusing on elements of management, business and entrepreneurship. Each business school has its own MBA suited to the character of that institution. Sometimes MBA degrees come with a promise that once a student graduates, they are guaranteed a certain level of salary which places them in the top tier of elite earners. MBA courses typically cost twice the amount of a typical master's degree, which makes them available only to those who are financially secure. In this sense, students taking an MBA course self-select into a pool of individuals and institutional promises which are set to place them in high-paying jobs. There are also executive MBA qualifications, which are often funded by commercial organisations, seen as a form of professional development. Moreover, research has found that there are gendered divides and effects present for those taking MBA courses. Sinclair (1995) has found that MBAs are taught based on outdated knowledge, specifically on gendered assumptions of how a manager should behave, leaving female students feeling disenchanted by their learning. Disenchantment with MBA teaching is widespread, and there has been a decline in the number of women enrolling in these qualifications as a result. Certainly, in these cases, it is important for academics to iteratively reflect on whether what is being taught truly reflects modern best practices and do not replicate unconscious biases. It is important that curricula 'moves with the times', is as inclusive as possible and draws from a rich array of sources ranging from multiple perspectives.

Chapter Summary

Within this chapter, knowledge hierarchies have been introduced; what they are, how they act and the way their influence can spread throughout marketing theory and practice. Hierarchical ideals spread easily within an ecosystem of academics, graduates, marketing professionals, advertising campaigns, through policy makers and grant funders and even via the design of academic marketing programmes. Within these hierarchies, some perspectives are valued more overtly than others. For example, most of the assumptions from the marketing literature originate from the theoretical canon of the Global North and from pro-business and capitalist theoretical assumptions. Scaling politics label and position certain parts of the world subjectively against one another, as better or worse, and introduce cross-cultural differences as a negative rather than something to be embraced and collectively learned from. Following this interrogation into the origins of hierarchies of knowledge, this chapter has considered the ways in which marketing academia can change to become more inclusive, both in the ways students and academics approach the creation of reading lists and in the ways in which academics and students relate to each other in the classroom. The academy needs more students in the education system from diverse backgrounds. An increase in inclusivity-focused postgraduate scholarships from marketing companies could introduce greater diversity into academic faculty.

This chapter has demonstrated the systematic way that knowledge hierarchies are built up over time. In changing course, it is important to embrace alternative modes of world making, for example, through an ethic of care rather than a pro-business economy. In the future, as a first step it is imperative that the connection between capitalism and colonialism is widely acknowledged.

Case Study: Decolonising the Media

As demonstrated within the 'hierarchies of knowledge' chapter, drawing largely from the context of academia, complex entanglements of power exist within systems of production. Over time, relations and actions of power create scaling politics and hierarchies which structure how systems of production operate. Typically, within knowledge hierarchies, greater powers are held by the few and smaller powers are held by the many. Hierarchies of knowledge exist not only in academia but also in the media and communications industry. This case study will exemplify how mass media is hierarchical and how this is related to everyday marketing practice.

Mass media are technologies which disseminate information to a large audience, through communicating publicly via television, radio, internet, movies, newspapers and magazines. Advertising is a stand-alone form of mass media and a component part of most other forms of mass media, although its significant role is often overlooked. In simple terms, many forms of mass communication are funded partly or solely through advertising. Advertisers buy space 'on air' in commercial breaks, in the pages of newspapers, within webpages and in movie theatres to send marketing messages alongside other communications in the hope of connecting with their audiences. Without understanding the importance of advertising and its relationship with other media formats, it is hard to conceive how media systems function.

This is significant when thinking of hierarchies of knowledge because behind every carefully placed advertising message is a decision made by an individual with thoughts, feelings and prejudices. Advertisers' money is spent in placing adverts within media which are deemed to be suitable outlets. They will choose outlets which publish what they feel is the right information, or a good match in representing the companies wishing to promote themselves. Therefore, these decisions will never be neutral and can be inherently structurally biased. It is well known that different media outlets follow certain political agendas. For example, *The Daily Telegraph* is a long-term public supporter of the Conservative party and so companies that choose to advertise within this publication will be aware of, or also in support of, this.

Media biases can also work to support hierarchies of knowledge in the mass media. A media bias is when an outlet will cover a news story in a particular way, often with an unwillingness to present both sides of view on a certain matter. Media bias is common and, therefore, so is advertising bias – and these biases often serve to shape public opinion on a grand scale through mass communications. Traditionally, the media is white and privileges the viewpoints of the pro-business, rich, male elite in the same way that academia does. Fundamentally, it is important to understand the role of marketing within mass media systems to better conceive how marketing can be used in a responsible, rather than problematic, fashion.

Social media is especially economically dependent on the sale of advertising. Advertising is the majority source of funding for social media systems, so much so that almost all opportunities for consumers to connect with others are dependent on advertisers' willingness to pay for the use of these services. The reality is that without advertising spend, most content on the internet would not exist. This is tricky to fathom, as consumers typically think of the internet as a free space of fluid potential and readily believe the myth that the internet is still a consumer-controlled Wild West.

Additionally, when considering hierarchies of media, breaking down structural biases of race, gender and other marginalising factors is dependent on advertisers taking a broader worldview and sponsoring greater diversity of content. Not only this but it also depends on platform logics and the training of algorithms. For example, it has been proven that algorithms learn to more readily favour content from white, beige and light-brown individuals. In this vein, platform algorithms are designed with systematic, repeatable errors which privilege certain categories over others. Relatedly, consumers can also create replicating effects which bolster the bias within platforms. Importantly, alongside algorithms, consumers must also have a willingness to engage with greater diversity of content. This is also an important consideration in how successful certain categories of content may be in terms of generating advertising revenue. Clearly, the issue of content, platform design and advertising spend in generating a fair and ethical media system is a multi-layered and complex topic. Clearly, hierarchies of knowledge cannot be 'solved' by a single agent's actions towards greater online diversity and inclusion. Rather, hierarchies of media are dependent on the ethical responsibility and change in behaviour of a range of agents working collectively towards a harmonious media system where power is distributed with greater equity.

Zines and New Media Spaces

Zines and new media spaces are examples of how collectives can disrupt established media hierarchies. These media forms collectively foster action in pursuit of breaking down traditional media-focused hierarchies of knowledge. Zines typically begin as self-published, homemade print publications with a limited distribution. Typically created within and circulated through subcultural networks, Zines can act as 'resistive texts', or 'alternative media', that stand in direct opposition to mainstream cultural ideologies (Schilt, 2003). While historically, zines were a form of media typically created through gluing text and images together onto a master flat for photocopying, today, they have evolved into online platforms, with potential for greater reach in being recognised as an assembling force when coupled with other organizational practices, such as growing online communities.

There are many instances of zines becoming institutionally accepted media companies in the progression of a particular social agenda. For instance, the company *Dazed Digital*, responsible for the magazine *Dazed*, started life in 1991 as a zine; and the infamous *riot grrrl* movement actively encouraged young women to make zines in 'getting their voices heard' and progressing feminist ideologies within punk culture. More recently, *gal-dem*, a publication which seeks to address inequality and misrepresentation in journalism through platforming the creative and editorial work of young women and non-binary people of colour, has been heralded as a disruptive, award-winning collective, partnering with major media outlets and celebrities in pursuing their charge. By organizing their work around the pursuit of intersectionality and voicing marginalised groups, *gal-dem* has succeeded in retaining authenticity whilst also co-opting the very media they seek to de-rail. In transferring specific practices of production into the online space, employees of zines are re-booting organizing and activist practices through creating new forms of feminist visibility and representation, often through seeking genuine inclusivity rather than superficial change.

Seminar Exercises

Discussion Questions

Do you think traditional mass media will be popular indefinitely?

Can you think of some changes which could be made to mass media outlets to make them more inclusive?

Are hierarchies of knowledge always problematic, or can they be used in a positive way?

Do you think zines can truly make a difference? If you were going to make a zine, which topic would you focus on?

Group Exercise

Please search the internet and find the *gal-dem* site. As a group, can you search through the site and find the types of advertising being used? Do you think the advertising on the site reflects the values of *gal-dem*? Can you ideate and think of ways that media outlets could make money other than through advertising revenue?

Key Readings

Duncombe, S., 2008. *Notes from Underground: Zines and the Politics of Alternative Culture*. Microcosm Publishing.

Eckhardt, G.M., Belk, R., Bradford, T.W., Dobscha, S., Ger, G. and Varman, R., 2022. Decolonizing marketing. *Consumption Markets & Culture*, 25(2), pp. 176–186.

Egbeyemi, E., 2020. Case study: How gal-dem magazine succeeded where mainstream media failed. In M. Sternadori and T. Holmes (Eds.), *The Handbook of Magazine Studies* (pp. 393–399). John Wiley & Sons, Inc.

Hrynyshyn, D., 2017. *The Limits of the Digital Revolution: How Mass Media Culture Endures in a Social Media World*. ABC-CLIO.

Rosa-Salas, M. and Sobande, F., 2022. Hierarchies of knowledge about intersectionality in marketing theory and practice. *Marketing Theory*, p. 14705931221075372.

Internet Resources

https://*gal-dem*.com/
https://thecreativeindependent.com/guides/how-to-make-a-zine/

References

Agenjo-Calderón, A. and Gálvez-Muñoz, L., 2019. Feminist economics: Theoretical and political dimensions. *American Journal of Economics and Sociology*, 78(1), pp. 137–166.

Arshad, R., 2020. *Decolonising and Initial Teacher Information*, available at: https://www.ceres.education.ed.ac.uk/2020/08/19/decolonising-and-initial-teacher-education/

Askegaard, S. and Östberg, J. eds., 2019. *Nordic Consumer Culture: State, Market and Consumers*. Springer.

Belk, R.W., 1988. Third world consumer culture. *Research in Marketing*, 4(1), pp. 103–127.

Bonsu, S.K., 2009. Colonial images in global times: Consumer interpretations of Africa and Africans in advertising. *Consumption Markets & Culture*, 12(1), pp. 1–25.

Brownlie, D. and Saren, M., 1995. On the commodification of marketing knowledge: Opening themes. *Journal of Marketing Management*, 11(7), pp. 619–627.

Chatzidakis, A., Hakim, J., Litter, J. and Rottenberg, C., 2020. *The Care Manifesto: The Politics of Interdependence*. Verso Books.

Chatzidakis, A., Larsen, G. and Bishop, S., 2014. Farewell to consumerism: Countervailing logics of growth in consumption. *Ephemera: Theory and Politics in Organization*, 14(4), pp. 753–764.

Denegri-Knott, J., Witkowski, T.H. and Pipoli, G., 2013. Marketeando: Domesticating Marketing Education the "Peruvian way". *Journal of Macromarketing*, 33(1), pp. 41–57.

Eckhardt, G.M., Belk, R., Bradford, T.W., Dobscha, S., Ger, G. and Varman, R., 2022. Decolonizing marketing. *Consumption Markets & Culture*, 25(2), pp. 176–186.

EM Steenkamp, J.B., Batra, R. and Alden, D.L., 2003. How perceived brand globalness creates brand value. *Journal of International Business Studies*, 34(1), pp. 53–65.

Flick, U., 2018. *Designing Qualitative Research*. Sage.

Francis, J.N., 2022. Rescuing marketing from its colonial roots: A decolonial anti-racist agenda. *Journal of Consumer Marketing*.

Grier, S.A., Thomas, K.D. and Johnson, G.D., 2019. Re-imagining the marketplace: Addressing race in academic marketing research. *Consumption Markets & Culture*, 22(1), pp. 91–100.

Gummerus, J., 2015. *The Nordic School-Service Marketing and Management for the Future*. Hanken CERS.

Gurrieri, L., Prothero, A. and Bettany, S., 2022. Feminist academic organizations: Challenging sexism through collective mobilizing across research, support and advocacy. *Gender, Work and Organization*, pp. 1–22.

Iqani, M., 2016. *Consumption, Media and the Global South: Aspiration Contested*. Springer.

Jafari, A., 2022. The role of institutions in non-Western contexts in reinforcing West-centric knowledge hierarchies: Towards more self-reflexivity in marketing and consumer research. *Marketing Theory*, 22(2), pp. 211–227.

Joonas, R., Joel, H. and Douglas, B., 2018. Screening marketing: Videography and the expanding horizons of filmic research. *Journal of Marketing Management*, 34(5–6), pp. 421–431, DOI: 10.1080/0267257X.2017.1403112.

Kaynak, E. and Hudanah, B.I., 1987. Operationalising the relationship between marketing and economic development: Some insights from less developed countries. *European Journal of Marketing*, 21(1), pp. 48–65.

Kravets, O. and Varman, R., 2022. Introduction to special issue: Hierarchies of knowledge in marketing theory. *Marketing Theory*, 22(2), pp. 127–133.

Sandikci, O., 2022. The scalar politics of difference: Researching consumption and marketing outside the west. *Marketing Theory*, 22(2), pp. 135–153.

Schilt, K., 2003. "I'll resist with every inch and every breath" girls and zine making as a form of resistance. *Youth & Society*, 35(1), pp. 71–97.

Schucan Bird, K. and Pitman, L., 2020. How diverse is your reading list? Exploring issues of representation and decolonisation in the UK. *Higher Education*, 79(5), pp. 903–920.

Sinclair, A., 1995. Sex and the MBA. *Organization*, 2(2), pp. 295–317.

Veletsianos, G., 2016. *Social Media in Academia: Networked Scholars*. Routledge.

Westwood, R., 2006. International business and management studies as an orientalist discourse: A postcolonial critique. *Critical Perspectives on International Business*, 2(2), pp. 91–113.

9
MARKETING, SPACES AND PLACES

Space is normally taken-for-granted, treated as the static physical container where marketing and consumption activities take place. Marketing management approaches most often treat space as a logistical challenge, covered by the typical distribution concerns incorporated into the 'P' of place in the marketing mix. Hence, when the importance of space and place is acknowledged, the focus tends to be limited to store atmospherics and servicescape design. With an emphasis on sensory stimulation and store layout, such perspectives usually adopt information-processing models to look at stimuli input and their resultant consumer outputs in terms of emotional and behavioural responses. Importantly, however, the cultural significance of space and place tend to be overlooked by these models. Disciplines across the social sciences and humanities recognise that space and place are not static entities but are instead dynamic and constantly evolving. Spaces become 'places' when they hold meanings the people who use or inhabit them.

The rise in destination marketing in recent years attempts to maximise and, indeed, influence the shared meanings about specific countries, regions or cities in order to create place-based identities that appeal to tourists. Often, the meaning of places like these are contested by various stakeholders (urban planners, residents, tourists, politicians, commerce and so forth) as different interests clash and sometimes try to suppress other voices. Nor is this type of contestation solely in relation to destination marketing. A botched refurbishment by the management of a shopping centre in Ireland alienated many local consumers who perceived it to have lost its special ambience and associated symbolic meanings (Maclaran and Brown, 2005).

This chapter focuses on the many dynamics of turning marketing spaces into places and how we can analyse and understand these dynamics holistically. First, we begin by taking a closer look at how we form attachments with places we know and how they can become an important part of our identity. Then we go on to discuss how marketers encourage place attachment through particular branding strategies. We consider the spectacular nature of much contemporary retail and set this in its historical context, showing how specific forms of retail have evolved in terms of creating a sense of place. After highlighting the significance of theming, especially in relation to newer

DOI: 10.4324/9781003201151-9

forms of retail, such as flagship brandstores, we continue with a discussion of the social and, sometimes, therapeutic roles commercial
locations may perform. Finally, we look in more detail at the different
kinds of spaces within which consumption takes place and introduce
key theorists and concepts on consumption *in* space.

Place Attachment and Identity

We build attachments to places throughout our lives, usually starting with our home environment (house or neighbourhood) and
radiating outwards from that as we grow up, move away and get to
know other places, whether for temporary or more permanent stays.
These places – be they workplaces or holiday resorts, countries or
local villages, churches or pubs – can become highly significant to us
and contribute strongly to our sense of who we are. The term 'place
attachment' encapsulates such feelings of familiarity and belonging
that we develop around the meaningful places in our lives. How we
experience the places in our lives varies greatly depending on a host
of factors.

In his seminal work, *Place and Placelessness*, the geographer
Edward Relph (1976) identifies a continuum of experiential place
intensity that ranges from direct experience on one end to abstract
thought at the other. Some spatial experiences will be instinctive and
bodily, whereas others will be cerebral and intangible. The former are
more likely to be taken-for-granted understandings of place and the
latter more analytical and reflective. Thus, we may move around the
rooms in our home in habitual ways that elicit little reflection, taking
for granted the contours and contents. In contrast, we may be awe-
struck by the magnificence of a Gothic cathedral and self-consciously
reflect on the beauty of its lofty spires. Many other spatial experiences will be nuanced mixtures of these two extremes. The point is
that understanding the subjective lived experiences that people have
in particular places is essential to appreciate the dynamics inherent
in place.

Many heterogenous spatial encounters in everyday life have the
power to order our actions and intentions. Our actions and thoughts
in the sacred space of a church are likely to be very different to those
we have on entering a pub. Whereas the former may awaken feelings of reverence that encourage us to bow our heads and retreat
into silent prayer, the latter may provoke feelings of conviviality that
encourage us to seek connections to others around us, rather than
to a transcendental entity. Of course, how we react in and to a space
will also depend on our own socio-cultural background that heavily
influences how we interpret the space. In the examples just given, we
will only bow our heads if religiously-inclined, and the pub experience
may be very different, depending, for example, on whether we are
male or female. As a woman walking alone into a traditional English
bar, where men often congregate on stools at the counter, we may
feel alienated by the gendered nature of the space and disinclined to
approach the bar to order a drink.

Thus, we can see how place influences identity not only in relation to material factors such as the built, physical environment or natural landscape it contains but also on account of social interactions that occur there. The relationship between people and their environment is always a dynamic and interactive one which encompasses a myriad of social, cultural, psychological, environmental, economic and political factors that are in continual interplay. As a consequence, our relationships with places can take many diverse forms, depending on the positive or negative associations that they engender in us and whether we experience affection, alienation or simply indifference to a place. As we have just seen in the example of the pub, the same space may provoke very different reactions in people, depending on their own socio-cultural backgrounds, as well as how they interpret their ongoing experiences there. Relph (1976) uses the term 'insideness' to denote the degree of attachment that a person or group has with a place. So in the instance of the pub, the men at the bar feel safe and secure because they are regulars, insiders who know the place well, whereas we as outsiders (and women) feel vulnerable and threatened. The term 'outsideness' encapsulates these feelings of alienation, a sense of being separate and apart.

At its simplest, 'outsideness' can be the homesickness we feel when we move to a new location. In practice, these two poles – insideness and outsideness – represent a dialectical process through which we experience differing spatial intensities. It plays a significant role in our self-concept, and like other aspects of identity, it helps us differentiate ourselves from others ('I'm a Londoner' and so forth). Place identity also gives us an anchoring point, lending a sense of rootedness that makes us feel more secure. It is not only our sense of individual self to which place contributes but also our social identity. Social identity is also usually tied to specific places that make us feel connected to certain reference groups (nation, neighbourhood, family, ethnic or religious group).

Apart from influencing our identity, places also establish their own identity, a special sense of place (genius loci) that allows somewhere to be differentiated from other places. Place identity is a complex mixture of memories, perceptions, interpretations and feelings. As we will see in the next section, there are three key components that various theorists on space (e.g. Relph, 1976; Lefebvre, 1991; Soja, 1996; Agnew, 2005) identify, and although they all use different terms for these, they are broadly agreed that these include: 1) the physical setting with its material contents; 2) the activities and events that take place within the space; and 3) the meanings created (both individual and group) through people's experiences and intentions in relation to the space. Whereas the first has to do with physical structures and objects, the second concerns people's phenomenological (lived) experiences. The third is more abstract and covers the ideologies embedded in a space (e.g. the masculine culture of the bar counter). Relph (1976, p. 64) also usefully distinguishes between authentic and inauthentic senses of place, seeing the former as 'a direct and genuine

experience of the entire complex of the identity of places – not mediated and distorted through a series of quite arbitrary social and intellectual fashions about how that experience should be, nor following
stereotyped conventions'. We will see as we continue in the next section that there is often a danger of marketers creating inauthentic
places and contributing to what Relph describes as *placelessness*, the
eradication of what is distinct about a place through standardisation
of its elements.

Destination Marketing and Branding

Destination marketing – promoting a town, city, region or country –
is probably the first thing that springs to mind when we think of
the intersection of place and marketing. Destination marketing has
grown enormously over the last two decades, fuelled by the huge
growth in the tourism and services industries sectors. A major aspect
of destination marketing is developing a place identity and communicating this to potential visitors, investors or residents to influence
their decisions about where to travel, invest in or live. At the heart of
destination marketing lies the concept of place branding (i.e. encod-
ing a place with a particular image, associations and values that differentiate it from other places and give it a unique identity). In such
ways, marketing communications attempt to encourage a sense of
place attachment in various audiences being targeted.

Often, place branding efforts can go awry, however, reflecting only
one constituency's perceptions of a place and failing to engage other
stakeholders. To explain this type of failure in terms of Relph's (1976)
terminology: by trying to create feelings of insideness for visitors,
you may alienate the original inhabitants (insiders), bringing them a
sense of outsideness and a place with which they can no longer identify. Unless they appreciate such dynamics, marketers risk creating an
image that fails to resonate with anyone who has a vested interest
in the place. Traditional marketing approaches overlook the many
complexities inherent in the concept of place, treating place instead
as if it were a product whose essence can be distilled into a single
meaning and communicated to a target market. In so doing, marketers ignore a key distinction between places, such as cities or regions,
and conventional products: rather than being owned by one individual or organisation, they are composed of different public and private
ownerships (Warnaby and Medway, 2013). In addition, traditional
approaches see identity as static, something that can be manipulated
at will through a new logo and a catchy promotional message. They
are usually the output of top-down decision-making processes (usually at local council/government level in conjunction with a consult-
ant) that decide what positive aspects to emphasise about a place and
what negative ones to mask. Place branding's role in this process is to
encapsulate this identity and communicate its relevance effectively
to various audiences.

Locals widely derided a city branding exercise for Belfast, Northern Ireland, even going so far as to describe it as 'putting lipstick on a

gorilla' (Brown et al., 2013, p. 1251). Admittedly, Belfast City Council and their consultants did not have an easy mission to rebrand Belfast, a city long tainted by 'the troubles', years of religious conflict and terrorist slaughters. However, many commentators accused the resultant heart-shaped B logo – duly accompanied by 'Be' messages such as 'Be vibrant' and 'Be inspired' – of whitewashing the town's history and producing a copycat city stereotyping. They noted its remarkable similarity to promotional logos used for two English towns, Barrow-in-Furness and Blackburn, who used also the tilted B in a similar heart-shaped fashion, as well as its likeness to Milton Glaser's iconic 'I Love New York' logo from 1977. Yet, somewhat surprisingly, despite its many vociferous critics, the rebranding of Belfast has been a success, precisely, Brown and Shultz II (2013) conclude, because it was an innocuous, middle-of-the-road choice that offended no one, a significant advantage in a city whose fighting spirit is legendary.

So although marketers often ignore the complexities underpinning place relationships, sometimes this may be deliberate, as in the case of Belfast, where they sought a blander alternative that papers over the cracks, so to speak, and masks differences. Despite the seemingly positive outcome against all the odds – no doubt on account of Belfast's uniquely troubled history – this case is a good illustration of what Relph (1976) refers to as 'mass identities of places', identities designated by opinion-makers rather than by the communities that live there. This leads to an inauthentic sense of place in Relph's view, one mediated and even distorted by marketers as they apply textbook principles in creating a cultural transformation package to differentiate the city and increase visitor numbers, as Patterson and Hodgson (2011, p. 297) so succinctly put it in their study of the city branding of Liverpool:

> The tried and tested format of such a makeover, to a cynic at least, involves: scouring the history books for points of hometown distinction; celebrating a sense of place by making local landmarks more tourist friendly, perhaps by installing a touch-screen kiosk or two, erecting plinths in honour of famous locals from the past and present, renovating and renewng public architecture, shopping precincts and generally polishing the town's jewels, whatever they might be, for the purposes of public display. Ultimately, the goal is to create a more palatable and exciting place tale.

Pursuing a makeover formula like this becomes a zero-sum game if every city does it as, ultimately, a formulaic approach erodes any real cultural differentiation. The commodification of the city to such an extent can destroy its soul, with its 'form and spirit remade to conform to market demand, not residents' dreams' (Holcolm, 1999, p. 69). In celebrating difference, marketers may in fact be imposing uniformity. For example, Manchester's Canal Street celebrates gay culture, Birmingham's Jewellery Quarter testifies to its English heritage, while Dublin's Temple Bar signals Irish artistic endeavours. Despite their cultural distinctiveness, each area is crammed with bars, restaurants and retail that erode difference and give them more in common, all

ultimately facilitating a hedonistic consumerist experience that car-
ries little differentiation. It is in this sense that Warnaby and Medway
(2013, p. 358) highlight how 'the very act of place marketing can dilute
and weaken the unique appeal of the place product', overlooking
deeper, more engrained symbolic significances that inhabitants hold
dear in the search for touristic thrills.

To retain a more authentic sense of place, one that reflects the
genuine experiences of its inhabitants, Kavaratzis and Hatch (2013)
propose an identity-focused place branding framework. Moving
away from a top-down perspective, the authors acknowledge place
as dynamic and polyphonic with many different stakeholders. Theirs
is a participatory model that encourages ongoing dialogue between
all stakeholders but especially local communities. Three key pivotal
points are in continuous interplay – culture, identity and image – to
co-create the brand identity among all interested parties. This pro-
cess-based model recognises that as people interact with their surroundings, their understandings of place are constantly produced and
reproduced. Consequently, place identity never remains static and
should involve ongoing negotiation between all stakeholders. The
place branding exercise becomes part of this process. By allowing
local cultural meanings to surface, the process ensures inhabitants
feelings are respected and participants gain confidence over time as
they see their own experiences reflected back to them.

Spectacular Retail Environments

Cities are often marketed as sites of spectacular consumption that
include the city's architectural heritage (museums, cathedrals, cas-
tles, etc.) intermingled with more contemporary consumptionscapes,
such as shopping malls, that also make a visual statement. Spectacular
consumptionscapes such as these are a crucial part of city branding,
providing key visitor attractions. Think of one of the world's largest
shopping and entertainment complex, the Dubai Mall, with 1,200-
plus retail outlets, which makes Dubai one of the world's top international destinations. Each consumptionscape creates its own sense of
place as well as contributing to the overall 'place of the city'. Shopping
malls, festival marketplaces like Covent Garden and London and flagship brandstores like Prada and Louis Vuitton are designed to inspire
a sense of awe, as well as acting as cultural resources for individualised identity projects. Although we tend to regard the intertwining of
commerce and culture as a relatively new phenomenon, this is not
strictly accurate. City planning has a long history of fantasy-inspiring
retailscapes. Nineteenth-century shopping arcades and departments
stores were the precursors of the modern shopping mall.

Shopping Arcades

Glazed shopping arcades were the first major retailing innovation to
take place with the onset of industrialisation. Creating a public space
that was sheltered from both weather and traffic, lavishly designed

galleria brought new ways to sell the burgeoning number of luxury products flooding the market. Major European cities each developed their own spectacular arcades. Paris, in particular, was famed for the creative elegance of its many arcades such as the *Galeries de Bois*, one of the earliest arcades constructed in the 1780s. Architecturally, arcades made much use of atriums, marble paneling and highly ornate fixtures and fittings that, together with an abundance of greenery, conveyed opulence and awoke desire. In its conception, the arcade was very much a fantasy-provoking realm, a space designed to offer shoppers undisturbed browsing of extravagant displays of merchandise. Today in Paris, one can still admire the faded grandeur of a few surviving arcades. (At their height, they totaled 150 in the city, although only 20 remain today.) Now mainly devoted to bric-a-brac shops, they draw tourists who seek immersion in their nostalgic ambience.

The Department Store

The advent of the department store in the mid-1800s heralded the demise of the arcades, and its arrival was certainly one of the defining moments in the development of consumer culture. The department store introduced many innovations to the retail trade: a status-free environment where all shoppers were treated as equal, pricing of merchandise to replace individual bargaining, free entrance without the moral obligation to buy which dominated the atmosphere of other shops and the right to exchange goods or obtain refunds. Perhaps the most significant innovation for modern retailing was the encouragement to browse around the shop, to wander and enjoy the experience without feeling committed to a purchase. Reekie (1993, p. 4) describes the lavish settings of early department stores, such as *Bon Marché, Galeries Layfayette, Printemps, Bloomingdale's, Selfridges* and *Harrods*, as 'palaces of consumption' because of the irresistible temptations that they offered to strolling shoppers. Stores such as these also prided themselves on a continual supply of novelty merchandise, sending buyers around the world in search of remarkable items. While the department store has largely become a redundant form of retail, famous stores like the aforementioned still thrive today, a crucial part of the cityscapes to which they belong, with their illustrious histories acting as major tourist draws.

Significantly, department stores were the forerunner for what Ritzer (1999, p. 42) terms 'the new means of consumption', whereby social relations have become profoundly altered, now more often expressed through interactions with objects rather than with people. The department store brought about a cultural change, unveiling a world where commodities began to symbolise the search for experience, rather than possession representing an end in itself. The emphasis on the spectacular features of consumerism was all part of this experiential development, creating illusionary 'dreamworlds'

(Williams, 1985), places that transported their visitors away from everyday reality and into a fantasy realm.

The idea of 'shopertainment' (Hannigan, 1998) – the convergence of retail and entertainment that is so prevalent today – also found its origins in department store tradition. Many department stores in the late 1800s provided free entertainment to lure shoppers into their midst. Sometimes they would have orchestra music, art shows or other cultural diversions. Siegel-Cooper, famous for having the largest store in the world when it opened its New York branch in 1896, ran a six-week-long 'Carnival of Nations' (Hannigan, 1998). In a flamboyant attempt to outdo its rivals, the highlight of the carnival was an exotic Turkish harem and parade of Turkish dancing girls. Tearooms – a slightly more mundane way to encourage clients to linger – were also common in department stores, encouraging shoppers to socialise and relax over assorted teas and cakes. This tearoom tradition is still celebrated in London department stores such as Fortnum & Mason's and Harrod's, although now largely catering for tourists to the city.

The Shopping Mall

Drawing on design features from both these predecessors – arcades and department stores – shopping malls play a pivotal role in contemporary consumptionscapes. Shopping is the foremost leisure activity (after television), and families go for a day out to the mall in the same way that they might have gone to the seaside 50 years ago. As our previous example of the Dubai Mall evidenced, malls have developed on ever grander scales since first introduced to retailing in the 1950s. Now they regularly mix a variety of leisure activities within one complex to keep customers entertained there as long as possible. The challenge for marketers is to give each mall its unique sense of place. Often, this is done through theming the environment in some way, a topic that we will discuss more in the sections that follow.

Shopping mall design borrowed heavily from the fantastic aspects of department stores and their theatrical nature. Victor Gruen designed the first enclosed mall in 1956 in Southdale, Minnesota, to protect shoppers from harsh weather. He introduced the notion of shopping complex as a world onto itself, where there could be a respite from the cares and toils of everyday life. Southdale's impressive atrium was filled with a fabulous profusion of flowers (including orchids, magnolias and azaleas) which bloomed all year round in what was called the 'Garden Court of Perpetual Spring'. Envisioning the mall as a new type of urban public space, Gruen encouraged the creation of a controlled environment that emulated the buzz and excitement of the city but without its attendant nuisances. The principles that guided the Southdale Mall design quickly became the blueprint for shopping centres across America and beyond.

As regards a sense of place, a major difference between mall developments and earlier marketplace types, such as bazaars, Parisian arcades and departments stores, is that the latter thrived in the heart of the city. In contrast, malls are often located in city suburbs and have to work much harder to create their own sense of place. Gigantic malls – like the West Edmonton Mall, Canada, and the Metro Centre, Gateshead, England – reflect less their local surroundings in terms of demography and geography, instead drawing on a cultural legacy of centuries of recreational and theatrical entertainment (Davis, 1991). Malls like these combine two sets of spatial practices and understandings: those that characterise the performance of leisure spaces and those that characterise the performance of commercial sites. On one hand, the mall epitomises the retailer's intention to sell goods and is designed to promote purchasing. On the other hand, the mall is also a physical space where individuals seek a certain urban ambience (Gottdiener, 1997). In other words, the mall is both an economic space organised as an exchange-nexus and a social arena that possesses characteristics of both leisure sites and public spaces.

Major mall developments, like the West Edmonton Mall and The Mall of America, have maximised this cultural form. For example, the West Edmonton Mall, completed in 1986, is one of the world's largest shopping and indoor leisure complexes and Alberta's top tourist attraction with more than 800 stores and an estimated 30-million-plus visitors a year. Claiming to be inspired by the traditional urban bazaars of Persia where 'shopping and entertainment were plentiful and operated in tandem', the mall covers 5.3 million square feet, making it the size of a small city. Size matters when it comes to shopping malls, with each making its own unique claims in this respect – check out the SM Mall of Asia's website that claims its construction used 2 million bags of cement as well as 44,000 gallons of paint and included installing 1.9 million floor tiles!

As already noted, separation from the city makes it essential for a mall to develop its own unique place-based identity. This separation, as well as the implied journey, become part of the fantasy aspects, giving the illusion of a voyage to another world. Creating a sense of displacement is, therefore, a key spatial practice that also conveys the feeling of between two contrasting worlds. A theatrical approach to mall management heightens this effect. In his detailed study of the *Malling of America*, Kowinski (1985) describes the principles of retail drama, where a fantasy world is managed and orchestrated to persuade customers to buy. The tenant mix is a fundamental part of the show and is selected carefully to reinforce the overall image of the mall. The drama analogy is carried through to merchandising and displays as crucial parts of the acts. Customers are not only the audience but also the actors, playing key roles in the action.

It cannot be assumed, however, that malls in Western life perform the same roles as they do in other global contexts. For example, a study of shopping malls in India revealed how young consumers use malls to feel modern and part of global consumer culture (Varman and Belk, 2012). In doing so, they overcome feelings of stigmatisation due to their colonial past and current poverty. Even though they cannot afford the goods so spectacularly displayed before them, they change their behaviours and dress styles when in these malls to masquerade as potential customers.

Themed Shopping Environments

As we can see from the previous sections, contemporary retail is more about telling stories. Shopping structures, such as department stores, malls, shopping centres and so forth, become discursive statements that invite interpretation. Postmodern retail design acknowledges this and often makes use of open-ended narrative structures that are deliberately ambiguous, allowing multiple interpretations. This process encourages consumers to engage in their own subjective fantasising and meaning creation. Perhaps the best examples of postmodern retail are the plethora of themed environments to be found in the contemporary marketplace: flagship brandstores such as ESPN zone (Kozinets et al., 2002); brand museums (Sherry, 1998); Irish pubs (Patterson and Brown, 2002); festival marketplaces (Maclaran and Brown, 2005); and many shopping malls, restaurants, hotels and other leisure venues. These elaborately designed locations create spectacular environments that appeal to consumers' imaginations and emphasise the experiential elements of the product or service they are offering. Making a crucial contribution to Hannigan's (1998) concept of the 'fantasy city' or the 'postmodern metropolis', they enchant and entice visitors to linger and immerse themselves in their surreal ambiance.

Over the last 20 years, there has been a major growth in the development of themed stores that encourage consumers to engage in a relationship with their brands. The spiritual aspects of such stores can even be likened the emotions inspired by cathedrals, with their dazzling displays being like shrines, where consumers can come to worship the brand. Similarly, highlighting a form of shopping motivation that is ideological, as opposed to simply utilitarian or hedonistic, Borghini et al. (2009) identify how *American Girl Place's* brand ideology is manifested in focal areas of the store. This encourages intergenerational female bonding and the creation of a family identity by combining commerce with a sense of domesticity.

Themed stores can thus evoke much more than basic sensory responses to their richly imaginative surroundings. These quasi-spiritual or moral elements accord with Pine and Gilmore's (1999) notion of transformational experiences, whereby a customer is changed in some way as a result of his or her experiences. Whereas the memory of sensory stimuli fades in time, these authors argue, transformations are more permanent and inspirational. 'Mindscapes' like these are at the forefront of themed environments, according to Kozinets et al. (2002), because they combine entertainment, therapeutics and spiritual growth.

Nevertheless, the importance of corporeal effects is often overlooked in conceptualisations, such as just discussed, that tend to privilege cognitive effects. Indeed, bodily impulses often precede cognition, resulting in intuitive, taken-for-granted responses that link actions to perceptions rather than the other way round. Drawing on embodied theory, a study of the Hollister brandstore experience explains how the body can play a significant role in experiential consumption (Stevens et al., 2019). Four crucial elements are depicted in what the authors describe as 'The Immersive Somascape Experience': 1) sense activation (instore multi-sensory stimulation), 2) corporeal relationality (meeting and interacting with other bodies), 3) brand materialities (store architecture, layout design and décor) and 4) (dis) orientation (how one moves in specific ways). Through these various corporeal understandings of their experience, many consumers achieve a very embodied sense of emplacement in a space.

Part of a themed environment's ability to transcend everyday reality and, indeed, to have a longer-lasting transformational effect is how it conveys a sense of elsewhereness, a sense of liminality (being between two worlds) that has long been associated with the marketplace more generally. Likewise, it has been noted that the illusionary elements of shopping mall design often make more pronounced these inherent liminoid characteristics. Such references draw on the works of two famous anthropologists, Arnold van Gennep (1960) and Victor Turner (1969). The former introduced the concept of liminality in his study of rites of passage, rites that mark societal transitions from one lifestage to another (puberty, marriage, death, etc.), transitions composed of three separate stages: separation, liminal period and reassimilation. At the first stage, the person undertaking the ritual leaves behind their current social status before entering into a liminal phase where they are 'betwixt and between' identities. Finally, the initiate emerges with a new social status to be reassimilated into society. Victor Turner further developed this work (1969, 1974), particularly in relation to understanding of the liminal period of transition and its relevance to industrialised society. He distinguished between liminal activity as practiced through rituals in pre-industrialised societies and liminoid activity that has developed in contemporary society to differentiate work from play and from which, Turner believes, transformations can grow. Noting that individuals are socially and structurally ambiguous during the liminal (or liminoid) phase, Turner developed his idea of anti-structure, whereby liminal individuals, on account of their betwixt-and-between status, develop a sense of communitas through their shared experiences.

Turner's ideas have been very influential within marketing and consumer research, with regards to both understanding essentially anti-structural, extraordinary consumption experiences (e.g. Kozinets, 2002) and more mundane, structural ones that are performed within scripted and ritualised settings, such as brandstores (e.g. Kozinets et al., 2002; Borghini et al., 2009) and retail environments (Maclaran and Brown, 2005). More recently, however, Lanier and Rader (2015) have noted that current research has almost entirely focused on the structural/anti-structural dimension of consumer experiences, ignoring another key dimension, that is, function and anti-function (Merton, 1957). The former refers to the manifest, intended consequences of a certain consumption activity, whereas the latter refers to the more latent and unintended ones. Lanier and Rader (2015) observe that less attention has been paid to anti-functional consumer experiences, which they further distinguish between stochastic and adventurous ones. Stochastic experiences are those that are still highly structured and scripted but can have unintended consequences, such as gambling in a casino. A key difference from Turner's anti-structural experiences is that they tend to be highly individualistic. Adventurous experiences are also individualistic, but they tend to refuse both any kind of structure and a pre-determined consequence. Although they are often as extraordinary as anti-structure experiences (e.g. visiting the Burning Man festival), they differ in their insistence on not having a functional outcome. A perfect example would be backpacking in a less known and unsafe tourist destination with a view to experience excitement and danger. From Lanier and Rader's (2015) analysis, it is clear that stochastic and adventure experiences remain less explored and understood by place marketers.

The Social Role of Place

In contrast to spectacular retail, there are also many more mundane places that are meaningful to consumers and that facilitate social interaction and a sense of community. Often, we form emotional attachments to everyday commercial locations, such as coffee shops, bars and even grocery stores. We may rely on such places to help us establish routines (morning coffee, nightly pints, weekly shop) and make us feel more rooted in place. They can enhance our social life, providing gathering points where we spend time with others. Sometimes referred to as 'third places' (Rosenbaum, 2006), pubs, coffee shops and other leisure spaces, such as gyms, provide a place between home (first place) and work (second place). An important defining characteristic of third places is that they are somewhere we can take out time, relax and interact with others. Fast-food restaurants are, therefore, unlikely to meet this requirement, as they encourage customers to move quickly through their establishments, rather than lingering to socialise, with layout designed to be functional as opposed to atmospheric. The coffee shop where everyone meets in the iconic US sitcom *Friends* and the pub in *Cheers* are perfect examples of third places.

Traditionally, social scientists assumed that retail environments are too uniform and regularly remodelled to allow any meaningful form of social and symbolic interaction. However, through retailers' ongoing attempts to enhance liminality, authenticity and creativity in their environments (as illustrated previously), consumers have begun to develop significant emotional bonds to commercialised third places. There is now growing consensus that place attachment to commercial locations is entirely possible and it occurs particularly when they provide experiences that go beyond what consumers believe the market usually offers (Debendetti et al., 2013). More specifically, Debendetti et al. (2013) illustrate that attachment to bars and restaurants often emerges from a blend of familiarity, authenticity and security, which is altogether akin to a sense of 'homeyness'. Importantly, homeyness not only arises from the various spatial features of the commercial space but also from the way in which proprietors and employees interact with customers, allowing them to feel unique and appreciated, for example, through engaging in genuine conversations, allowing backstage access and offering unexpected gifts. In turn, consumers often 'give back' to their treasured commercial spaces, through practices such as volunteering, tipping and acting as their informal brand ambassadors.

A sense of homeyness, therefore, is a key state or liminal feeling that can bridge the divide not only between private and public spaces but also commercial and non-commercial ones. Accordingly, consumers often invest in product constellations that reproduce a sense of personalisation and domesticity not only in their homes and second spaces, such as their workspaces (e.g. Tian and Belk, 2005), but also in public and commercialised spaces, such as sports events and music festivals (e.g. Bradford and Sherry, 2015). For philosopher Edward Casey (1993), this is because of two fundamental modes of 'dwelling-in-place' that date back to antiquity: that is hestial and hermetic. Whereas the hestial mode of dwelling is private, self-enclosed and inward-looking, the hermetic mode remains public, open and outward-directed. Importantly, Casey sees them as complementary modes of dwelling, that is, we enjoy residing in a particular place (the exemplar hestial place being the home), but we also appreciate traveling and wandering (exemplar hermetic places being airports, restaurants, hotels and other consumptionscapes). As noted previously, however, consumers often attempt to reassert the hestial in otherwise hermetic places and with that, a sense of familiarity and domesticity, for instance, by having a favourite spot in one's local pub or by personalising and decorating one's tent whilst attending sports and music festivals. It is often through hestialising practices that more specific forms of place attachment and place identity can develop.

Rather than reasserting the private into the public, however, some consumer activists attempt to do the opposite, that is, embrace the 'public' or a more collectivised and political ethos in what otherwise may be deemed as individualised place-making. For instance, the radical and anti-structural nature of some public spaces (from Kozinet's Burning Man festival to Chatzidakis et al.'s guerrilla park in Exarcheia) often allows consumers to challenge taken-for-granted assumptions and to develop alternative forms of community and sociality that are devoid of market logics. At stake is the development of new subjectivities that challenge possessive individualism and atomised logics and practices. (This is explained in more detail in Chapter 5.)

The Therapeutic Role of Place

We have just seen how commercial locations can play a significant role in consumers' everyday lives, satisfying the need for human interaction as well as offering specific goods and services. Now we explore

how servicescapes can also offer therapeutic benefits by bringing restorative (physical) and relational (social) resources together
(Rosenbaum et al., 2020). The built environment and its material
contents (i.e. architecture, layout and design features) can provide
restorative resources to help alleviate mental fatigue, whereas relational resources can be found in other customers and employees.
Therapeutic servicescapes successfully meld the two and do not have
to be prestigious brandstores, or even strongly themed, to achieve
such effects as Rosenbaum et al. (2020) illustrate through their study
of a local grocery store.

Deepening our conceptualisation of therapeutic servicescapes,
Higgins and Hamilton (2019, p. 1230) argue that they offer 'consumption settings where emplaced market-mediated performances compensate for sociogultural dilemmas'. These authors identify three
categories of dilemmas for which servicscapes can offer compensa-
tion: 1) providing opportunities for play and escape from corporate
life and the alienation this can generate (e.g. Tough Mudder events,
rave nights), 2) facilitating connections to nature that bring a sense
of healing and renewal (white water rafting, wilderness retreats) and
3) conveying spirituality to atone for the absence of conventional
religious authority (the Burning Man festival or themed brandstores/
malls as discussed earlier). Theorising from a three-year ethnography of the Lourdes pilgrimage servicescape, Higgins and Hamilton
(2019) note therapeutic servicescapes to be composed of three key
elements: *ideological homogeneity* (being with like-minded people),
evocative spaces (environments that, whether natural or built, are
highly symbolic) and *restorative emotional scripts* (the generation of
wellbeing through positive expression of emotions).

Towards a Typology of Spaces

Arguably, because of a deeper appreciation of the social role of
place, more recent research highlights the numerous ways through
which consumption is implicated in the production and social construction of any kind of space, from shopping malls and flagship
stores to urban bars and restaurants, residential neighbourhoods
and national parks. Drawing on this observation, Castilhos and Dolbec (2018) have attempted to provide a more systematic typology
of spaces and how certain logics and practices of consumption are
excluded/included within them, identifying four main types – that
is, public spaces, market spaces, emancipating spaces and segregating spaces. These are in turn largely constituted by two underlying dynamics, first, being a contradiction between negotiation and
consensus and, second, a contradiction between participation and
subjugation (see Figure 9.1). *Public spaces* include streets, squares,
urban and national parks, mountains, beaches and waterfronts
among others. They are, by their very inception, public goods or
'commons' that are participatory and inclusive of different social
groupings. However, they are also continuously contested by the
variety of stakeholders that inhabit them or represent them, from

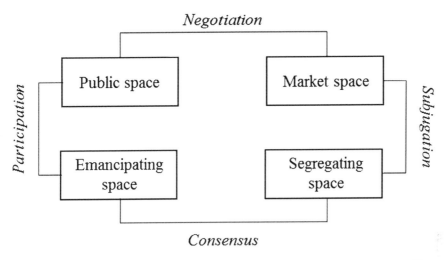

Figure 9.1 Castilhos and Dolbec's typology of spaces (2018, p. 156)

local and national authorities to various commercial actors, citizen groups and not least, consumers. For example, Visconti et al. (2010) identify different ideologies of public space consumption (e.g. individualistic versus collectivist) and how these in turn affect the kind of street art found in different urban neighbourhoods. Likewise, public spaces are increasingly designed or revamped with specific (consumer) groups in mind and not others. As evident in this chapter, *market spaces* are those that are most examined by consumer researchers. Unlike public spaces, they are owned and/or governed by commercial actors only (or mostly) and they are exclusionary, in the sense that only consumers of particular socio-economic and cultural groupings are allowed. However, as we have seen previously, commercial actors often attempt to 'democratise' their market spaces with a view to enhance their authenticity and ultimately, consumer satisfaction and place attachment.

Castilhos and Dolbec (2018) also identify *segregating spaces* such as houses, gated communities, private clubs, ghettos and favelas. They differ from market spaces in the sense that they may be owned and/or governed not by commercial interests alone but by social actors who are actively invested in consensual spaces that fit their private interests. Like market spaces, they are exclusionary but not on the basis of class, race, age and gender (to name a few variables) rather than market logics alone. However, consumption is also central in segregating spaces, in so far as particular practices and rituals foster a sense of community and homogeneity, both enabling and hindering certain commercial opportunities. Finally, *emancipating spaces* are spaces of subversion and resistance to hegemonic ideas of public space consumption. Similar to segregating spaces, they are produced upon consensus, but unlike them, they are participatory and open to everyone who is actively engaged in overturning the status quo, either temporarily, as in the case of the Burning Man festival

(Kozinets, 2002), or permanently, as in the case of the urban neighbourhood of Exarcheia (Chatzidakis et al., 2012).

Theorising Consumption *in* Space

Castillhos and Dolbe's typology exemplifies a move away from treating space (solely) as the object of consumption (e.g. consuming or not-consuming themed stores, shopping malls, tourist destinations, etc.) to understanding space as the context of any consumption activity. That is, all consumption is *in* space and consumers, both knowingly and unknowingly, are implicated in the construction of space. Perhaps more profoundly, consumer logics and practices are also somewhat 'produced' or at least depend upon the kind of space(s) they inhabit. This highlights the need to develop more nuanced and multi-dimensional understandings of how consumers experience space. In line with the so-called 'spatial turn' in social sciences, various anthropologists and sociologists have attempted to develop more sophisticated frameworks, drawing on seminal spatial theorists such as Henri Lefebvre (1991), Ed Soja (1996) and David Harvey (2004). Common in such approaches is the conceptualisation of different variants of space, for instance, the descriptive, the phenomenological and the social constructivist (Chatzidakis et al., 2018) and the embodied, affective, discursive and relational (e.g. Low, 2016), to name a few.

Chatzidakis (2017) has recently attempted to apply a triadic understanding to the Exarcheian space, drawing on three key dimensions: material, symbolic and socio-spatial. Focusing on the *material* space, he mentions how even factors such as the size of the building blocks and road intersections affect the kind of social interaction and mobilisation that a particular area allows. Frequent road intersections, for instance, allow for the quick spread of communication and activity, such as rioting, which would be impossible in areas with higher exposure and visibility. Importantly, Chatzidakis (2017) discusses how the Exarcheian marketplace is also specific to the particular material and aesthetic features of the area. All shops are small, independent and somewhat rustic, whereas there is a disproportionate amount of bookstores, print shops and record shops, catering to the area's countercultural sensibilities. Bar and restaurant names include 'Molotov', 'Kalashnikov Garden' and 'Necropolis', contrasting with a generation of new 'happy' cafes and restaurants that opened after the early 2000s. Focusing on *symbolic* space, Chatzidakis mentions how the neighbourhood is legendary for its range of affective and embodied experiences. For instance, people often talk about the particular 'air that one breathes when entering Exarcheia', a sense of 'tension' and 'urgency' that contrasts with the significantly calmer and less politicised surrounding neighbourhoods. This is because, in many ways, the area is explicitly positioned against the production of individualised and apolitical 'consumers' that frequent highly commoditized spaces, such as retail parks, shopping districts and malls. What is at stake is the production of new subjectivities and ways of thinking that are devoid of the consumption-centric social order. Accordingly, the area is fertile ground for the production of alternative consumption logics and practices, centred on voluntary simplicity, solidarity and alternative trading economics, time banks, gifting bazaars, numerous DIY projects, collective cooking events and no-ticket cinema screenings among other things. Ultimately, as Chatzidakis puts it, consumption *in* the Exarcheian space reflects and reproduces logics of normative and 'aesthetic revisioning' (Soper, 2008) that stand in opposition to those of mainstream consumer society and are felt alike upon both fans and despisers of the area.

Finally, akin to Castilhos and Dolbec's (2018) understanding of public and emancipatory space, Exarcheia can be viewed as the *socio-spatial* product of competing stakeholders, including residents, street artists, marketplace actors and city and state planners. For instance, multinational retail chains, such as Starbucks, are anything but welcome in the area, and the real threat of being firebombed keeps them well outside the neighbourhood's borders. Likewise, symbols of conspicuous consumption, such as expensive cars, often get vandalised. Perhaps more strikingly and certainly more illustrative of the area's countervailing logics to public space consumption is Exarcheia's 'park' or 'Navarinou park' and which operates on the principles of mutuality, solidarity, anti-commercialisation and gift economy. Altogether then, what Chatzidakis's (2017) study highlights is the multiple ways in which space frames (if not produces) any kind of consumption activity and is in turn framed by it. What may seem as natural and desirable in some spaces (e.g. carrying a Gucci bag) may be frowned upon in others and may even prove dangerous. Likewise, the way in which we think and fantasise about consumption is dependent upon the options we have in our everyday whereabouts and the various material, symbolic and social cues we get from our environment. Put differently, our consumption logics and practices both constitute and are constituted by our marketplaces and public spaces.

Furthermore, recent research on the intersection of space and consumption has attempted to move beyond the 'visual', with a view to explore the different ways in which senses, such as smell and sound, interpenetrate our consumption in space. For instance, Canniford et al. (2018) counter-propose smell as a key gateway to feeling, practicing and producing space. Specifically, the function of smell is threefold. First, smell encodes space in so far as particular spaces are associated with specific odours and not others. For instance, the deodorised ambience of a department store, the lack of lingering smell in a professional trading floor and the sweaty smell of a gym floor. Second, smell identifies bodies with spaces, for example, when specific 'country smells' are associated with people that carry them around, literally or metaphorically. Finally, smell 'moves spaces'. That is, it helps punctuate movements and changes in spaces. For instance, various professional districts are associated with the smell of junk or takeaway food after dark, whereas rural spaces are characterised by winter and summer smells as well as Saturday and weekday smells.

As Henshaw et al. (2016) note, similar observations about the olfactory identity of different times and places have long been exploited by place marketers, if only intuitively. More generally, Canniford et al. (2018) and Henshaw et al. (2016)'s studies are part of recent ethnographic attempts to advance more 'multi-sensorial' understandings of consumption in and of space and to treat time and space as inextricably linked (Chatzidakis et al., 2018).

Summary

Moving beyond a simplistic understanding of place as one of marketing's 4 Ps, this chapter explores the various dynamics of turning spaces into places. First, we took a closer look at how place attachments and place-related identities develop before considering how marketers attempt to influence such processes through place branding and marketing efforts. Subsequently, we considered the spectacular nature of much contemporary retail and set this in its historical context, showing how specific forms of retail have evolved in terms of creating a sense of place. We then moved on to consider the social role of places and a typology of spaces that accounts for the different ways in which everyday consumption is implicated in these. Finally, we concluded with an attempt to develop a more multi-dimensional understanding of consumption *in* (rather than of) place.

Case Study

Eating Dans le Noir?

Dans le Noir? is a themed restaurant franchise where you eat in the dark. It has 13 locations around the globe including; France, Belgium, Luxembourg, Switzerland, UK, Spain, Russia, New Zealand and Egypt. Its name – Dans le Noir? – deliberately provokes the question of who is in the dark. Customers are looked after by blind serving staff who move dextrously in the darkened surrounds, where sighted consumers find themselves completely disorientated and immobilised. A visit to the restaurant is highly organised, orchestrating a ritualistic process to take the patron through the eating-in-the-dark experience as efficiently and safely as possible. This experience can be broken down into a four-stage structure that is inherent in rites of passage (see Van Gennep, 1960):

1 Preparation

   On arrival at the restaurant, guests enter the fully-lit bar area where they wait in anticipation of their eating experience. Staff offer them colour-coded menus: green (vegetarian), red (meat), blue (fish) or white (surprise). Then they ask customers to leave their bags, watches and phones in lockers. This simulates the preparation of initiates for a rite of passage. As customers leave the customary trappings of the civilised world behind, they are being metaphorically stripped of their social status. In final preparation, they also visit the bathroom, a type of purification ritual before immersion in the dark. This stage creates feelings of excitement, anticipation and unease among visitors as they assemble for their departure into the dark.

2   Separation

Customers form a line behind the blind staff member who will lead them into the eating area. They must pass along a darkened corridor that acts as a threshold between the two worlds (light/dark, abled/disabled). To undertake this journey, they each place their left hand on the shoulder of the person in front. At the head of this human chain, the blind server assumes authority (like a ritual elder, Turner, 1969), leading his customers slowly into the dark. The touching required at this stage begins to prepare diners for the process of physical disabling that is to follow, and many experience symptoms of physical anxiety, such as racing hearts or butterflies in the stomach.

3   The Liminoid Phase

As they are led to their table in complete darkness, diners suddenly find themselves quite helpless, trying to ascertain where their eating utensils are and who is next to them. The blind servers became the able-bodied people in this environment, moving with an air of confidence and calm that is in sharp contrast to the disorientated fumblings of their customers. This is the topsy-turvy world associated with liminal spaces where role reversals are typical (Bakhtin, 1968). Touch becomes the most important sense, and patrons touch everything around them to establish the parameters of the new world in which they find themselves. Often, this is messy, as they spill drinks or food over themselves and others. Much eating takes place with hands, and there is an overall sense of regression to childhood, a feeling that also heightens the loss of status in this liminal stage and of being transformed.

4   Reassimilation

Finally, the eating experience is over and customers are led back into the light. Now the light blinds them as they blink and try to readjust to their return. For many, it has been a challenge that they are proud to have survived, while, for others, it has been a more empathetic experience and they return full of admiration for the blind serving staff. Consistent with having completed a ritual process, everyone feels a little different, even transformed in some way, as they reflect on their eating in the dark and how much they have taken their own sighted world for granted.

Seminar Exercises

Discussion Topics

1   Think of a place to which you are attached and discuss the ways in which this place makes you feel an insider. Who could be termed the outsiders?

2   Go to www.*youtube*.com/watch?v=Xu4szbNFPwM&spfreload=10. Following Turner, would you describe this as a structure or anti-structure consumption experience? Subsequently, think of the different senses involved in this consumption experience. How would you analyse this from a multi-sensorial perspective?

3   Identify a commercial location that you frequent and that could be described as a 'third place', elaborating on the social role it plays in your life and in the life of others who go there. How is place attachment achieved within that place?

4   Place marketers are quickly catching up with place-making research as evident in http://lifeathome.ikea.com/home/. Go to the website and have a look at the section titled 'place'. How is this linked to ideas of 'homeyness' and hestialising third place? Can you think of any counter-arguments to the idea of extending the home 'beyond the four walls of a residence'?

Group Exercises

1   Identify (from the internet, papers or your own local knowledge) and detail a recent case of city branding. How authentic or inauthentic do you think the result of this branding exercise has been? Justify your answer by making reference to Relph's (1976) theories on this.

2   Think of the neighbourhood that you live in.

   i   How does it affect your consumption logics and practices, and how is it in turn affected by them?
   ii   Try to analyse this in relation to Chatzidakis's (2017) three dimensions, that is, material, symbolic and socio-spatial.
   iii Can you apply a more multi-sensorial perspective?

Internet Resources

Dans le Noir? https://london.danslenoir.com/en/home/
IKEA, http://lifeathome.ikea.com/home/.
SM Mall of Asia, www.smsupermalls.com/mall-directory/sm-mall-of-asia/information/

Key Readings

Castilhos, R. B. and Dolbec, P. Y. (2018), 'Conceptualizing spatial types: Characteristics, transitions, and research avenues', *Marketing Theory*, 18(2), 154–168.

Chatzidakis, A. (2017), 'Consumption in and of crisis-hit Athens,' In D. Dalakoglou and G. Aggelopoulos (Eds), *Critical Ethnographic Approaches and Engaged Anthropological Perspectives*, London: Routledge.

Kavaratzis, M. and Hatch, M. J. (2013), 'The dynamics of place brands: An identity based approach to place brand theory', *Marketing Theory*, 13(1), 69–86.

Warnaby, G. and Medway, D. (2013), 'What about the 'place' in place marketing?' *Marketing Theory*, 13(3), 345–363.

References

Agnew, J. (2005), 'Space: Place (81–96),' In P. Cloke and R. Johnston (Eds), *Spaces of Geographical thought: Deconstructing Human Geography's Binaries*, London: Sage.

Bakhtin, M. (1968), *Rabelais and His World*, Cambridge: MIT Press.

Borghini, S., Diamond, N., Kozinets, R. V., McGrath, M. A., Muniz, A., Jr. and Sherry, J. F., Jr. (2009), 'Why are themed brandstores so powerful? Retail brand ideology at American girl place', *Journal of Retailing*, 85(3), 363–375.

Bradford, T. W. and Sherry, J. F. Jr. (2015), 'Domesticating public space through ritual: tailgating as vestaval', *Journal of Consumer Research*, 42, 130–151.

Brown, S., McDonagh, P. and Shultz II, C. J. (2013), 'A brand so bad it's good: The paradoxical place marketing of Belfast', *Journal of Marketing Management*, 29(11–12), 1251–1276.

Canniford, R., Riach, K. and Hill, T. (2018). 'Nosenography: How smell constitutes meaning, identity and temporal experience in spatial assemblages', *Marketing Theory*, 18(2), 234–248.

Casey, E. S. (1993), *Getting Back into Place*, Bloomington: Indiana University Press.

Castilhos, R. B. and Dolbec, P. Y. (2018), 'Conceptualizing spatial types: Characteristics, transitions, and research avenues', *Marketing Theory*, 18(2), 154–168.

Chatzidakis, A. (2017), 'Consumption in and of crisis-hit Athens,' In D. Dalakoglou and G. Aggelopoulos (Eds), *Critical Ethnographic Approaches and Engaged Anthropological Perspectives*, London: Routledge.

Chatzidakis, A., Maclaran, P. and Bradshaw, A. (2012), 'Heterotopian space and the politics of ethical and green consumption', *Journal of Marketing Management*, 3(4), 494–515.

Chatzidakis, A., McEachern, M. G. and Warnaby, G. (2018), 'Consumption in and of space and place: Introduction to the special issue', *Marketing Theory*, 18(2), 149–153.

Davis, T. C. (1991), 'Theatrical antecedents of the mall that ate downtown', *Journal of Popular Culture*, 24(4), 1–15.

Debendetti, A., Oppewel, H. and Arsel, Z. (2013), 'Place attachment in commercial settings: A gift economy perspective', *Journal of Consumer Research*, 40(5), 904–923.

Gottdiener, M. (1997), *The Theming of America: Dreams, Visions, and Commerical Spaces*, Boulder: Worldview Press.

Hannigan, J. (1998), *Fantasy City: Pleasure and Profit in the Postmodern Metropolis*, London and New York: Routledge.

Harvey, D. (2004), 'Space as a Keyword,' In *Marx and Philosophy Conference*, London: Institute of Education, www.inter-accions.org/sites/default/files/space-as-key-word-david-harvey.pdf

Henshaw, V., Medway, D., Warnaby, G. and Perkins, C. (2016), 'Marketing the 'city of smells'', *Marketing Theory*, 16(2), 153–170.

Higgins, L. and Hamilton, K. (2019), 'Therapeutic servicescapes and market-mediated performances of emotional suffering', *Journal of Consumer Research*, 45(6), 1230–1253.

Holcolm, B. (1999), 'Marketing cities for tourism,' In D. R. Judd and S. S. Fainstein (Eds), *The Tourist City*, New Haven: Yale University Press, pp. 54–70.

Kowinski, W. S. (1985), *The Malling of America*, New York: William Morrow & Co.

Kozinets, R.V., Sherry, J. F. Jr, DeBerry-Spence B., Duhachek, A., Nuttavuthisit, K. and Storm, D. (2002), 'Themed flagship brand stores in the new millennium: Theory, practice, prospects', *Journal of Retailing*, 78, 17–19.

Lanier, C. D. and Rader, C. S. (2015), 'Consumption experience an expanded view', *Marketing Theory*, 15(4), 487–508.

Lefebvre, H. (1991), *The Production of Space*, Oxford: Blackwell.

Low, S. M. (2016), *Spatializing Culture: The Ethnography of Space and Place*, Oxon: Routledge.

Maclaran, P. and Brown S. (2005), 'The center cannot hold: Consuming the utopian marketplace', *Journal of Consumer Research*, 32, 311–323.

Merton, R. K. (1957), *Social Theory and Social Structure*, Glencoe: The Free Press.

Patterson, A. and Brown, S. (2002), 'Reading writer, quaffing quiddity and rejoicing Joyceans: unpicking the packaging of an Irish icon,' In S. M. Broniarczyk and K. Nakamoto (Eds), *Advances in Consumer Research* 29, Valdosta: Association for Consumer Research, pp. 504–509.

Patterson, A. and Hodgson, J. (2011), 'Re-imagining the city of liverpool as a capital of consumption,' In A. Bradshaw, P. Maclaran and C. Hackley (Eds), *European Advances in Consumer Research*, Duluth: Association for Consumer Research, pp. 298–303.

Pine, B. J. and Gilmore, J. H. (1999), *The Experience Economy: Work Is Theatre and Every Business a Stage*, Boston, MA: Harvard Business Press.

Reekie, G. (1993), *Temptations: Sex and Selling in the Department Store*, Sydney: Allen and Unwin.

Relph, E. (1976), *Place and Placelessness*, London: Pion.

Ritzer, G. (1999), *Enchanting a Disenchanted World: Revolutionizing the Means of Consumption*, Thousand Oaks: Pine Forge Press.

Rosenbaum, M. S. (2006), 'Exploring the social supportive role of third places in consumers' lives', *Journal of Service Research*, 9(1), 59–72.

Rosenbaum, M. S., Friman, M., Ramirez, G. C. and Otterbring, T. (2020), 'Therapeutic servicescapes: Restorative and relational resources in service settings', *Journal of Retailing and Consumer Services*, 55, 102078.

Sherry, J. F., Jr. (1998), 'The soul of the company store: Nike town Chicago and the emplaced brandscape,' In J. F. Jr. Sherry (Ed), *Servicescapes: The Concept of Place in Contemporary Markets*, Lincolnwood: NTC Business Books, pp. 109–146.

Soja, E. W. (1996), *Thirdspace: Journeys to Los Angeles and Other Real-and-Imagined Places*, Cambridge: Blackwell.

Soper, K. (2008), 'Alternative hedonism, cultural theory and the role of aesthetic revisioning', *Cultural Studies*, 22(5), 567–587.

Stevens, L., Maclaran, P. and Brown, S. (2019), 'An embodied approach to consumer experiences: The Hollister brandscape', *European Journal of Marketing*, 53(4), 806–828.

Tian, K. and Belk, R. W. (2005), 'Extended self and possessions in the workplace', *Journal of Consumer Research*, 32, 297–310.

Turner, V.W. (1969), *The Ritual Process: Structure and Antistructure*, Ithaca: Cornell University Press.

Turner, V.W. (1974), *Dramas, Fields, and Metaphors: Symbolic Action in Human Society*, Ithaca, NW: Cornell University Press.

Van Gennep, A. (1960), *The Rites of Passage*, Chicago: University of Chicago Press.

Varman, R. and Belk, R.W. (2012), 'Consuming postcolonial shopping malls', *Journal of Marketing Management*, 28(1–2), 2–84.

Williams, R. H. (1985), *Dream Worlds: Mass Consumption in Late Nineteenth-Century France*, Berkeley and Los Angeles: University of California Press.

10

THE GLOBALIZED MARKETPLACE

Introduction

Our lives are extraordinarily intertwined with those of people living in distant lands; we are living in an interdependent world. We are influenced by an increasingly globalised spread of information, goods and ideas. The food we eat, the clothes we wear, the music we listen to and the books we read are infused with the views and experiences of distant others, so, too, are the ideas we are exposed to about culture, politics and religion. These processes of globalization have been advanced by developments in transportation and digital technology. The world is now seemingly smaller than ever and we are all now citizens of a global society. Research shows that while global flows of goods grew rapidly in the period 1980–2008, their growth as a share of the global economy stabilised at this point. Currently, we are seeing growth globally in flows of services, international students and intellectual property. The biggest growth area, however, has been data flows which grew by 50% in the period 2010–2019 (McKinsey Global Institute, 2022). Data flows were particularly pronounced in 2020–2021, as remote working and business operations relied on them in the face of the Covid-19 pandemic, where travel was almost impossible. In summary, global flows are continuing apace, but the global patterning of these flows is slowly changing.

While globalization has had a whole host of effects on economies, politics and cultures, of particular interest to marketers and consumer researchers is the way in which this increasingly globalised marketplace impacts on our everyday experiences of consumption. This chapter uses two contrasting stories of globalization to explore its impact on consumers and consumer culture. These stories are one of glocalization and one of grobalization (Ritzer, 2004, p. xiii). Grobalization describes the process, whereby the drive towards constant growth (i.e. to keep on increasing sales and profits) pushes organisations to expand into more and more areas of the globe and impose themselves on localities. Whereas glocalization occurs when the interaction of the global and the local produces something new – the glocal. The final section discusses alternatives to these stories, exploring how individuals and communities are organising themselves in

DOI: 10.4324/9781003201151-10

the face of globalization. First, however, it is important to examine what we mean by globalization and its accompanying processes, as there is significant disagreement and debate surrounding these terms and their effects. This discussion is followed by a brief consideration of the rise of global brands as central to processes of globalization.

What is Globalization?

While globalization can be seen as an economic, a political and a cultural process, it is generally agreed that economics tends to be the driving force behind it. Recent times have seen the opening up of world markets to allow increased flow of capital, goods and technologies across national borders; this has resulted in the interdependence of markets across the globe. The emergence of institutions such as the World Bank, International Monetary Fund and the World Trade Organisation are clear evidence of a global economy. To encourage international trade, governments have set up preferable trading arrangements which have bolstered the rise of multinational corporations (MNCs), such as McDonald's, Nike, Samsung and Sony. Closer to home, the global reach of these companies means that we now eat American fast food, wear Chinese clothes, talk on Korean mobile phones and drive Japanese cars. These companies also source their head office and technical staff from the global marketplace, producing a group of relatively placeless transnational workers. Politically, governments have increasingly began to work together to manage trade and the economy. For example, institutions such as the European Union (EU) bind together European countries and the North American Free Trade Agreement (NAFTA), which joins Canada, North America and Mexico together. Global political pressure groups have also emerged to deal with issues affecting the environment and human rights, such as Amnesty International, Greenpeace and the World Wildlife Fund. However, in developed countries, it is perhaps culturally that we experience the most obvious impacts of globalization in our everyday lives (Lash and Lury, 2007). Our cultures are becoming more mixed through migration and infused with values and ideas from other cultures. We are also seeing the emergence of global standards in fashion, food, films and sport. The dominance of a shared global football culture is a good example of this (Tiesler and Coelho, 2013), with teams, such as Manchester United, having more fans outside than within the UK and players, such as David Beckham, becoming global celebrities in their own right. Brands themselves also embody values which travel globally. Coke is probably the most obvious example of this. The company even promotes a global universalism and harmony as their key brand value (Ger and Belk, 1996).

However, the previous discussion suggests that globalization is a relatively uncontested process and this is far from the case. Debates on globalization have raged long and hard over the past few decades. Broadly speaking, there are proponents and opponents of the phenomena, with each side identifying different accompanying dynamics and sets of processes to support their case. One of the more positive proponents of globalization is the journalist and political economist Philippe Legrain. In his 2002 book, *Open World: The Truth About Globalization*, he argues that globalization is a positive, liberating force that results in an open world where goods, services and information are exchanged freely and where people can move freely across borders. Similarly, Thomas Friedman in his 2005 book, *The World Is Flat*, argues that globalization is an inevitability that societies should not resist and one that is creating an increasingly level playing field. Drawing on the free market economics of Hayek, Adrián Ravier views globalization as:

> the process that arises spontaneously in the market and acts by developing a progressive international division of labour, eliminating restrictions on individual liberties, reducing transportation and communication costs, and increasingly integrating the individuals that compose the 'great society'.
>
> (Ravier, 2009, p. 2)

This concept of the 'great society' Ravier is referring to originates from Lyndon B. Johnson's radical reforms in 1960s America to improve education and medical care and reduce widespread poverty. In this sense, Ravier sees globalization as a positive force, improving quality of life and bringing benefits to all.

Critics of globalization point to a series of unwanted effects of the process, including the increased power of multinational corporations putting democracies at risk, the cost to the environment of privileging corporate imperatives over any others and the dilution and gradual dissolution of local cultures across the globe. More generally critics argue that the process of globalization is trenchantly unequal in its effects, as Held and McGrew observe:

> Since a significant segment of the world's population is either untouched by globalization or remains largely excluded from its benefits, it is a deeply devisive and, consequently, vigorously contested process. The uneveness of globalization ensures it is far from a universal process experienced uniformly across the planet.
>
> (Held and McGrew, 2000, p. 4)

The Rise of Global Brands

The process of branding is at the heart of multinational corporations' attempts to globalise their operations. Brands are important here in two senses: as facilitating globalization from a production point of view and also from a consumption point of view in providing a shared global language for consumers around the globe.

In terms of *production*, brands act as vehicles for the spread of globalization, functioning as mediators of the supply and demand of products and services. They frame the activities of the market, and they organise the very logics of global flows of products, people, images and events (Lury, 2004). So central are brands to processes of globalization that Celia Lury (2004) sees brands as the 'logos of the global economy'. Brands have immense value for companies in their own right. This is typically termed brand equity and is based on the fact that well-known brand names can significantly increase the sales of products and services. For example, the Apple brand was identified as the number one global brand in 2022, valued at 482,215$m followed by Microsoft at 278,288$m and Amazon at 274,819$m (Interbrand, 2022, Best Global Brands).

Perhaps because brands are the most visible element of multinational corporations, they have been at the heart of critiques of globalization. Naomi Klein's book *No Logo: Taking Aim at the Brand Bullies* is probably the most well-known of these critiques. Klein ties the huge expansion of multinationals closely to the invention of the brand:

> The astronomical growth in the wealth and cultural influence of multi-national corporations over the last fifteen years can arguably be traced back to a single, seemingly innocuous idea developed by management theorists in the mid-1980s: that successful corporations must primarily produce brands, as opposed to products.
>
> (Klein, 2001, p. 3)

Klein charts the impacts of the rise of global brands (and by association MNCs) on experiences of work in both developed and developing countries and on local cultures and public space. In their recent Best Global Brands report, Interbrand highlights the increasing influence of global brands in our lives, seeing brands as 'Acts of Leadership'; 2022 saw the fastest rate of growth in brand values ever recorded. There is an emerging brand 'super league' with a small number of high-value super brands. For example, in 2022, the top ten brands made up 53% of the total value of the top 100 brands. These super brands are also extending their influence by diversifying. For example, Apple now helps us to connect, do, belong, play, pay and thrive (Interbrand, 2022), which means that big brands are increasingly penetrating more and more areas of our lives as consumers.

Klein describes the 'race to the bottom', where MNCs contract out production to the lowest bidder, resulting in extreme inequalities, as factory workers in developing countries are forced to work faster, longer hours in poor and often-dangerous sweatshop conditions to meet the terms of these contracts. While Klein reported on these issues back in 1999, death and injury is still common, resulting from illegal working practices and poorly maintained factories. In November 2012, a fire broke out at the Tazreen Fashions garment factory in the Ashulia industrial area 24 km north of the Bangladeshi capital of Dhaka. The factory manufactured clothes for global brands such as Walmart, C&A, Sears and KiK. More than 1,150 people were inside the factory at the time, 117 employees died and more than 200 were injured in the fire. The blaze broke out in the open-air ground floor, where large mounds of fabric and yarn were illegally stored. Managers and security guards on some floors reportedly ordered employees to ignore the fire alarm and continue to work. In addition, windows were secured with iron grilles, making it impossible for some employees to escape. In the years following the fire, one of the key issues highlighted by worker and human rights organisations is the convoluted and opaque supply chain which makes it difficult to police compliance with international labour standards. Suppliers often use multiple subcontractors to meet orders. This means that when an accident occurs, buyers can deny responsibility. After the Tazreen blaze, retailers said they had not authorised production at the factory, saying that suppliers had subcontracted production without informing them. Indeed, the hugely complex web of subcontractors.

The attraction of global brands to *consumers* is undoubtedly that they make them feel like global citizens. Consumers view these brands as symbols of cultural ideals and use them to create an imagined global identity (Holt et al., 2004, p. 3). 'Like entertainment stars, sports celebrities and politicians, global brands have become a lingua franca for consumers all over the world' (Holt et al., 2004, p. 2). Brands like Samsung, Coca-Cola, Apple and Mercedes speak a global language that can be understood by all. Brands like these are symbolically very powerful. For example, in a survey of 7,000 people in six different countries (Germany, Australia, India, Japan, UK and the US), 88% identified the brand logos of McDonald's and Shell, whereas only 54% recognised the Christian cross (Sponsorship Research International).

One of the reasons brands can impact so powerfully on individuals is their ability to create reassurance and familiarity. Authors have developed the concept of the brandscape to describe the interplay between brands and the sites and spaces they inhabit (Klingman, 2007; Salzer-Mőrling and Strannegård, 2007; Wood and Ball, 2013), as Wood and Ball suggest: 'brandscapes can be viewed as more or less successful organisational attempts to inscribe spaces and their inhabitants in their own terms' (2013, p. 59). Thus, 'control' here is not only about encouraging shoppers to visit several stores as they pass through the mall or to linger longer through the manipulation of the environment. Brands act at a significantly deeper level, as Askegaard (2006, p. 98) observes: 'Branding as a (global)ideoscape . . . provides the ideological basis for the establishment of new meaning systems, new practices and new identity forms for the members of the consumer culture'. As such, Thompson and Arsel (2004) develop the construct of the 'hegemonic brandscape'. Using the case of Starbucks, they argue that it is through the development of oppositional meanings (i.e. the anti-Starbucks discourse) that local coffee shops are constituted. As such, these local cafes depend on these hegemonic meanings for their identity as 'other'. In other words, these global brands significantly influence the smaller local operations because they set the terms of the game (i.e. they set the norms regarding what a coffee shop or food retailer should look like, norms against which all coffee shops or supermarkets, etc., are measured).

Grobalization: The Death of the Local and the Scripting of Consumption

The American sociologist George Ritzer coined the term 'grobalization' to capture the way in which corporations' drive to grow and expand at all costs results in imperialistic ambitions which stifle and colonise other parts of the globe (Ritzer, 2003, 2004). Ritzer (1993) argues that this has made possible through the process of McDonaldization. He uses the fast-food chain McDonald's as the ultimate example of what he sees as a new period in the organization of production. Essentially, this new period began in the 1920s, when Henry Ford produced standardised cars on a mass scale using assembly line machinery and semiskilled labour. McDonaldization represents the final globalized expression of this process of rationalization, one which involves *efficiency, predictability, calculability* and *control*. These processes result in a drive towards time saving at all costs, the reproducibility and standardisation of goods and production processes (labour) all through increased control of smaller and smaller aspects of production. Take McDonald's as an example:

- *Efficiency* is equated with time saving – finding ways to take orders, cook and serve the food as quickly as possible. This is achieved, for example, though tightly timed interactions with customers and the breaking down of food preparation into small, discreet tasks, avoiding duplication and leading to operational efficiency.
- *Predictability* is equated with standardization of the product and service so that wherever a customer enters a McDonald's, they will receive the same product and have the same experience. This is achieved, for example, through scripting of staff-customer interactions and the uniform restaurant interiors. Standardisation is also applied to the workforce so workers' tasks are highly routine and repetitive.
- *Calculability* is equated with the ability to use objective measures wherever possible in the business. So, for example, sales quantity and service speed are prioritised over food taste and quality.
- *Control* is achieved through the previous processes but also the replacement of human labour with technology. McDonald's kitchens are highly automated, for example, with conveyer ovens and toasters. In some restaurants, McDonald's is replacing sales assistants altogether with touch-screen kiosks for ordering food.

Ritzer argues that these principles have spread beyond McDonald's to other corporations (such as Benetton, The Body Shop and Starbucks) but also that they have begun to dominate more and more sectors of American society (i.e. education, healthcare and the media). But perhaps most crucially, these principles have spread through processes of globalization to other country contexts. While these principles have spread *through* globalization, it is also important to note that these principles have also *enabled* corporations to globalise their operations.

Through these processes of McDonaldization and grobalization, Ritzer argues that we are increasingly moving from 'something to nothing'. In his book *The Globalization of Nothing*, Ritzer defines 'nothing' as 'generally centrally conceived and controlled forms that are completely devoid of distinctive and substantive content' (2004, p. xi). He argues that it is much more easy to globalize that which is centrally conceived and controlled. He also argues that it is easier to globalize largely empty forms than those that are loaded with distinctive local content. He discusses four types of 'nothing' which are non-places, non-things, non-people and non-services. He argues that these forms have proliferated precisely because they involve certain conveniences and efficiencies. Non-places are characterised by sameness and homogeneity which are easy to control, reproduce and market. The mega mall might be thought of as a non-place because it is centrally owned and managed and the environment is highly controlled – from the lighting and air-conditioning to the behaviours allowed within it. (Malls are heavily policed largely through the use of surveillance cameras.) The environment of shopping malls are deliberately designed to manipulate shoppers' behaviour by provoking specific moods and dispositions (Ritzer, 1993). The spaces themselves are also structured to facilitate a flow of people which provides optimal exposure to the goods on offer. The range of shops you might find in the mega mall would probably include a series of global brands and associated mass-produced goods which you might find in any mall in any country context. This uniformity and lack of distinctive content means that if dropped into a mall at random, you may have little idea which country you are in. In many cases, local sites and spaces have become replaced by non-places. In the UK context, this can be seen in the closure of independent high-street shops and cafes, as shoppers gravitate to Aldi, Primark and Starbucks.

Perhaps these non-places are popular, as they place few expectations on the consumer; they require very little of the self as individual. In these highly controlled and controlling spaces, the consumer knows exactly what they are expected to do. There is little room for uncertainty, or surprise. In fact, any ambiguity is eliminated because it has the potential to produce inefficiencies. In particular, the spaces embody the *predictability* principle of Ritzer's McDonaldization thesis. Auge (1995) identifies non-places as including supermarkets, train stations, airports and hotels, arguing that in non-places, individuals are connected in a uniform manner and creative social life is very limited if not non-existent.

> a person entering the space of non-place is relieved of his usual determinants. He becomes no more than what he does or experiences in the role of passenger, customer or driver. Perhaps he is still weighed down by the previous day's worries, the next day's concerns; but he is distanced from them temporarily by the environment of the moment. Subjected to a gentle form of possession, to which he surrenders himself with more or less talent or

conviction, he tastes for a while – like anyone who is possessed – the passive joys of identity loss, and the more active pleasure of role-playing.

(Auge, 1995, p. 103)

Here, consumers are reduced to automatons, mindlessly reproducing the imperatives of multinational corporations through their daily work tasks and consumption choices. Lifestyles are sold pre-packaged, safe and devoid of any real distinctive local content. The scripting of consumption by corporations effectively stamps out any creativity and individuality.

Glocalization: A Return to Local, Creative Consumption

Ritzer's second story of globalization he terms 'glocalization'. To better understand this as a process, he observes that it is synonymous with heterogenisation and hybridity. While grobalization leads to world that is becoming more and more similar or homogenous, for example, through the spread and dominance of global brands, glocalization suggests that when these global brands meet the local culture, something new and hybrid is formed. So glocalization suggests that rather than the world becoming more homogenous, local differences are still important and they perpetuate heterogeneity. So, for example, the language of global brands is not absorbed uniformly by consumers. It is read and understood by them in relation to their own localised culture and circumstances. Research also shows that global brands have different meanings for the same consumers in different local contexts (i.e. when consumers travel abroad, the meanings of global brands change for them) (Bengtsson et al., 2010).

All of the above suggests that brands are co-created as much by consumers at the local level as by marketers working in the head offices of MNCs (Pongsakornrungsilp and Schroeder, 2011). There is evidence to suggest that consumers value personalised and authentic retail spaces rather than bland, de-humanized environments. In response to this, many multinationals are attempting to re-humanize their products at the shopfloor level by using ethical and fairly traded products (The Bodyshop) and insisting that products are sourced locally (Tesco's regional buying offices which reduce food miles and encourage local producers). While the retail landscape has seen the rise of standardized and discount stores (such as Aldi, Lidl, Gregs and Primark in the UK), it has also seen an increase in speciality and niche chains, for example, family-run service stations stocking locally produced and artisan products (Gloucester and Tebay services), independent microbreweries and pubs and farmers markets to name but a few. Many of these operations have sprung up in response to the over homogenization of the retail landscape and a frustration at the uniformity of what is on offer, combined with a reflexive approach to retailing that attempts to think through the impact of the business on workers, customers and the local population alike. Indeed, Ger (1999,

p. 65) argues that local corporations can 'out-localize' global firms by mobilizing local cultural capital in international marketing contexts.

It can be argued that grobalization narratives over emphasise the processes of production, suggesting that corporations that merely deliver a pre-packaged consumer experience misses out on the productive behaviours of consumers at the local level. Consumer researchers have long been mindful of the whole range of practices consumers engage in to personalise and transform goods and services at the point of consumption. This work recognises that consumers are creative and playful in their translation of good and services from the shopfloor into their own homes and lives. Researchers have emphasised that the work of consumption often occurs in partnership with organisations – as a form of 'co-creation' of meanings (Prahalad and Ramaswamy, 2004). If this is indeed the case, it contradicts the idea that consumers are mindlessly absorbing the meanings that multinationals are folding into their goods and services during production. Consumers have significant agency and are not merely pawns of multinational corporations (Eckhardt and Mahi, 2004). Work on co-creation suggests that the relationship is two way, with consumers both receiving and creatively interpreting brand meanings but also having input into the various stages of the production process, including product and packaging design, advertising and store interiors. This trend again contradicts that idea that multinationals can grow and expand globally merely by imposing their values on local populations. Numerous examples abound of instances where local populations knowingly and deliberately re-appropriate the meanings of global brands. For example, Caldwell's (2004) study of McDonald's in Russia explores the way in which Russian consumers domesticate the meanings of McDonald's foods and restaurants to create new nationalistic identities. Yazıcıoğlu (2010) finds that in the reterritorialization of rock in Turkey, global symbols are reinterpreted by individuals to establish local meanings. Likewise, Takhar et al. (2012) highlight how a global imaginary of 'Indian-ness' is consumed at the local level through the film genre Bollywood to produce a range of new hybrid identifications.

Eckhardt and Mahi's (2012) work on consumption in India finds that in negotiating tensions between local cultural traditions and globalised consumption meanings, consumers create their own discourses which in turn shape the marketplace. As such, flows of meanings are certainly not one way and top down. Askegaard and Eckhardt's (2012) study of 'glocal yoga' similarly reveals the multi-directional flows of culture in globalization. They find that yoga practices are re-appropriated in the Indian context 'after a process of sanctioning in (most often) the Western hotbed of consumer culture production' (p. 46). Here, discourses of yoga and yoga practice in the West are re-appropriated to form new South Asian discourses on yoga. In these examples, we see global flows of culture which involve a two-way interaction of the global and the local where 'local consumptionscapes become a nexus of numerous, often contradictory, old, new and modified forces' (Ger and Belk, 1996, p. 271). Wilk (1995) similarly highlights the paradox of globalization in his study of beauty pageants in Belize. This format is embedded locally, invested by specific local meanings by unique local groups in the community, while at the same time, winners still conform more to a 'New York standard of beauty than that of Belize City', being tall and fair skinned. Kjeldgaard and Nielsen (2010) similarly find that global gender identity narratives interact with locally saturated cultural categories of gender in the Mexican telenovela *Rebelde*.

In a study of McDonald's in Israel, Ram (2004) usefully identifies a split between structural-institutional and symbolic-expressive levels of globalization. He argues that homogenization occurs at the structural-institutional level but that the symbolic-expressive level still allows for heterogeneity, diversity and local difference. In his example of the Golani Junction McDonald's in Israel, falafel is included on the menu, the hamburgers are larger than usual and the local Air Force brigade banner is used rather than the McDonald's golden arches. Ram observes, therefore:

> On the symbolic level, the 'difference' that renders the local distinctive has managed to linger on. At the same time, on the structural level, that great leveller of 'sameness' at all locales prevails: the falafel has become McDonaldized; the military has privatized food provisioning; and Air Force 'Ms' can hardly be told apart from McDonald's 'M'.
>
> (Ram, 2004, p. 24)

Thus, it remains that the global tends to subsume the local and mobilize it for its own ends (Belk, 2000).

In summary, the either-or argument of the consumer as a creative agent as in the story of glocalization or as mindless automaton as in the story of grobalization is oversimplified, as Sassatelli observes (2010, p. 177):

> Thus we do not find ourselves facing a split between a free and active consumer and a McDonaldized one: for example, in response to global commodities, consumers can either negotiate standardization through propping up local cultural repertoires and traditional hierarchies, or they can embrace the elements of universalism which mass culture always contains to unhinge the inequalities embedded in their traditions.

However, while recognising that globalization can prompt creative responses, we should bear in mind that it remains a process that people of the world certainly do not participate in on equal terms. For the privileged minority, it certainly delivers, but for a subaltern majority, its outcomes are, at best, distant and, at worst, pernicious in effect. Rather than delivering a democracy of consumption opportunity, global consumption influences tend to produce social inequality, class polarizations, stress, materialism and threats to health and the environment (Ger and Belk, 1996). For a majority that live on the margins of global flows of capital, the consumption dream passes them by. They are more likely to participate on the global stage as sellers of labour than consumers of a cornucopia of globalised goods (Belk, 2006; Varman and Vikas, 2007).

Emerging Alternatives

In closing, it is useful to consider some of the alternative narratives of globalization that have begun to emerge. Recent work within critical marketing recognises the ways in which marketing ideology and practice shapes global markets (Bjerrisgaard and Kjeldgaard, 2013). Commentators have argued that the global spread of 'marketing think and marketing speak', in fact, 'the globalization of the very idea of marketing', acts as a vehicle for the spread of neoliberalism. In the wake of the Covid-19 pandemic, commentators are also arguing for a complete re-wiring of how we think about globalization (Rodrik, 2020). As we have seen previously in relation to the brand, marketing ideology also shapes our view of the consumer by subjectifying consumers in particular ways (Fougère and Skålén, 2013). Marketing communications and brand values are increasingly designed to address consumers as global citizens. Taken as a whole, this work argues that painting the consumer as sovereign, promoting market choice as a form of liberation and markets themselves as democracies within which the consumer-citizen freely operates is problematic. Sassatelli argues that it is possible to see consumer sovereignty in an alternative light:

> as something other than consumer choice as predicated on the variables singled out by neoclassical economics and free market ideologies alike (i.e. price and quantity). The value-for-money logic does not hold when the target is not only individual satisfaction, but (also) a set of public goods.
>
> (Sassatelli, 2010, p. 187)

The question remains as to how in practice we might achieve this focus on public as opposed to private goods. Chatzidakis and colleagues put forward a politics of degrowth as one answer:

> It is about simple living and localisation of production and consumption, as opposed to a globalised economy. In a de-growth society small, self-organised communities would produce and consume what is needed, and the wealth that is produced would not be defined in economic terms, but through quality of life, social relations, equality and justice.
>
> (Chatzidakis et al., 2014, p. 760)

On the ground, a whole host of initiatives have sprung up which contrast starkly with the globalised world of the multinational corporation. The Slow Food Movement is one good example which was set up in response to the dominating influence of supermarkets, fast-food chains and agribusiness. Originating in Italy in 1986, the movement initially focused on regional traditions, good food and a slow pace of life. Since its inception, the movement has grown significantly and now has over 100,000 members in more than 130 countries (Andrews, 2008). It has evolved to develop a comprehensive politics of food to include a celebration of the local and local food systems; education of the dangers and risks of fast food, factory farms and monoculture; and lobbying for organic farming and lobbying against the use of pesticides and genetic engineering. The Fairtrade movement has similarly targeted global systems of food provision, offering minimum prices to small producers and ensuring the protection of workers' rights and the environment. These are just two examples of a whole raft of initiative which essentially go against the grain of grobalization and all that it stands for. Other examples include farmers markets, co-operatives and ethical finance initiatives. These initiatives frame the consumer as a political actor within the wider net of production, recognising that they can be key to effecting wider social change.

Summary

This chapter has explored two sides to the story of globalization. In the story of grobalization, processes of globalization have the ability to stifle local consumer culture, replacing local difference with a bland sameness. Here, global brands have the power to manipulate the consumer into mindlessly responding to their call to consume. On the other hand, in the story of glocalization, processes of globalization produce something new and innovative where the global meets the local. Here, the consumer is seen as an active agent creatively translating global brand meanings into something new in his or her own local context. The reality is that neither of these narratives tells the whole story. Focusing solely on grobalization and the sameness it delivers confers too much power on the multinational and too little on the individual consumer by emphasising production over consumption. This story also misses out on the importance of local specificity and difference. However, focusing solely on glocalization means that we over celebrate the agency of the consumer and fail to recognise the very real power wielded by the multinationals. One potential solution to this problem (as suggested by Ram, 2004) is to recognise that globalization operates at different levels: the structural-institutional and the symbolic-expressive. While homogenization occurs at the structural-institutional level, the symbolic-expressive level still allows for heterogeneity, diversity and local difference. A second solution is one which has been promoted by consumer researchers. Rather than sticking to either or binaries, we should recognise the multi-directional flows of culture and the co-creative capacities of consumers and producers.

Case Study: The Rise of Emerging Market Brands: The Case of Corona Beer

The picture of encroaching McDonaldization and American imperialism needs attenuating as emerging markets become ever more visible on the world stage. The term 'emerging markets' itself is a complex one. Researchers at the International Monetary Fund, Arizala and Yang (cited in Duttagupta and Pazarbasioglu, 2021) have generated a measure based on GDP, population, per capita GDP, share of world trade and share of world external debt. From this measure, they identify the following 20 emerging economies: Argentina, Brazil, Chile, China, Colombia, Egypt, Hungary, India, Indonesia, Iran, Malaysia, Mexico, the Philippines, Poland, Russia, Saudi Arabia, South Africa, Thailand, Turkey and the United Arab Emirates. More affluent economies the IMF identifies as 'advanced economies' and less affluent as 'developing economies'.

The global scene continues to be dominated by brands based in the United States (49 of the top 100 global brands in 2022 – Interbrand), but the picture is slowly changing. The top 100 brands list in 2022 also includes Chinese brands Huawei and Xiaomi, South Korean Samsung, Hyundai and Kia, and Mexico's Corona Beer. The usual approach in marketing textbooks would be to explore what happens when a global brand from an advanced economy enters an emerging or developing market; however, as a handful of studies emphasise, in the future, we are likely to see many more brands moving the other way, from emerging economies to more advanced ones. In their book *Brand Breakout: How Emerging Market Brands Will Go Global*, Kumar and Steenkamp (2013) argue that this is a trend on the rise. One of the interesting facts they put forward is that while emerging markets' GDP has grown significantly in recent years, their brands have failed to keep apace in terms of recognition and awareness in the global economy, particularly in advanced market contexts. However, it seems that it is only a matter of time given the increased focus in emerging markets on growing manufacturing, innovation and marketing capabilities. There is evidence to suggest that strong brands from emerging markets are outperforming those in developed markets. A study by the North American bank RBC that explored stocks of market-leading brands across countries found that since 2016, 'China, India, Brazil, Malaysia and Indonesia have a superior average return on equity (ROE) compared to the average ROE of developed market brands' (RBC, 2020, p. 1). In a model developed from their reading of a series of studies of brands from emerging markets, Gupta et al. (2015) identify seven key success factors for emerging economy brands to include: CEOs vision, organisational capability, organisational policies, international resources, local reputation, differentiation strategy and product quality.

One interesting example that helps to illustrate this trend is the Mexican emerging economy brand Corona Beer. Corona were placed 80th in the Interbrand Best Global Brands list in 2022, being one of only six emerging economy brands in the list. Corona's brand value has doubled in the period 2010–2022 and has grown by 12% in the last year to 7,764$m. Production of Corona Beer began in 1925 at Cerveceria Modelo S.A., the largest brewery in Mexico. In spite of challenges during the Great Depression during the 1930s, the beer quickly became popular, and within ten years, it was the best-selling beer in Mexico. Grupo Modelo began exporting to the United States in 1976, using US agents to distribute Corona Beer in this market. Later, when expanding its internationalisation strategy, the Modelo Group entered into distribution contracts with local companies who had knowledge of local markets and distribution channels. In 2013, Grupo Modelo merged with Anheuser-Busch InBev. Corona Beer is now exported to 180 countries worldwide. Corona developed a brand image that connected to sunshine and beach life, as the current global vice president for Corona recently commented the brand was 'born on the beach', with campaigns such as 'Find Your Beach' and most recently in 2022, 'Sunshine, Anytime'.

Corona Beer has an innovative approach to marketing. From the start, the beer was packaged in a unique clear glass bottle with strong 'made-in-Mexico' branding and an image of a crown ('Corona' means crown in Spanish). The beer is now popularly drunk with a slice of lime wedged in the bottle neck. There are a variety of stories for why this is the case, ranging from lime acting as a disinfectant and rust remover (rust left by the bottle caps) to keeping flies out of the beer to improving the taste. Whatever the case, the brand has embraced the trend. For example, in 2017, Corona became the official sponsor of the University of Texas Longhorns with the slogan 'Horns Up, Limes In'. Again, demonstrating an innovative ability to communicate the brand values via a variety of mediums. In 2021, to reinforce its message of sustainability, Corona launched a new form of recyclable packaging using the barley straw which is leftover from the harvest of the barley seed used in the beer's production. Most recently, in the summer of 2022, Corona announced that it will be opening an island off the coast of Cartegena in Colombia, 'Corona island', which the brand has leased from the Colombian government. Corona's intention in promoting the island as a peaceful resort where guests can re-connect with nature is to reflect and communicate its commitment to sustainability whilst also reinforcing its longstanding brand associations with beach life, relaxing and spending time with family and friends. The brand worked with Oceanic Global (an international non-profit) on sustainable elements of the island to include a focus on sustainable design and construction of buildings to blend in with the landscape and also sustainable energy production and food sourcing. The brand has announced that visitors will be limited to small numbers to protect the island's fragile ecosystem.

During the Covid-19 (also known as Coronavirus) pandemic, Corona Beer, due to the unfortunate name association, was the butt of a series of jokes on social media which quickly went viral. The name association was also reported to prompt some negative associations in consumers' minds. However, Corona's marketing team consistently debunked the circulating myths with substantiated statistics and the brand survived and even thrived in this period. Most recently in the summer of 2022, there have been concerns that the company could be prohibited from using water due to droughts in Mexico's northern region. However, the brand secured the support of the current president, Andres Manuel Lopez Obrador, for their brewing operations.

Case Study Sources

Carroll, N (2022) Corona on earning permission to 'stretch' beyond traditional marketing, *Marketing Week*, August 9.

Florence, F (2020) How Corona built brand equity in spite of the pandemic, *Marketing Week*, June 9.

Zheng, Y; Wang, L; Zhao, S; Hu, W (2022) Product sales and unintentional name association with the coronavirus pandemic, *Journal of the Agricultural and Applied Economics Association*, Vol. 1 (2), p. 136–150

Seminar Exercises

Discussion Topics

1 Identify the key features of grobalization and glocalization and discuss how each perspective sees the consumer. Reflecting on your own experiences, which view of the consumer do you identify with most strongly?
2 Discuss the problems with focusing either on grobalization or glocalization.
3 Thinking about a global brand of your choice, discuss why global brands might impact so powerfully on consumers.
4 With reference to the case study on Corona Beer, identify the key elements of their marketing strategy and discuss how these have helped the brand succeed on the global stage.

Group Exercises

1 Identify a global fast-food restaurant or coffee shop (i.e. McDonald's, Kentucky Fried Chicken, Starbucks, Café Nero, etc.) and compare it with a local, independently run operation you are familiar with.

  i Discuss the extent to which each operation might be seen as global or as local (think about brand values, product range and quality, store environment – i.e. music, lighting and interior design – and staffing/service).
  ii Consider which one you would rather visit and why.
  iii Discuss why you think people are sometimes drawn to global brands as opposed to local ones.

2   Read the paper 'The Starbucks Brandscape and Consumers' (Anti-corporate) Experiences of Glocalization' (full reference listed in key readings).

i   What criticisms have been made of Starbucks' business in the past? Why do you think Starbucks has been such a target for protest and criticism?

ii   What is 'glocalization'? What evidence of this process can you find in the article?

iii   How do the authors describe a 'hegemonic brandscape'?

iv   What are 'experiential brands'? And why do you think they are particularly powerful in influencing consumers?

v   What are the two types of consumers described in the paper? And how do they each describe Starbucks? Create a list for each group (think here also about the use of the language of aesthetics/style for one group and the use of the language of politics for the other group). How might their descriptions relate to their identity (i.e. who they want others to see them as)?

vi   Referring to the discussion section of the paper, what 'desires' are the two groups acting on?

Internet Resources

Interbrands – Best Global Brands Survey, https://interbrand.com/best-brands/
The Global Policy Forum, www.globalpolicy.org/globalization.html
The Globalist – An online magazine onthe global economy, politics and culture, www.theglobalist.com/
The International Monetary Fund – www.imf.org/en/home

Key Readings

Klein, N. (1999, 2001) *No Logo: Taking aim at the Brand Bullies*. Knopf Canada: Picador.
Ritzer, G. (2004) *The Globalization of Nothing*, London: Sage.
Sassatelli, R. (2010) 'Chapter 8 contexts of consumption', in *Consumer Culture, History, Theory, Politics*, (the useful section runs from pp. 174–192), London: Sage.
Thompson, C. and Arsel, Z. (2004) 'The Starbucks brandscape and consumers' (anticorporate) experiences of glocalization', *Journal of Consumer Research*, 31, 631–642.

References

Andrews, G. (2008) *The Slow Food Story: Politics and Pleasure*, London: McGill – Queens University Press.
Askegaard, S. (2006) 'Brands as a Global Ideoscape', in J. E. Schroeder and M. Salzer Mörling (Eds), *Brand Culture*, pp. 91–102, London: Routledge.
Askegaard, S. and Eckhardt, G. M. (2012) 'Glocal yoga: Re-appropriation in the Indian consumptionscape', *Marketing Theory*, 12(1), 45–60.

Auge, M. (1995) *Non-Places: An Introduction to Supermodernity*, London: Verso.

Belk, R. W. (2000) 'Wolf brands in sheep's clothing: Global appropriation of the local', in J. Pavitt (Ed), *Brand New*, pp. 68–69, London: Victoria and Albert Museum.

Belk, R. W. (2006) 'Out of our sight and out of our minds: What of those left behind by globalism?' in J. N. Sheth and R. Sisodia (Eds), *Does Marketing Need Reform?* pp. 209–216, Armonk: M.E. Sharpe

Bengtsson, A., Bardhi, F. and Venkatraman, M. (2010) 'How global brands travel with consumers: An examination of the relationship between brand consistency and meaning across national boundaries', *International Marketing Review*, 27(5), 519–540.

Bjerrisgaard, S. M. and Kjeldgaard, D. (2013) 'How market research shapes market spatiality a global governmentality perspective', *Journal of Macromarketing*, 33(1), 29–40.

Caldwell, M. L. (2004) 'Domesticating the French Fry Mcdonald's and consumerism in Moscow', *Journal of Consumer Culture*, 4(1), 5–26.

Chatzidakis, A., Larsen, G. and Bishop, S. (2014) 'Farewell to consumerism: countervailing logics of growth in consumption', *Ephemera*, 14(4), 753–764.

Duttagupta, R. and Pazarbasioglu, C. (2021) 'Miles to go: Emerging markets must balance overcoming the pandemic, returning to more normal policies and rebuilding their economies', *International Monetary Fund*, 2021.

Eckhardt, G. M. and Mahi, H. (2004) 'The role of consumer agency in the globalization process in emerging markets', *Journal of Macromarketing*, 24(2), 136–146.

Eckhardt, G. M. and Mahi, H. (2012) 'Globalization, consumer tensions, and the Shaping of consumer culture in India', *Journal of Macromarketing*, 32(3), 280–294.

Fougère, M. and Skålén, P. (2013) 'Extension in the subjectifying power of marketing ideology in organizations a foucauldian analysis of academic marketing', *Journal of Macromarketing*, 33(1), 13–28.

Friedman, T. (2005) *The World is Flat: The Globalised World in the Twenty First Century*, London: Penguin.

Ger, G. (1999) 'Localizing in the global village: Local firms competing in global markets', *California Management Review*, 41(4), 64–83.

Ger, G. and Belk, R.W. (1996) 'I'd like to buy the World a coke: Consumptionscapes of the less affluent World', *Journal of Consumer Policy*, 19(3), 271–304.

Gupta, S., Balmer, J. M. T. and Low, B. (2015) 'Brands in, from and to emerging markets: The role of industrial relationships', *Industrial Marketing Management*, 51, 4–10.

Held, D. and McGrew, A. (2000) *The Global Transformations Reader*, Hoboken: Wiley.

Holt, D. B., Quelch, J. A. and Taylor, E. L. (2004) 'How global brands compete', *Harvard Business Review*, 82(9), 68–75.

Interbrand (2022) *Best Global Brands Ranking*, https://interbrand.com/best-brands/

Kjeldgaard, D. and Nielsen, K. S. (2010) 'Glocal gender identities in market places of transition: Marianismo and the consumption of the telenovela Rebelde', *Marketing Theory*, 10(1), 29–44.

Klingman, A. (2007) *Brandscapes: Architecture in the Experience Economy*, Cambridge: MIT Press.

Kumar, N. and Steenkamp, J. B. E. (2013) *Brand Breakout: How Emerging Market Brands Will Go Global*, New York: Palgrave Macmillan.

Lash, S. and Lury, C. (2007) *Global Culture Industry: The Mediation of Things*, Malden: Polity.

Legrain, P. (2002) *Open World: The Truth about Globalization*, London: Abacus.

Lury, C. (2004) *Brands: The Logos of the Global Economy*, London: Routledge.

McKinsey Global Institute (2022) *Global Flows: The Ties that Bind in an Interconnected World*, November 15, www.mckinsey.com/capabilities/strategy-and-corporate-finance/our-insights/global-flows-the-ties-that-bind-in-an-interconnected-world

Pongsakornrungsilp, S. and Schroeder, J. E. (2011) 'Understanding value co-creation in a co-consuming brand community', *Marketing Theory*, 11(3), 303–324.

Prahalad, C. K. and Ramaswamy, V. (2004) 'Co-creating unique value with customers', *Strategy and Leadership*, 32(3), 4–9.

Ram, U. (2004) 'Glocommodification: How the global consumes the local-McDonald's in Israel', *Current Sociology*, 52(1), 11–31.

Ravier, A. O. (2009) 'Globalization and peace: A hayekian perspective', *Libertarian Papers*, 1(10), 1–18.

RBC (2020) 'The future of emerging markets: Brands', *RBC Insights*, September 6, https://www.rbcgam.com/en/ca/article/the-future-of-emerging-markets-brands/detail

Ritzer, G. (1993) *The McDonalization of Society*, Thousand oaks, CA: Pine forge Press.

Ritzer, G. (2003) 'Rethinking Globalization', *Sociological Theory*, 21(3), 193–209.

Rodrik, D. (2020).'Globalisation after Covid-19: My plan for a rewired planet', *Prospect*, May 4, https://www.prospectmagazine.co.uk/magazine/dani-rodrik-globalisation-trade-coronavirus-who-imf-world-bank

Salzer-Mörling, M. and Strannegård, L. (2007) '"Ain't Misbehavin": Consumption in a Moralized Brandscape', *Marketing Theory*, 7(4), 407–425.

Takhar, A., Maclaran, P. and Stevens, L. (2012) 'Bollywood cinema's global reach: Consuming the "diasporic consciousness', *Journal of Macromarketing*, 32(3), 266–279.

Tiesler, N. C. and Coelho, J. N. (2013) *Globalised Football: Nations and Migration, the City and the Dream*, London: Routledge.

Varman, R. and Vikas, R. M. (2007) 'Freedom and consumption: Toward conceptualizing systemic constraints for subaltern consumers in a capitalist society', *Consumption, Markets and Culture*, 10(2), 117–131.

Wilk, R. (1995) 'Learning to be local in Belize: Global systems of common difference', in D. Miller (Ed), *Worlds Apart: Modernity through the Prism of the Local*, pp. 110–131, London: Routledge.

Wood, D. M. and Ball, K. (2013) 'Brandscapes of control? Surveillance, marketing and the co-construction of subjectivity and space in neo-liberal capitalism', *Marketing Theory*, 13(1), 47–67.

Yazıcıoğlu, E. T. (2010) 'Contesting the global consumption ethos: Reterritorialization of rock in Turkey', *Journal of Macromarketing*, 30(3), 238–253.

Index

Printed in the United States
by Baker & Taylor Publisher Services